MW01140063

# The Foundations of American Jewish Liberalism

American Jews have built a political culture based on the principle of equal citizenship in a secular state. This durable worldview has guided their political behavior from the founding of the United States to the present day. In *The Foundations of American Jewish Liberalism*, Kenneth D. Wald traces the development of this culture by examining the controversies and threats that stimulated political participation by American Jews. Wald shows that the American political environment, permeated by classic liberal values, produced a Jewish community that differs politically from that of non-Jews who resemble Jews socially and from Jewish communities abroad. Drawing on survey data and extensive archival research, the book examines the ups and downs of Jewish attachment to liberalism and the Democratic Party and the tensions between two distinct strains of liberalism.

Kenneth D. Wald is Distinguished Professor Emeritus of Political Science and the Samuel R. "Bud" Shorstein Professor Emeritus of American Jewish Culture and Society at the University of Florida. He is the author of *Religion and Politics in the United States* (8th edn.); *Politics of Cultural Differences; Private Lives, Public Conflicts*; and *Crosses on the Ballot*.

## Cambridge Studies in Social Theory, Religion, and Politics

Editors

David E. Campbell, University of Notre Dame
Anna M. Grzymala-Busse, Stanford University
Kenneth D. Wald, University of Florida
Richard L. Wood, University of New Mexico

Founding Editor

David C. Leege, University of Notre Dame

In societies around the world, dynamic changes are occurring at the intersection of religion and politics. In some settings, these changes are driven by internal shifts within religions; in others, by shifting political structures, institutional contexts, or by war or other upheavals. Cambridge Studies in Social Theory, Religion, and Politics publishes books that seek to understand and explain these changes to a wide audience, drawing on insight from social theory and original empirical analysis. We welcome work built on strong theoretical framing, careful research design, and rigorous methods using any social scientific method(s) appropriate to the study. The series examines the relationship of religion and politics broadly understood, including directly political behavior, action in civil society and in the mediating institutions that undergird politics, and the ways religion shapes the cultural dynamics underlying political and civil society.

Mikhail A. Alexseev and Sufian N. Zhemukhov, *Mass Religious Ritual and Intergroup Tolerance: The Muslim Pilgrims' Paradox*

Luke Bretherton, *Resurrecting Democracy: Faith, Citizenship, and the Politics of a Common Life*

David E. Campbell, John C. Green, and J. Quin Monson, ⸙ *Seeking the Promised Land: Mormons and American Politics*

Ryan L. Claassen, *Godless Democrats and Pious Republicans? Party Activists, Party Capture, and the "God Gap"*

Darren W. Davis and Donald Pope-Davis, *Perseverance in the Parish? Religious Attitudes from a Black Catholic Perspective.*

Paul A. Djupe and Christopher P. Gilbert, *The Political Influence of Churches*

Joel S. Fetzer and J. Christopher Soper, *Muslims and the State in Britain, France, and Germany*

François Foret, *Religion and Politics in the European Union: The Secular Canopy*

Jonathan Fox, *A World Survey of Religion and the State*

Jonathan Fox, *Political Secularism, Religion, and the State: A Time Series Analysis of Worldwide Data Anthony*

Gill, *The Political Origins of Religious Liberty*

Brian J. Grim and Roger Finke, *The Price of Freedom Denied: Religious Persecution and Conflict in the 21st Century*

Kees van Kersbergen and Philip Manow, editors, *Religion, Class Coalitions, and Welfare States*

Mirjam Kunkler, John Madeley, and Shylashri Shankar, editors, A Secular Age *Beyond the West: Religion, Law and the State in Asia, the Middle East and North Africa*

Karrie J. Koesel, *Religion and Authoritarianism: Cooperation, Conflict, and the Consequences*

Ahmet T. Kuru, *Secularism and State Policies toward Religion: The United States, France, and Turkey*

Andrew R. Lewis, *The Rights Turn in Conservative Christian Politics: How Abortion Transformed the Culture Wars*

Damon Maryl, *Secular Conversions: Political Institutions and Religious Education in the United States and Australia, 1800–2000*

Jeremy Menchik, *Islam and Democracy in Indonesia: Tolerance without Liberalism*

Pippa Norris and Ronald Inglehart, *Sacred and Secular: Religion and Politics Worldwide*

Amy Reynolds, *Free Trade and Faithful Globalization: Saving the Market*

Sadia Saeed, *Politics of Desecularization: Law and the Minority Question in Pakistan*

David T. Smith, *Religious Persecution and Political Order in the United States*

Peter Stamatov, *The Origins of Global Humanitarianism: Religion, Empires, and Advocacy*

# The Foundations of American Jewish Liberalism

KENNETH D. WALD

*University of Florida*

CAMBRIDGE
UNIVERSITY PRESS

# CAMBRIDGE
## UNIVERSITY PRESS

University Printing House, Cambridge CB2 8BS, United Kingdom

One Liberty Plaza, 20th Floor, New York, NY 10006, USA

477 Williamstown Road, Port Melbourne, VIC 3207, Australia

314–321, 3rd Floor, Plot 3, Splendor Forum, Jasola District Centre, New Delhi – 110025, India

79 Anson Road, #06–04/06, Singapore 079906

Cambridge University Press is part of the University of Cambridge.

It furthers the University's mission by disseminating knowledge in the pursuit of education, learning, and research at the highest international levels of excellence.

www.cambridge.org
Information on this title: www.cambridge.org/9781108497893
DOI: 10.1017/9781108597388

© Cambridge University Press 2019

First published 2019

Printed and bound in Great Britain by Clays Ltd, Elcograf S.p.A.

*A catalogue record for this publication is available from the British Library.*

*Library of Congress Cataloging-in-Publication Data*
NAMES: Wald, Kenneth D., author.
TITLE: The foundations of American Jewish liberalism / Kenneth D. Wald, University of Florida.
DESCRIPTION: Cambridge, United Kingdom ; New York, NY : Cambridge University Press, [2019] | Series: Cambridge studies in social theory, religion, and politics
IDENTIFIERS: LCCN 2018042084 | ISBN 9781108497893 (hardback)
SUBJECTS: LCSH: Jews – United States – Politics and government. | Liberalism – United States – History. | United States – Ethnic relations. | BISAC: POLITICAL SCIENCE / Government / General.
CLASSIFICATION: LCC E184.36.P64 W35 2019 | DDC 305.892/4073–dc23
LC record available at https://lccn.loc.gov/2018042084

ISBN 978-1-108-49789-3 Hardback
ISBN 978-1-108-70885-2 Paperback

*To the Next Generation ....*
    *Zohar Lyn*
    *Jackson Cole*
    *Zuriel Laeb*
    *Gavin Hayes*

# Contents

# Figures

# Tables

# Acknowledgments

I worked on this book for a long time before I realized I was writing a book. The ideas expressed here emerged slowly, in fits and starts, germinating while I was thinking about other topics and doing other things. Because my debts accumulated over decades, I suspect I don't remember them all. I hope those contributors I neglected to mention will nonetheless recognize their fingerprints on the manuscript. I don't know about raising a child but it certainly took a village for me to write this book.

The seeds for this project were planted during my graduate career in the Department of Political Science at Washington University in St. Louis. Thanks to a talented faculty, I learned that people's political values and behavior are shaped in part by the places where they live and the people whom they live among. I learned other valuable lessons – that sophisticated statistical models must be anchored in strong theory, that every research project is a case study of something, and that history is essential to understanding contemporary politics.

After decades studying the role of religion in politics, I eventually turned my attention to Judaism. My ideas incubated during sojourns as a visiting scholar at the Centennial Center for Politics and Policy in Washington, DC; the Hebrew University of Jerusalem; Haifa University; the Frankel Center for Judaic Studies at the University of Michigan; the Weatherhead Center for International Affairs at Harvard University; and the Tanenbaum Center for Jewish Studies at the University of Toronto. I was also helped considerably by grants from the Memorial Foundation for Jewish Culture, the Society for the Scientific Study of Religion, and the US–Israel International Education Fund, which appointed me a Fulbright Senior Lecturer.

The University of Florida supplemented these appointments with sabbatical or leave pay and a Faculty Enhancement Opportunity award. When I finally made this book my major project, I was able to draw on funds from my appointment as the first Samuel R. Shorstein Professor of American Jewish Culture and Society. Thanks to Bud Shorstein for his generosity and to Jack Kugelmass and Sandra James from the University of Florida Center for Jewish Studies.

I am also indebted to other institutions that nurtured the project by providing access to essential quantitative materials. For providing machine-readable data sets, I'm grateful to the Roper Center for Public Opinion Research, the Berman Jewish Data Bank, the Berman Jewish Policy Archive, the Association of Religion Data Archives (ARDA), the Pew Research Center, the Dataverse Project, and the Inter-University Consortium for Political and Social Research. I also benefitted from the access to proprietary survey data graciously provided me by the Public Religion Research Institute (PRRI), GBA Strategies, the Solomon Project, Knowledge Networks, and J Street. Steven M. Cohen, Jim Guth, Shibley Telhami, Eric Uslaner, and Clyde Wilcox kindly loaned me a variety of datasets. Among the friends and colleagues I bothered for advice about other kinds of material, let me acknowledge Stephan Brumberg and Melissa Klapper, who were especially helpful.

Somewhat ironically, I grant, the qualitative component of my work depended heavily on electronic access to Proquest's historical collection of American Jewish newspapers, the invaluable Hathi Trust, and the comprehensive Jewish National and University Library. I also was enriched by time I spent immersed in documents at various brick and mortar archives. The staffs of the American Jewish Archives in Cincinnati, the Center for American Jewish History in New York, the library of the Katz Center for Judaic Studies in Philadelphia, and the New York City Municipal Archives provided expert guidance and congenial environments. To sate my compulsiveness about sources, I've bothered a great many librarians at other institutions and appreciate their patience. At the Price Library of Judaica at the University of Florida, Rebecca Jefferson, Emily Madden, and Katarina Rac went far beyond their duties to help me identify and locate fugitive materials. So did Colleen Seale, an astounding reference librarian. The Interlibrary Loan service of Smathers Library has always responded promptly to my sometimes bizarre requests for materials scattered around the globe.

Among the audiences who heard me expound on various aspects of this project, willingly and unwillingly, I'm particularly grateful to the students in my various courses and seminars at the University of Florida who taught me so much. I also appreciated the opportunity to prepare a paper on this topic for the Association of Religion Data Archives and to expound my thesis on Tony Gill's "Research on Religion" podcast. All these venues gave me a chance to sharpen my arguments.

Thank you to Kristen Soltis Anderson, Joseph Eskin, Diana Forster, Heather Lear, Tom Reynolds, Enrijeta Shino, and Bryan D. Williams, research assistants who often figured out what I wanted before I understood it myself.

Apart from those already named, various friends and colleagues deserve gratitude for their comments, questions, and challenges. Let me note the assistance and valuable insights provided by Deborah Dash Moore, Paul Djupe, Marc Dollinger, Ira Forman, Zvi Gitelman, Emmanuel Guttman, Rabbi David Kaiman, Laurence Kotler-Berkowitz, Geoffrey Levey, Peter Medding, Marsha Rosenblit, Lee Sigelman, Patricia Sohn, Elizabeth A. Stuart, Eric Uslaner, and Herb Weisberg. David G. Dalin and Jonathan Sarna provided an important psychological boost by pushing me to get this thing finished. Badredine Arfi and Michael Martinez have been model colleagues, sharing their wisdom in conversations and responding graciously when I pestered them about technical matters. My lifelong research collaborator, David Leege, has influenced me (mostly for the better) in ways I can't even discern.

Lew Bateman and Sara Doskow both encouraged me to submit the manuscript to Cambridge University Press, a decision that has paid dividends. The CUP editorial team of David Campbell, Anna Grzymala-Busse, and Richard Woods has been wonderful to work with and I also appreciate the helpful comments from two external readers. During the production process, I enjoyed working with Joshua Penney, Terry Kornak, Sri Hari Kumar, Danielle Menz, Jim Diggins, and a great many people who I don't know by name. Depending so heavily on the kindness of strangers, I feel a bit like Blanche Dubois, only less tragic.

I want to acknowledge the contributions of Robin Lea West, my wife and resident memory expert. She patiently endured (and sometimes enjoyed) my long periods of isolation in my study and my absences on research trips and speaking engagements. When I wanted to try out an idea, she was usually the first audience and her reactions often let me know I still needed to turn inchoate thoughts into relatively coherent arguments. Even if I wasn't entirely sure she was right, my father did tell me on my wedding day to listen to my wife. That advice has paid off when I've followed it.

I dedicated an earlier book to my two wonderful daughters, neither of whom ever read it. (It's been published in eight editions so they've had plenty of time.) I'm trying to break that tradition by dedicating this volume to my grandchildren in hopes they will feel obliged to outshine their mothers by reading it. Even though only one of them is currently reading and the youngest could consume the book only by gnawing on it, I remain hopeful that the chapters will become bedtime stories.

# PART I

# THE PROBLEM(S) OF AMERICAN JEWISH LIBERALISM

# I

# America Is Different

The United States is the only nation in the world which, from the moment of its birth, gave the Jew all the rights and the privileges of citizenship, placed him upon a par of equality with his neighbor, and recognized him as an integral and essential part of the nation.

–Ferdinand Isserman, "Keeping America," 1937 (p. 4)

On June 5, 1868, Cincinnati's Bene Israel congregation laid the cornerstone for a new synagogue building at 8th and Mound Streets. Following a venerable custom, the celebrants deposited a time capsule in the foundation stone. According to contemporary accounts, they filled a metal box with a copy of the first Jewish sermon preached in the city, a congregational history, coins from the Roman era in Palestine, a roll of contributors to the new building, and a list of Cincinnati's Jewish institutions (*Cincinnati Inquirer*, June 6, 1868, 1; Philipson 1915, 453). They also placed an unexpected object among the relics and mementos in the box: a copy of the United States Constitution.

Why did they think the Constitution belonged with the other memorabilia in the cornerstone of their synagogue? On its face, the decision was curious. The US Constitution consigned religious organizations to the private realm, forbidding the state from either rewarding or punishing citizens for their religious views and prohibiting the nation from adopting any official religion. There was no reference to God or other religious language in the entire document. Given that state and religion were so clearly separated in the national charter, why would a Jewish religious organization choose to store a copy of it among its precious keepsakes?

Interring the Constitution alongside other sacred objects could have been a rebuke to anti-Semites who habitually charged Jews with greater loyalty to their own "nation" than devotion to country.[1] By placing the Constitution in the bedrock of their new tabernacle just three years after the end of the Civil War, perhaps the congregation merely intended to reaffirm its loyalty to the Union. I believe, however, that the congregants had a deeper motive in planting the US Constitution in the groundwork of their new building.

By 1868, the American Jewish community had come to consider the Constitution as part of the underpinning of Judaism in the United States. By creating a secular state that disclaimed any religious identity, the Constitution provided conditions that enabled Judaism to thrive in the new nation. Beyond religious freedom, the Constitution gave Jews equal citizenship and an ownership share in the country. As a prominent Jewish leader told President John Quincy Adams in 1820, the United States provided Jews with "perfect civil and religious liberty," enabling them to thrive in America as nowhere else (quoted in Kleinfeld 1999, 70).

In the United States under the Constitution, for the first time in centuries, Jewish well-being thus depended neither on the patronage of a prince nor on an evanescent spirit of toleration. Whether they intended to or not, the Bene Israel members who sealed the Constitution in the base of the new building effectively declared that the Jewish stake in America rested symbolically and literally on a constitutional foundation.

In the following pages, I demonstrate that American Jews have attributed their success to a political climate steeped in classic liberalism and have therefore given priority to defending the political system that made it possible. They developed a political culture that reinforced their interpretation of the American Jewish experience, emphasizing above all else the importance of maintaining the principle of equal citizenship in a secular state. The culture first emerged in nascent form at the time of the founding of the United States in the late eighteenth century and was largely consolidated by the end of the nineteenth century. The political culture based

---

[1] The old building was full of objects attesting to the congregation's patriotism. The area above the ark was dominated by a tableau featuring an American eagle with the Ten Commandments in its talons (*Cincinnati Enquirer*, June 6, 1868, 1). Just above the eagle's head, there was an American flag inscribed with God's reminder to Moses that the Jews had been borne from Egyptian slavery to freedom on an eagle's wings. As the guests recessed from their old building for a short walk to the new structure, a band played the national anthem.

on classic liberalism continues to define the foundational political priority of American Jewry today.

Political scientists use the concept of "political culture" to denote core beliefs about politics and government among the members of a population. The ideas that compose a political culture are important because they generate "rules that govern behavior in the political system" (*International Encyclopedia* 2008). In all aspects of their political decision-making – identifying and framing political issues, developing strategies and tactics for action, articulating their concerns in public discourse, defining their political interests – American Jews have operated within the framework of a distinctive political culture. For stylistic purposes, I will sometimes refer to political culture as a "political ethic," worldview, or perspective. I distinguish political culture from ideology, which I take to define the direction rather than the content of political beliefs. I do not use the concept of "political theology" because it suggests a worldview that locates political authority in God or the divine (Lila 2007). The political culture developed by American Jewry explicitly rejected this connection.

## WHY THIS BOOK?

Although scholars have delved deeply into the American Jewish experience, they have given relatively short shrift to the explicitly political dimensions of Jewish life in the United States. That omission is curious given that virtually all accounts recognize that American Jews identified democracy and equality as a source of the exceptionally positive situation they enjoyed in America. But in most research on American Jewry, the political system has been a backdrop, not the main story. Mentioning the democratic character of the United States has become a ritual invocation rather than a means to investigate systematically how a Jewish politics was created and sustained in the United States.

Traditional histories of American Jewry give little emphasis to how Jews responded to the favorable political conditions in North America by crafting a political worldview and deploying it when they needed to mobilize the community against developments that threatened their standing. Enfleshed in newly formed organizations charged with defending the community's interest, this political culture provided a discourse that articulated grievances in a way that reinforced Jewish claims to belong fully to the nation. The Jewish political culture was the operational link between the design of the American polity and the subsequent political behavior of American Jews. Overlooking this critical intervening variable amounts to denying the agency of American Jews in the ongoing work of their own emancipation.

The failure to emphasize the importance of the American political context has also left unsolved the key puzzle in the study of modern American Jewish political behavior. Jews today rank among the most pro-Democratic and politically liberal constituencies in the United States. This fact contradicts the dominant academic theories of voting that attribute political behavior principally (though not exclusively) to economic interests. As a relatively wealthy, highly educated, and upper-status community, Jews should be more Republican and politically conservative than other Americans. They are not and, in fact, are decidedly more Democratic and liberal than the electorate as a whole *and* more so than that portion of it that shares similar socioeconomic traits. Scholars have attempted for more than sixty years to resolve this anomaly without taking account of the unique qualities of the American political system.

In this volume, I draw out the consequences of the American emphasis on the Enlightenment values of liberty and equality for the development of a political worldview by American Jews. I focus closely on the kind of democracy that American Jews favored, the way they constructed an image of citizenship and the secular state, how this image was transmitted to newcomers, and how it sometimes generated conflict over political issues but also provided guidelines to help the community when it entered the public square on behalf of its interests. This study focuses on the political worldview crafted by American Jews and how that perspective, encompassed within a distinctive political culture, continues to shape their otherwise puzzling politics.

*The Foundations of American Jewish Liberalism* differs from other works about American Jewish politics in three respects: time frame, theoretical lenses, and methodological pluralism.

Although he acknowledges earlier historical roots, Henry L. Feingold (2014) considers American Jewish political culture as essentially a twentieth-century phenomenon. Most scholars follow the timeline adopted by Beth Wenger (2010) in her chronicle of how American Jews constructed their heritage in the United States. She emphasizes the period from the late nineteenth century through the early 1950s when Jews embraced the principle of "Americanization." This meant pushing newcomers toward acculturation, encouraging them to adapt to the norms of the United States outside the synagogue. In looking for the underpinnings of American Jewish liberalism, I begin much earlier – at the founding of the United States in the late eighteenth century – and the analysis extends through the presidential election of 2016. The Jewish embrace of liberal political values began much earlier than is commonly supposed and still matters greatly today – even if the meaning of "liberal" has changed over the course of American history.

This study also differs by its social scientific perspective. I treat the political experience of American Jews as a case study of how a very small group, its members often despised as outsiders and aliens, managed nonetheless to carve out a political role enabling adherents to advance their interests in a majoritarian political process. Although their religious heritage was largely responsible for their status as strangers and outsiders, it was incidental to the process by which American Jews developed a distinctive political role. Hence, where appropriate, I invoke general theories of political behavior rather than emphasizing strictly "Judaic" explanations to account for the distinctive features of American Jewish political action. Such an approach is more accurate, I contend, and also enables me to bring this study into conversation with other research on ethnic and religious political activism.

The work is anchored principally in three such theoretical approaches: contextual analysis, political opportunity structure, and threat perception. I deploy other frameworks when necessary to place the American Jewish experience in comparative perspective. I realize that viewing Jewish political life via these theoretical angles may strike some observers as producing an "overly schematic" account running roughshod over the intricacies of the American Jewish experience (Fetter 2016). Although this may result in a less fine-grained approach, it provides a basis to explain a wider range of cases than a more insular, Judeo-centric account. Given my commitment to developing theory about political mobilization by ethnoreligious minorities in general, I am comfortable with that trade-off.

Finally, because they complement one another, the book uses both qualitative and quantitative methods of analysis. Recognizing that qualitative data may be more helpful in hypothesis formation and quantitative tools more appropriate for hypothesis testing, I have never perceived conflict between them (Brady, Collier, and Seawright 2017). Nor do I put much stock in arguments that one approach is intrinsically superior to another.

To understand the gestation of American Jewish liberalism, I thus dug deeply into all sorts of written materials: books and articles, memoirs, reports, organizational records, private correspondence, newspapers, sermons, lectures, and the like. Reading these archival sources exposed me to the assumptions, concepts, and imagination of the people who contributed to the liberal political tradition within American Judaism. The experience was not unlike an in-depth interview. I also compiled numerous quantitative datasets using systematic surveys of Jewish (and, at times, non-Jewish) respondents and other kinds of numerical information. These sources were subjected to various forms of statistical analysis. I incorporated this material because I do not believe that qualitative methods alone can plumb "the soul or psyche" of Jews, where, it is said, we will find the buried secrets of Jewish political behavior (Feingold 2014, ix, xv). Rather, we need to test systematically the intuitions arising from qualitative analysis to ensure that they are more than fanciful impressions. Using both methods enables me to assess the impact of a liberal political culture on the attitudes and behavior of American Jews.

In undertaking this project, I had no ambition to write a comprehensive history of American Judaism, a task that has been ably handled by several scholars. Nor is this book meant to be a full history of American Jewish politics. Rather than cover every significant political choice point, I focus more narrowly on issues and controversies that contributed to the formation, institutionalization, and evolution of the dominant political worldview that contemporary American Jews inherited from their eighteenth- and nineteenth-century ancestors. I leave out pieces of the story less vital to my central concern.

## PLAN OF THE BOOK

The remaining chapters in Part I identify the central intellectual puzzles posed by the contemporary political behavior of American Jews. Chapter 2 discusses how Jews' strong commitment to the Democratic Party and political liberalism violates dominant theories of American political behavior and then assesses the "Judaic" theories that scholars have developed to explain why American Jews are so politically exceptional. Apart from my uncertainty that these theories do in fact explain the anomaly of American Jewish liberalism, such approaches raise more puzzles than they solve, being unable to explain (a) why American Jews are politically unique among Jewish communities around the world; and (b) why the attachment of American Jews to the Democratic Party and political liberalism oscillates over time. Because these ad hoc explanations do not account satisfactorily for the anomalous political behavior of American Jews, Chapter 3 begins the work of developing a new perspective on American Jewish political behavior. It attempts to unpack the common scholarly observation that "America is different" for Jews by asking how and why it is different. This leads to a discussion of the importance of two social science approaches, the theory of political context and the concept of political opportunity structure.

With the theoretical building blocks in place, Part II traces the development of the American Jewish political culture from the American founding through World War II. Chapter 4 concentrates on how the pioneers of the American Jewish community embraced the classical liberal values underlying the political architecture of the US Constitution. Chapters 5 through 7 trace the subsequent development of the Jewish political culture, covering, respectively, the early national period, the state of the culture at the end of the nineteenth century, and how the culture operated on crucial public issues during the first half of the twentieth century.

The chapters in Part II address liberalism as an idea, a set of norms that strongly conditioned the way Jews dealt with various political issues. Until the 1930s, Jewish political culture was not firmly attached to any single political party. In a fluid political economy, organized Jewry worked with whatever party was in power when an issue of Jewish interest or concern arose. Individual Jewish voters were divided along party lines. Although that changed in the 1930s when Jews joined with other groups in the New Deal electoral coalition, their attachment was less to classic liberalism than to support for the welfare state and other public programs associated with Franklin Roosevelt's Democratic administration. It's worth remembering that even under Roosevelt, the Democrats were a socially conservative party focused primarily on economic concerns and reluctant to address questions of race or gender.

Part III examines the fusion between Jewish political culture and the Democratic Party that became particularly marked in the postwar era and beyond. Chapter 8 examines the post–World War II tensions between Jews and the Democrats that seemed likely to disrupt the Jewish attachment to both liberalism and its political carrier, the Democratic Party. In Chapter 9, I show that these breaches were healed or overlooked when most Jews perceived an immediate threat to their status and well-being from the new coalition between the Republican Party and politicized Christianity in the late 1970s. Conflict over church and state, a critical issue in the formation of Jewish political culture, returned to the political agenda and cemented the connection between Jews and the Democratic Party. As Chapter 10 shows, that concern was reinforced during the presidential campaign of 2016.

Please keep some caveats in mind while reading this book. First, this study is *not* meant as a critique, positive or negative, of the American Jewish political culture. I wish to understand how this culture arose and its impact on Jewish political action, but I don't take a stand on whether contemporary Jewish political behavior is wise or not. That important philosophical question cannot be answered with data. Second, I am agnostic about whether the pro-Democratic skew in Jewish voting – so powerfully reinforced in 2016 – will last over the long haul. As political scientists like to say, predicting the present is hard enough without trying to forecast the future. Finally, when I talk about Jews, I usually mean ordinary Jews, what I would call "Jews in the pews" if Jews attended synagogue at the same rate that other Americans go to church. In any case, when talking about Jewish political behavior, I mostly refer here to the Jewish rank-and-file. Jewish elites play an important role in this study but the focus remains on the politics of the Jewish masses. That is my dependent variable.

## JEWS IN THE UNITED STATES: A BRIEF OVERVIEW

To understand why Jews behave politically as they do, it's important to know some basics about them: the size of the community, basic traits, origins, and development. Hence I conclude this chapter with a profile of the Jewish community in the United States and a brief account of its origins.

Agencies of the US government do not ask residents to disclose their religious affiliation or identification, depriving us of official information about the size of the Jewish population. Even if the government could put such questions on the census or surveys, that would not eliminate the challenge because Jews don't agree on the markers of Jewishness. And even if the organized Jewish community could somehow achieve consensus on who is a Jew and who isn't, individuals would remain free to identify as Jews without paying any attention to Jewish or secular authorities. After all, as the Hebrew Bible teaches in Exodus 32, Jews are a "stiff-necked" people no easier to herd than cats.

Considering the individualism that permeates American thinking, it's not surprising that people develop their own standards to define Jewishness or any other religious identity. In the traditional definition, individuals are Jewish by birth to a Jewish mother or conversion by a recognized rabbi. But when asked who they would more likely classify as Jewish – a person who has a Jewish mother but does *not* practice Judaism or somebody whose mother *isn't* Jewish but who regularly attends synagogue – barely a quarter of self-described American Jews endorsed the traditional criteria of birth to a Jewish mother (*Los Angeles Times* Poll, 1988, 6).[2] Many American Jews think of Jewishness principally as a matter of ethnic and cultural heritage rather than religious commitment (*Los Angeles Times* Poll, 1988, 6). More than a few of these who do have a Jewish heritage based on the traditional criteria select "no religion," atheist, or agnostic when asked their religious identity in surveys.[3]

Asked by researchers what makes someone a "good" Jew, most self-identified Jews endorse qualities that have very little to do with the standards set by rabbinic authorities. For example, when the Pew Research Center asked Jewish respondents which aspects of being Jewish were central to their own identity, respondents ranked "observing Jewish law" next to last among the nine options presented to them (Pew Research Center 2013). Because of the elasticity in the way people define Jewish identity, Barry Kosmin (1992, 30) quipped, everyone can be a "Jew by choice" (a term often used to describe converts to Judaism).

That makes it difficult to develop firm estimates about the size of the American Jewish community. Despite these ambiguities and the use of different techniques to locate Jews, most demographers estimate the American Jewish population at around 6.5 to 7 million people or roughly 2% of the entire US population (Sheskin and Dashefsky 2017; Tighe et al. 2013). How significant is this community? In absolute terms, the *number* of Jews has been fairly static over the last half century, and there are today about as many Jews as Presbyterians (Pew Research Center 2015, 102). On the other hand, the Jewish *share* of the total American population has dropped significantly because the non-Jewish population has grown so much faster than the Jewish community. But even that claim is challenged by studies that identify an additional 6 million or so Americans who are not counted as Jews in the demographers' estimates based on birth or conversion but who are "Jewishly-connected" or have some legitimate tie to Jewish heritage (Tobin and Groeneman 2003).

Although *Look* magazine inspired panic among Jewish organizations with its 1964 article about "the vanishing American Jew," it turns out that

---

[2] Asked the same question in a parallel survey, 43% of Israeli Jews took the traditional position.

[3] The Pew Research Center (2013, 7) indicates that somewhere between a fifth and a quarter of individuals who identify as Jews and claim Jewish ancestry and/or upbringing nonetheless report themselves as having no religion. Previous research suggests that most members of this subpopulation consider themselves ethnic or cultural Jews.

people raised as Jews are much more likely to retain that identity as adults than people from other religions are to retain theirs (Pew Research Center 2015, 39). While Jewish leaders fret about continuity in the size of the Jewish population, the American public thinks there are far more Jews than demographers have identified. Ordinary Americans estimate the Jewish population share at 10% or even higher (Herda 2013). If that were the case, there would be one Jew for every two Catholics in the United States and it would be much easier to study them.

Regardless of trends in population growth or decline, American Jews remain distinctive in many ways (Smith 2005). Jews are, on average, older, with higher rates of marriage and smaller families. Owing to their predominantly European heritage, they are disproportionately white and non-Hispanic. They are distributed spatially in a very different way than the population as a whole: Jews are much more likely to reside in large urban and metropolitan areas and in the northeastern United States. Jews possess, on average, higher socioeconomic status as well. This is the result of their high levels of formal education, high-status occupations, and, largely as a result, higher than average incomes and net wealth. Subjectively, Jews are more likely than other Americans to define themselves as middle and/or upper class.

These are tendencies, not iron laws, so one can find Jews from Nebraska (like the author), Jews with large families, poor Jews, and Jews of Latino and African-American heritage. Jews may well be acculturated to American society, but they still stand out from the rest of the population in demographics and socioeconomic status and, as we will see, in politics.

## HOW DID THEY GET HERE?

Celebrating in 1905 the 250th anniversary of Jewish settlement in the United States, a distinguished rabbi addressed his audience at New York's Carnegie Hall as "you whose sires escaped from German scorn, you or yours from Russian hate, mine from Spanish Inquisition" (Mendes 1906). Although he scrambled the chronological order, the rabbi did identify correctly the three major sources of Jewish migration to what became the United States.

As far as we know, Jews first arrived in the Western Hemisphere as part of Columbus's crew when the explorer docked somewhere in the Caribbean in 1492. Very few identifiable Jews set foot upon what would become the United States for another century and a half and none established a permanent community. In 1654 two ships sailed into the harbor of New Amsterdam, capital of the Dutch colony of New Netherlands (today's New York), carrying a group of twenty or so Jews from Recife, Brazil who became the Jewish founding fathers.

These immigrants to the New Netherlands colony were descendants of Jews who had lived in Spain and Portugal during the Middle Ages. Under the Muslim caliphate that reached the Iberian Peninsula early in the eighth century, Jews often enjoyed considerable autonomy and tight integration into society despite their minority standing. They developed a Spanish and Arabic-inflected variant of Hebrew, Ladino, and often acquired Spanish and Portuguese surnames. Jews with this heritage became known by the adjective "Sephardic," a term derived from the Hebrew word for Spain. This relatively happy era of Jewish history in Iberia was punctuated by occasional periods when Catholics displaced Muslim rulers and imposed less benign conditions than Jews had usually enjoyed under Islamic rule (Menocal 2002).

The period of religious pluralism ended decisively after the *Reconquista*, the consolidation of Christian power in the Iberian Peninsula under Ferdinand and Isabella in the late fifteenth century.

The Catholic monarchs began enforcing religious uniformity, culminating in the expulsion of unconverted Jews and Muslims from Spain in 1492 and, a few years later, from Portugal as well. Holland, with its reputation for tolerance and its location on key trading routes, beckoned to many of the Spanish and Portuguese exiles, who established Jewish communities in the Netherlands and became major actors in international trade. Some of their descendants ventured to South America when Brazil came under the colonial rule of the Netherlands in 1630, hoping to expand their trade under Dutch protection. Once the colony fell back into Portuguese hands in 1654, the renewed Inquisition traveled across the Atlantic to Portuguese possessions in South America. Dutch Jews promptly sailed north from Recife in search of safe haven.

Given their Dutch connections, the Jewish emigrants of 1654 reasonably enough expected to receive asylum from the Dutch colony in North America. Denied permission to settle in New Amsterdam by Governor Peter Stuyvesant, they won the right of residence in 1655 on the orders of the Dutch West India Company, which held the colonial charter. One of the pioneering immigrants, Asser Levy, even sued for and was awarded the rank of burgher, entitling him to the rights of suffrage, public office, and other civic honors (DeLancey 1886). Almost a century later, when Great Britain had acquired New Netherland and rechristened it New

York, the British Parliament granted citizenship under liberal terms to foreign-born aliens residing in British North America. During the Revolutionary War, the New York colonial assembly went further by guaranteeing freedom of religion to all inhabitants "without discrimination or preference." The precarious foothold first won in 1655 became more secure but Jews remained a tiny community at the outbreak of the American Revolution, with an estimated population of at most 2,500 people. Most resided in port cities along the Atlantic.

The major growth of the Jewish population in the United States was subsequently driven by three major flows of immigrants. Jacob Rader Marcus (1958) argued that each major wave produced distinct communities with unique "political, economic, social, cultural, and religious life." Although these periods do not correspond closely to the traditional cutpoints of American history, Rader showed that they demarcated major shifts in the American Jewish experience. I follow Marcus in tracing the composition of the Jewish population using the three epochs he defined: Sephardic Jewry (1654–1840), German and other central European Jews (1841–1920), and the *Ostjuden* of eastern Europe (1852–1920).

The first wave, arriving during the colonial period, included some British Jews and residents of British Caribbean colonies but was composed primarily of Sephardic Jews from Spain, Portugal, and Holland or their colonies.[4] The earliest synagogues in the American colonies mostly followed the Sephardic model of worship and often described themselves as synagogues "in the Portuguese [or Spanish] manner." Their religious values were deeply rooted in the classic period of medieval Judaism and did not stray in practice from what became Orthodox Judaism. These pioneering Sephardim were eventually outnumbered by Jews from other locales in part because the Spanish Jews (as they were often called) quickly assimilated and their children intermarried with Ashkenazic (Western or European) Jews as well as with Christians.

Even so, one historian insists, the Sephardim set the tone for American Jewish life well into the eighteenth century even when they were outnumbered by Jews with different ethnic origins (Angel 1973). At the outset of the Revolutionary era, a Sephardic Jew who migrated from England to South Carolina became the first American Jew elected to public office and one of the first colonists to die in the War of Independence. A member of the Provincial Congress of the colony and a strong supporter of the

---

[4] The plural term, *Sephardim*, was commonly used to describe all Jews who did not come from a German or Yiddish-speaking area (Angel 1973, 77).

American Revolution, Francis Salvador died in 1776 during a skirmish between pro-independence soldiers and a joint force of British soldiers and Native Americans (Huhner 1905). Haym Solomon, born in Poland to Jewish refugees from Portugal, subsequently immigrated to New York, where he helped finance the Revolution. Uriah P. Levy, whose family had experienced the Spanish Inquisition, served with distinction during the War of 1812 and later became Commodore of the US Navy. Other notables with Sephardic ancestry include Emma Lazarus, a writer best known for her sonnet affixed to the Statue of Liberty, and her cousin, Benjamin Cardozo, the second Jewish member of the US Supreme Court. Although estimates differ (see Ben-Ur 2009), perhaps as many as 10% of contemporary American Jews have some degree of Sephardic heritage (Be'chol Lashon 2018).

The next major wave of Jewish immigrants, sometimes referred to in shorthand as the "Germans," came to the United States from central Europe principally during the middle years of the nineteenth century. During this time, the Jewish population grew from around 10,000 to nearly a quarter of a million. These newcomers came from the various Germanic states that were not yet consolidated and from lands under control of the Hapsburg Monarchy in Austria-Hungary. Although the largest Jewish community in Europe, German Jews did not acquire the rights of citizenship until the early nineteenth century, when the Napoleonic armies marched into central Europe, bringing with them a legal code that accorded Jews citizenship and equal rights. With the end of the Napoleonic Wars, most of the German states found ways to abrogate the laws imposed upon them by the French, a decision that was codified by the Congress of Vienna in 1815. Despite Jewish hopes that their emancipation would accompany the revolutionary movements that spread across Europe in 1848, the uprisings failed and *ancien regimes* were reconstituted. Many disappointed young Jews, seeing no future for themselves in the region, subsequently departed for the United States, where they were known as the Forty-Eighters (Korn 1949).

Many of these second-wave arrivals began new lives as itinerant peddlers on the southern and western frontiers. They traveled across the country, following rivers and railroads, often settling in smaller towns or outside the Northeast. Some became shopkeepers after amassing a modest amount of capital, and, in time, several built large enterprises based on mass merchandising techniques. German Jews founded businesses that became Levi Strauss, Sears & Roebuck, the *New York Times*, Hart Schaffner & Marx, Bloomingdale's, and Macy's. German Jewish immigrants from banking families relied on transnational connections that enabled them to develop important finance networks. Some accumulated considerable fortunes and the group played outsized roles in American commerce and investment, establishing firms such as Lazard Freres, Lehman Brothers, and Goldman Sachs. This class of entrepreneurs, known in New York as the "uptown Jews," led the development of many Jewish organizations and continued to occupy a disproportionate share of communal leadership positions well into the twentieth century.

Their religious life differed from the Sephardim who had preceded them. Many of the Germans, educated in the Enlightenment tradition when it reached central Europe in the late eighteenth century, became deeply engaged with the movement to modernize Judaism by adapting to modernity and embracing some of its values. Once in the United States, where the state did not regulate religion, they eliminated gender-segregated seating in synagogues, adopted the vernacular (German or English rather than Hebrew) as the language of worship and sermons, and discarded much of traditional Judaism such as the dietary laws. The movement known as Reform Judaism, imported from Germany, recast Judaism from a tribal faith to a universalistic religion. Reform developed as the first organized denomination within American Judaism.

A massive wave of Jewish immigrants from eastern Europe, the "Russians" in common parlance, poured into the United States from the mid to late nineteenth century until the adoption of restrictive immigration during the 1920s. None of the subsequent bumps in the Jewish population matched the size of this cohort or so affected the composition of the Jewish community. In absolute numbers, there were an estimated 250,000 Jews when the migration began and 4 million by the time Congress adopted severe national origins quotas in 1924. Fully three-quarters of the Jewish immigrants during this period arrived from eastern Europe (calculated from Joseph 1969, 93–94). By the outbreak of World War I, more than four out of five Jews in the United States had eastern European origins (Sarna 2004, 207). In 2001, a full century after the great wave of eastern European Jewry had crested, a majority of American Jews still claimed at least one grandparent who was born an *Ostjuden* and the percentage rose to almost 75% among those aged 55 and older.[5]

---

[5] Calculated from the Survey of Heritage and Religious Identification 2002. Available at www.jewishdatabank.org/Studies/details.cfm?StudyID=394. Per note 3, the figure includes individuals who described themselves as having a Jewish cultural/ethnic background even if they did not claim a Jewish religious affiliation. Any grandparent born in Poland, the Soviet Union, Romania, or eastern Europe was classified as eastern European.

Most of the Jewish immigrants in the third wave came from the Pale of Settlement, a common term for czarist Russia (which also encompassed most of present-day Poland and Lithuania), and the European territory that was part of the Ottoman Empire (principally Turkey and the Balkans). Jews in the Pale had faced increasing repression and impoverishment throughout the late nineteenth and early twentieth centuries. Periodic spikes in violence associated with murderous pogroms and the threat of forced enlistment in the czar's army produced intense pressure to emigrate. As a French observer commented in 1904, "If the Jews of Russia land on the shores of America by thousands every year, it is because the rigor of the Russian laws, intolerance and insecurity drive them ..." (Leroy-Beaulieu 1917, 35). Despite efforts to recruit them to join Jews in Palestine, then a province of the Ottoman Empire, or to form a Jewish nationalist movement in Russia, the largest proportion of Jewish emigrants chose North America.

In Europe, these Jews had been concentrated predominantly in the countryside, small towns, and villages or in densely populated ghettos in larger cities. As a rule, they were Yiddish speaking and unlikely to have obtained an education beyond a traditional Jewish *heder* (religious school). Their Judaism was also religiously traditional, comprising practices that eventually became defined as Orthodox.

The eastern Europeans arrived in the United States just as the nation was becoming a major industrial power requiring a significant number of factory workers and employees in smaller enterprises. The opportunity for work drew Jews to the centers of manufacturing and industry, concentrating in major cities throughout the Northeast and Midwest. Many entered the workforce as manual laborers with varying degrees of skill. With their experiences in small-scale business, they were well suited for positions in various industries (textiles and clothing being the foremost), and many assumed roles as small-scale entrepreneurs as well as workers in textile factories and workshops (Lederhendler 2009).

Having been denied anything beyond a rudimentary education in the lands of the czars, they wanted better for their children. Mary Antin (1912a, 53), arguably the most influential writer among the Russian Jewish immigrants from this period, noted how her father was transfixed by the free public schools available to his children:

Education was free. That subject my father had written about repeatedly, as comprising his chief hope for us children, the essence of American opportunity, the treasure that no thief could touch, not even misfortune or poverty. It was the one thing that he was able to promise us when he sent for us, surer, safer than bread or shelter.

Antin rejoiced to find in Boston's common schools "No application made, no questions asked, no examinations, rulings, exclusions; no machinations, no fees." Though making a living absorbed her father's energy, leaving no time for his own intellectual pursuits, he found vicarious satisfaction through his children's education and "would walk by proxy in the Elysian fields of liberal learning" (Antin 1912a, 59).

As migrants from "the heartland of Jewish nationalism and Jewish Orthodoxy" (Mendelsohn 1993, 49), eastern Europeans fueled the growth of American synagogues and Jewish political organizations in the late nineteenth and early twentieth centuries. Orthodox synagogues were established but without a strong right-wing political movement attached to them as in Poland and Russia (Mendelsohn 1993, 82). In the early years of immigration, the Jews from eastern Europe developed associations that were primarily mutual aid societies, often organized based on the immigrants' home towns (*landsmannschaften*), providing funds for burials, weddings, health insurance, and the other immediate needs of poor people not then the responsibility of government. As memorably sketched by Irving Howe in *World of Our Fathers* (1976), trade unions, fraternal orders, cultural programs, and a rich associational life developed in the Jewish areas of major urban centers.

The Russians from the third wave of mass immigration also brought with them a Yiddish culture that flourished for a time and a strong proclivity for left-wing politics, a reaction to their long experience as an oppressed people under czarist rule. The Russian Jews also provided the major American constituency for the Zionist movement that began at the tag end of the nineteenth century. Although conceived in western Europe by Theodore Herzl, an assimilated Viennese Jew, the idea of recreating a Jewish state in Palestine exerted its greatest appeal in the Pale and among the Russian Jewish immigrants. However, American Zionism in the main differed from its European variant in that it did not assume that Jews were a "national minority" in the United States who should prepare for emigration to Palestine. It was, Mendelsohn notes (1993, 58–62, 79, 132–139), something more akin to the ethnic nationalism of non-Jewish minorities such as the Irish and Poles devoted principally to providing aid and comfort to Jews elsewhere. (This topic is taken up in more detail in Chapter 7.)

Even though the passage of restrictive immigration laws in the 1920s did not completely shut the door for Jews seeking entry to the United

States, it significantly reduced the influx of newcomers who had accounted for the growth of the Jewish population throughout American history. The Johnson-Reed Act effectively denied entry to most Jews seeking refuge from the Nazis during the 1930s and 1940s but a significant number of survivors did manage to immigrate after World War II. In addition, between 1968 and 2000, an estimated 400,000 Jews made their way from Russia and the former Soviet Union to the United States (Cohen, Haberfeld, and Kogan 2011). Most arrived after 1989, when emigration restrictions were relaxed in Russia and the United States explicitly defined Russian Jews as refugees entitled to admission due to religious persecution (Rosenberg 2002). Despite these additions, the composition of American Jewry has changed only incrementally since the end of World War II.

As the third-wave immigrants and their children became accustomed to life in the United States, many achieved a measure of economic security and, particularly after their military service during World War II, took advantage of the opportunities provided by the GI Bill to obtain university education, postgraduate training, and inexpensive home mortgages. During the postwar era, they moved quickly into the middle class, suburbia, and the professions. In relatively short order, what had been a working-class population of modest means evolved into a middle-class community with better-than-average economic resources and a strong network of communal associations to meet their religious, social, and political needs (Goldscheider and Zuckerman 1984).

Some observers describe the period after World War II as a golden era when the American Jewish community came of age. Jews not only moved out of urban neighborhoods to the suburbs but, in time, fanned out across the United States. Jewish institutions like synagogues and community centers followed the population flows. Although the Jewish defense organizations inherited from earlier times persisted in their activities, Jews faced fewer hurdles to personal advancement and encountered less discrimination than in the past. They also became more publicly engaged in politics, both on their own behalf but also in support of various causes on the liberal agenda. Although they became more open about expressing their political interests in the post–World War II period, they did not stray far from the political culture that began to develop in the eighteenth century. As this book will show, the contemporary politics of American Jewry has continued to flow from the values and practices developed during the founding of the American Jewish community.

# 2

# Why American Jewish Politics Is Puzzling

American Jews earn like Episcopalians but vote like Puerto Ricans.
                                                    – Milton Himmelfarb

What is it about being rich and white that American Jews don't understand?
                                                    – Peter Sagal

To anyone who follows American politics closely, the attachment of Jews to the Democratic Party is hardly a revelation or state secret. When he considered opposing Israeli settlements in the West Bank in 1992, President George H. W. Bush worried about electoral retaliation from American Jews. His trusted adviser, James Baker, told Bush not to worry because "the Jews don't vote for us" – the "us" being Republicans (Gelb 1992). Popular culture in the form of Woody Allen's movies also conveys the message that Jewish politics "lean leftward" (Zeitz 2007, 39–40). The public seems to think so. According to a 2006 survey, more than twice as many American adults thought Jews were mainly Democrats rather than Republicans (41% to 18%), with the remaining third believing that they were evenly divided between the two parties (Campbell, Green, and Layman 2011, 45). Only the nonreligious were perceived to be more pro-Democratic.

As I noted briefly in the first chapter, American Jews' strong attachment to the Democratic Party in particular and liberalism in general constitutes an anomaly. The anomaly was nicely (if politically incorrectly) captured by the epigraphs at the beginning of this chapter. From a social scientific perspective, it makes no theoretical sense for most American Jews to vote as they do. Anomalies arise from conflicts between theory and the reality they are meant to explain. Scientific theories tell us that certain conditions are necessary and sufficient to produce a specific outcome. But sometimes we find outcomes *without* the conditions that theory tells us should cause them or we discover situations in which the conditions are in place but don't produce the expected outcome. That is precisely what seems to happen when American Jews cast their ballots. They have many of the social traits of Republican/conservative supporters but largely vote in a different manner and hold political views that tend to cluster on the left side of the ideological spectrum.

The first task of this chapter is to demonstrate the reality of the anomaly, first by showing the attachment of Jews to the Democratic Party, and then by using data to compare Jewish political behavior with the political choices of non-Jews who share the same social traits as Jews. The chapter then summarizes political science theories about voter choice, the conventional wisdom from which most American Jews routinely depart. Then it assesses the "Judaic" theories scholars have developed to try to account for the anomaly. I argue that these theories do not achieve their goals. Rather than explaining Jews' theoretically counterintuitive political behavior, they deepen the anomaly by generating two additional puzzles about American Jewish political behavior. This will set the stage for the introduction of an alternative theoretical approach to American Jewish political behavior in Chapter 3.

## JEWS ARE DEMOCRATS

In characterizing Jews as Democrats, I focus on partisanship because it is the best indicator of an individual's political identity and predicts to a high degree the political choices voters make and the issue attitudes they develop. That is why survey researchers routinely ask survey respondents whether they have forged a mental attachment to the Democrats, Republicans, or another political party. Even though many Americans claim to vote for the person and not the party, most readily identify with a political party.

In addition to a making a distinction between participants who say they identify with the Democrats or Republicans, these data also classify as partisans those respondents who said they were Independents but who acknowledged in a follow-up question that they "leaned" toward the Democrats or Republicans. Because many of these Independent leaners vote as if they were unalloyed partisans (Green, Palmquist, and Schickler

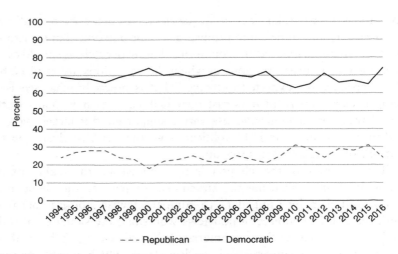

FIGURE 2.1 Party identification of Jewish registered voters, 1994–2016.
Source: Pew Research Center, "Party Identification Trends, 1992–2016," retrieved from: www.people-press.org/2016/09/13/party-identification-trends-1992–2016/#religion.

2002; Keith et al. 1992), I reserve the Independent label only for survey participants who do not lean toward either party.

From surveys of registered voters conducted by the Pew Research Center over the last twenty-three years, we see in Figure 2.1 just how disproportionately Jews identify with the Democrats. Over the last quarter-century, Jews have been two to three times as likely to identify with or lean toward the Democratic Party as the Republicans. Counting leaners, the Republican share of the Jewish electorate has never risen above 31 % and the Democratic share has never dropped below 63%. In absolute terms, the partisan identification gap between the two parties among Jews has been more than 40% and, occasionally, has reached or exceeded 50%. Jews are disproportionately Democratic in this fundamental indicator of political attachment.

In their strong identification with the Democrats, Jews differ strikingly from non-Jews. Figure 2.2 displays the level of identification with the Democratic Party exhibited by Jewish registered voters and the entire sample. In the twenty-three years that Pew has asked this question, Jews were on average 20% more Democratic than the entire population. Although the partisanship of both groups was relatively stable, the gap in Democratic identification between Jews and non-Jews sometimes

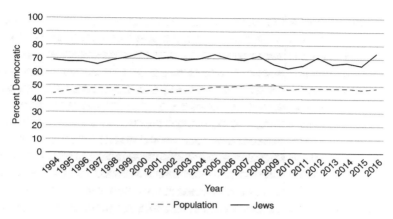

FIGURE 2.2 Democratic Party identification of Jews and the public as a whole, 1994–2016.
Source: Pew Research Center, "Party Identification Trends, 1992–2016." Retrieved from: www.people-press.org/2016/09/13/party-identification-trends-1992–2016/#religion.

dropped to 15% and rose to as high as 29%. Whatever number we choose, Jews have been much more inclined to call themselves Democrats than the rest of the population of registered voters for nearly the last quarter century.

Jews are not merely distinctive in partisanship but also constitute the most pro-Democratic white ethnoreligious constituency in the electorate. Figure 2.3 compares them to other ethnoreligious voting blocs using data from the Religious Landscape survey. Excluding African Americans, only three groups came close to or exceeded the level of Jewish identification with the Democratic Party: Hindus, Muslims, and Buddhists. Owing to the relatively small number of Hindus, Muslims, and Buddhists in the Religious Landscape study (as opposed to 847 Jews), we cannot be certain if these differences are due to sampling error. Compared to the large electoral blocs of Evangelical Protestants, Mainline Protestants, and Catholics, Jews stood out firmly in both their pro-Democratic skew and their low levels of identification with the Republican Party.

Among Jews, as among other voter groups, this cognitive partisanship translates into vote choice at election time. Figure 2.4 reports the Democratic share of the vote cast by Jews and by all voters in presidential elections from 1948 through 2008. The data for the first twenty years were reported by various private polls while the estimates from 1972 to 2008

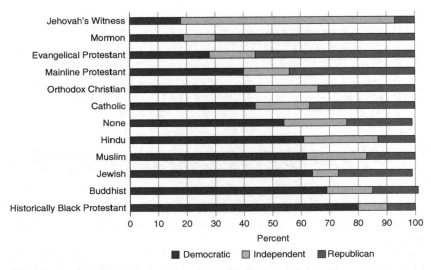

FIGURE 2.3 Party identification of adults in the United States by religion, 2014. Source: Party Affiliation by Religious Group from Pew Research Center, Religious Landscape Study (2014). Retrieved from: www.pewforum.org/religious-landscape-study/party-affiliation/.

are taken from the national exit polls conducted on Election Day by a consortium of news organizations. Because the exit poll data are the basis for vote projections on election night, they require massive samples in the tens of thousands. Until a change in design in 2010, these surveys had very large Jewish subsamples and thus are considered the gold standard for research on Jewish political behavior.[1]

Over the last sixty years, the pro-Democratic skew in voting among Jews was actually higher than we found for partisan identification among registered voters in Figures 2.1 and 2.2. Focusing on the two-party vote by removing third-party candidates who typically affected only a single election, the Democratic share of the Jewish vote over the last sixty-some years has ranged from a low of 60% to a high of 90%. Reaffirming the disproportionate nature of Jewish commitment to Democratic presidential candidates, the gap between Jews and other voters has been in the 20% to 30% range in most elections, always favoring the Democratic

---

[1] Apart from the large Jewish subsamples, the exit polls have the virtue of ensuring that the participants did in fact vote in the election. Interviewers are stationed in selecting polling stations and interview respondents selected by random processes. In more recent years, with early voting and more absentee ballots, the surveys have incorporated telephone surveys to access respondents who do not vote on Election Day.

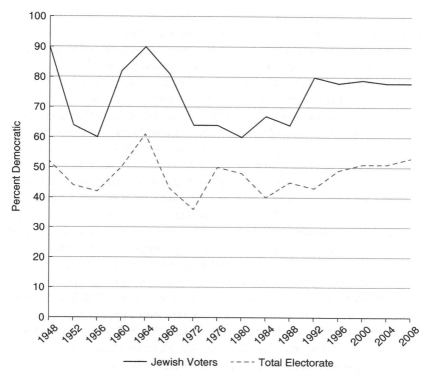

FIGURE 2.4 Self-reported presidential vote of Jews and the entire electorate, 1948–2008.
Source: Forman (2001, 153) for 1948–1968. Estimates for 1972–2008 are from the published results of national exit polls archived by the Roper Center.

nominee. We shouldn't be surprised by these results because self-described partisans and leaners typically vote for the party with which they identify.

## MEASURING THE ANOMALY

When compared to the general American population, as I noted in Chapter 1, Jews are older, and have higher rates of marriage and smaller families. They are disproportionately white and non-Hispanic. They are more likely to live in large urban and metropolitan areas and in the northeastern United States and to possess, on average, higher socioeconomic status as measured by formal education, occupational status, and income. These traits – not being Jewish per se – could account for the political differences we've observed between Jews and non-Jews. If Jews do hold the same political outlook as other Americans who share their social profile, there is no theoretical anomaly to explain.

To see if Jews truly deviate from the political patterns of people with the same social traits, I compare Jewish identification with the Democratic Party to the Democratic attachment of non-Jews who "look" like Jews. To accomplish this, I took two survey samples of American adults and matched them to corresponding samples of Jewish adults. That procedure generated samples of non-Jews who share a significant number of social, economic, and demographic traits with the Jewish population. I then compared the partisan distributions of Jews and the subset of matched non-Jews. Given the importance of these tests to the argument that Jewish political behavior is truly anomalous, I made the two tests somewhat different. Apart from drawing respondents from different surveys, I utilized the matching technique called propensity sampling in the first study and coarsened exact matching in the second study. The other differences were due to the datasets available to run the comparisons.

The first study looks at partisanship in the period from 1989 to 1994 using thirty-five surveys conducted for the *Roper Political Report*. Combining these surveys produced a dataset with approximately 69,000 survey respondents, of whom 2,279 selected "Jewish" when asked about their religious affiliation.[2] To select non-Jewish respondents from the dataset for comparison with Jews, the non-Jewish members of this dataset were matched to the Jewish members based on geography (state, region, city size, metropolitan residence), socioeconomic resources (employment, occupational status, education, income, labor union membership), demography (race, Hispanicity, household size, marital status, age, gender), and year of survey. There was an exceptionally close match, indicating that the two subsamples (Jews and matched non-Jews) were virtually indistinguishable on this vast array of background characteristics. Because the two surveys did not ask Independents the follow-up question about whether they leaned to one party or another, there are more nominal Independents in both the Jewish and non-Jewish matching samples.

The second study was derived from two surveys conducted by the Pew Research Center. A Jewish sample of approximately 5,000 was interviewed in 2013 for a special study of the American Jewish population and the matching non-Jews were selected from Pew's Religious Landscape survey of almost 40,000 participants in 2014.[3] In addition to socioeconomic

---

[2] These data were previously reported in Wald (2014).
[3] I deleted the Jewish respondents who were surveyed in the Religious Landscape study.

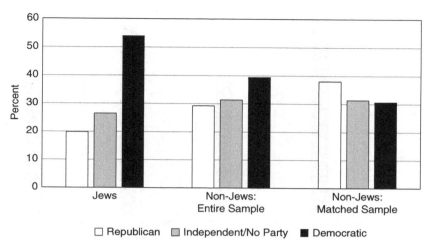

FIGURE 2.5 Party identification of Jews, all non-Jews, and non-Jews from a matched sample.
Source: Calculated from Roper Political Reports as described in Wald (2015), 8–9. There were 2,279 Jewish respondents, 66,573 non-Jews in the entire sample, and 2,279 non-Jews in the matched sample.

resources (education, income) and demography (race, Hispanicity, household size as a child and adult, marital status, age, gender, principal language, region), respondents were further matched on whether they were born in the United States and their voter registration status. Because there were significantly fewer non-Jewish respondents per Jewish respondent than in study 1, I could match only about two-thirds of the Jewish respondents with equivalent non-Jews. Nonetheless, the two populations used for the analysis were very much equivalent based on the standard tests of sample balance and, with more than 3,000 respondents in each sample, more than adequate to make a comparison. Because the Pew surveys asked self-described Independents if they leaned toward either of the major parties, the dependent variable is more nuanced than the partisanship question in study 1.

Figure 2.5 displays the party attachment of Jews and non-Jews from study 1. The first and second sets of bars compare Jews to *all* non-Jews in the sample. By looking at the first and third sets of bars, we compare the Jews only to the matched sample of non-Jews chosen for their similarity to the Jewish participants. (Because all Jews were successfully matched, their partisanship does not change.) Compared to the entire non-Jewish subsample, Jews were "only" 14.4% more Democratic in party identification.

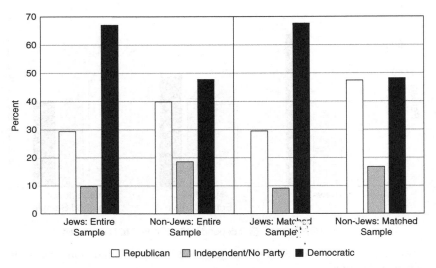

FIGURE 2.6 Party identification of Jews, all non-Jews, and non-Jews from a matched sample.
Source: Pew Research Center: *Religious Landscape Study* (2014); *Portrait of Jewish Americans* (2013). There were 5,132 Jews and 34,070 non-Jews in the entire sample. The two groups in the matched sample each numbered 3,217.

But when the comparison was narrowed to non-Jews who most closely resembled Jews, the pro-Democratic gap in Jewish partisanship *increased* to 23.2% and the percentage of Jewish Republicans was only half that of the selected non-Jews. Looking only at declared partisans, the pro-Democratic gap between Jews and their sociologically equivalent non-Jews grew to a chasm of more than 40%. The differences might have been even greater had the Roper organization used a question about partisan identification that separated out the Independents who leaned to one of the parties. Nonetheless, it's clear that Jews don't exhibit the same partisanship as other Americans who are, in the main, very much like them in all but religion.

Study 2 (see Figure 2.6), which used a different measure of partisanship, yielded patterns quite like those observed more than twenty years earlier in study 1. Comparing Jews surveyed in 2013 to all non-Jews in the 2014 Religious Landscape Study, Jews were 18% more Democratic and 11% less Republican, for a 29% gap in partisan identification. When Jews were contrasted with the matched non-Jews, the gap grew even wider.

Jews were 15% less Republican and 19% more Democratic for a total gap of 34% in favor of the Democrats.

Even with controls for differences in demography, socioeconomic resources, and other traits commonly linked to political behavior, Jews in both studies tilted appreciably more to the Democratic side of the party spectrum than other Americans of comparable backgrounds. Respondents with high levels of education, income, occupational status, and other specific traits are much more Republican than other respondents – unless they are Jews. These remarkable findings tell us that the partisan gap between Jews and non-Jews *increases* when Jews are compared to the non-Jews who most resemble them in social background (defined broadly). Jews are not merely *distinctive* in their partisanship; they are *anomalous*. The next section makes clear why this behavior is puzzling.

## VOTING AS RATIONAL CHOICE

Theories of rational political behavior predict that Jews will embrace the Republican Party and political conservatism. This is not a philosophical position but a deduction from the assumptions that underlie voting behavior research. As we just saw, non-Jews who shared the social and demographic characteristics of Jews were in fact more Republican than the entire electorate. That is what theories of rational voting behavior lead us to expect.

W. G. Runciman (1969, 94) once expressed concisely the central idea behind the dominant theory of voting when he insisted that "nothing needs to be explained about a South Wales miner voting Labour or a General Motors executive voting Republican" beyond the "simplest model of rational self-interest." He assumed that voters chose the party that offered them the best chance of securing their preferred policy outcomes. For political scientists who pioneered this approach, self-interest was largely driven by social class and economic benefits, making elections "the democratic expression of class struggle" (Anderson and Davidson 1943; Lipset 1960, chapter 7).

In the United States, political parties have offered incentives aimed at different segments of the electorate. The Democrats have historically represented the working class and lower middle class by promoting policies that favored trade unions, social welfare programs, unemployment assistance, public schools, and a progressive tax system. They have usually been rewarded with the plurality of votes cast by the working class, trade unionists, and their allies. More attentive to the needs of business and corporations, the Republicans have mostly resisted government regulation of business, and preferred lower taxes on corporations and income taxes that were not so steeply graduated. Republican candidates have routinely done better among business owners, managers, white collar workers, and upper-income voters in general.[4]

The world is always more complex than scientific models and it became apparent in the 1970s and beyond that these patterns had begun to change. Scholars are now divided between those who maintain that social class remains central to party alignments and voter choices and others who contend that class differences in voting have weakened appreciably, replaced by new lines of conflict based on race, culture, religion, and other forces. Many scholars take the middle ground, acknowledging the rise of partisan conflict and voter cleavages based on cultural issues but insisting that social class still drives voter choice, sometimes directly, sometimes indirectly (Evans 2000). Income rather than occupation has increasingly become a primary driver of voting choice, which may explain why occupational differences matter less in party choice (Van Der Waal, Achterberg, and Houtman 2007). Considering the strong ties between various indicators of social class and party identification/vote choice, the evidence suggests to me that economic differences still matter enormously in the electoral choices made by individual American voters and that the two major parties are still defined in large measure by their economic differences (Bartels 2008; Hout, Brooks, and Manza 1995; Stonecash 2000).

The political behavior of most groups is consistent with a class voting model. Over time, as they move up the economic ladder, voters usually move away from the Democrats and toward the Republicans. The New Deal, the Democratic response to the Great Depression in the 1930s, moved working-class constituencies such as white Southern Evangelical Protestants and Roman Catholics more firmly into the Democratic coalition and sharpened class differences in voting across the electorate (Shively 1971). Following World War II, legislation such as the GI Bill, federal guarantees for home mortgages, and various antidiscrimination laws helped move sizable numbers of Jews, Catholics, and white Evangelical Protestants into the middle class.

---

[4] Despite commentaries that suggest the parties flipped their electoral bases in 2016, the evidence suggests that the usual class divisions in presidential voting were apparent. See analyses by Carnes and Lupu (2017), Manza and Crowley (2017), and Silver (2016).

Beginning with the post–New Deal era of the 1960s, the patterns shifted in accord with expectations that affluence would reduce attachment to the Democrats over the long run. With new jobs, residences, neighborhoods, and opportunities, Roman Catholics followed the predictions of the model by falling away from the Democratic Party to a more centrist position on the political spectrum. Jews did not follow suit (Wald 2006), explaining why they are still seen as politically anomalous.

The failure of Jews to move permanently into the Republican Party en masse after the 1960s was not due to a lack of effort to change their partisanship. The assumption that Jews should vote their economic interests by supporting Republicans gained a public voice from the Neoconservative movement in the 1970s (Friedman 2005). Led by Jewish intellectuals who described themselves as former liberals who had been "mugged by reality," the Neocons (as they became known) argued that it was long past time for Jews to abandon the Democratic Party. According to the movement's intellectual leaders, Jews needed to start voting based on rational self-interest: This meant switching over to the GOP, which was more in tune with Jewish economic needs and foreign policy priorities.

Despite these efforts, the Neocons appeared to fade away much more rapidly than Jewish Democrats. One of the movement's founders, Norman Podhoretz (2009), expressed his frustration at the durability of the Jewish attachment to liberalism in a book described by one reviewer as a "document of his bewilderment ... that his brethren are not more like himself" but persist in their political errors because of "willful blindness and denial" (Wieseltier 2009). Social scientists have offered other theories about the Democratic preponderance among Jews. Though unsatisfactory in several respects as I will document in the text that follows, these alternatives do not treat American Jewish political behavior as a form of mental illness but as a challenge to be addressed with social theory.

## SOURCES OF JEWISH LIBERALISM: JUDAIC THEORIES

The durability of the Jewish/liberal/Democratic alignment has stimulated a cottage industry churning out theories to explain why most Jews in the United States still approach politics from a liberal/Democratic perspective. After summarizing those theories, I conclude that (1) they do not fully explain the puzzle of American Jewish liberalism, and (2) they actually deepen the anomaly of Jewish attachment to the Democratic Party by identifying two new puzzles.

In trying to account for American Jewish attachment to liberalism and the Democratic Party, scholars have mostly developed what I describe as "Judaic" explanations. The theories are "Judaic" in the sense that they locate the source of Jewish political liberalism in the distinctive experiences and culture of Judaism. Specifically, they contend that the religious values of Judaism, the historical experience of Jewish emancipation, and Jews' persistent minority status contribute to Jewish affinity with a left-liberal political outlook. These causal factors (apart from religious values) may not be intrinsic to Judaism but have become central to the Jewish experience because of historical circumstances. They are, in effect, the inheritance of Jews, even those far removed in time and place from the direct encounters that produced these orientations. I will first summarize and then offer brief critiques of each approach before identifying the common weaknesses they share.

## Values

In his pioneering research on Jewish political behavior, Lawrence Fuchs (1956) argued that Judaism had embedded within its theology specific values that translated well into the language of liberal politics. He emphasized three values in the Jewish tradition: learning (Torah), charity (*Tzedakah*), and, in what he acknowledged was an awkward label, nonasceticism, the belief that living a good life includes sensual pleasures that are not sinful by nature (178). While these values are not expressed only by Jews, he found that they were "more valued by most Jews than by most non-Jews" (184).

Charity, concern for the widow and orphan in the language of the Hebrew Bible, seemed to call for public programs to assist people in need, a welfare state in the language of modern liberalism. Jews reacted positively to many proposed public programs during the New Deal, he further explained, not only because the Depression had made their economic situation so dire but because their religious tradition emphasized communal responsibility for the poor. Beyond need, Jews' veneration of education, the professions, and intellectuality conferred legitimacy on plans hatched by credentialed experts. That many of the experts who designed New Deal programs were Jews, mostly New Yorkers with lengthy experience in government, no doubt added to the respect that Jews felt for these initiatives.

Fuchs argued further that the idea that life's pleasures are divine gifts to be enjoyed rather than feared tends to make Jews relatively more accepting of alcohol use and less censorious of behavior that other religious traditions regard as morally problematic. But more than that, the non-ascetic perspective means that Jews are particularly concerned with ensuring that individuals experience good lives and they see no positive virtue in deprivation. By emphasizing life in the here and now, not postponing the good life until heaven, Jews give priority to building a good society that addresses human social needs. Hence, Fuchs avers, Judaism is comfortable with liberalism because liberalism is compatible with deeply held Jewish religious values. This may well be the most common explanation of Jewish liberalism and why many Jews believe that liberalism is simply applied Judaism.

### The Heritage of Emancipation

Historical theories of Jewish liberalism emphasize the way Jews made sense of the political environment during the period of European Jewish emancipation from the late eighteenth through the early twentieth centuries. Emancipation meant that Jews were incorporated as citizens by the state. Jew were to be governed not by their own religious institutions, as in the ancient and medieval periods, but by the same political-legal system as every other resident. Most Jews relished the opportunity to expand their horizons by leaving the ghetto, both real and metaphorical, as full participants of the societies in which they lived.

The battles over the admission of Jews to citizenship, it has been suggested, left an impression on their subsequent political thinking. In most places, Jewish emancipation was resisted by the state church, the monarchy, big business, the craft guilds, the military, and other defenders of the social order who had opposed the Enlightenment. These opponents invoked different reasons for resisting emancipation: Jewish responsibility for the death of Jesus, fear of competition from Jewish businesses, and concerns to maintain the religious and ethnic purity of the state. By contrast, the advocates of Jewish inclusion were mostly liberals, socialists, journalists, trade unionists, and other supporters of social changes introduced by the Enlightenment. Some embraced the expansion of citizenship as a matter of justice while others, it is important to acknowledge, felt that Jewish exposure to modernity would hasten the collapse of what they saw as an outmoded and inferior religion. Even if they supported emancipation for the wrong reasons, Gentile critics of traditional Judaism were allies in a common cause.

From this experience, Jews learned that their friends were on the left side of the political spectrum, their opponents on the right. When European Jews traveled across the Atlantic to the United States or went elsewhere, they carried with them in their cognitive baggage a tendency to perceive the political system through a European political lens (Sorin 1985). Their natural political home was on the left, it was assumed, while the political right was thought to teem with anti-Semites and others who wanted to maintain Christian dominance in America. That tendency persists today, it has been claimed, in the visceral tendency of American Jews to favor more liberal movements and parties over their conservative alternatives.[5]

### Trauma

Social marginality theory, the final category of explanations for the left-wing disposition of Jews, stresses the political consequence of Jews' minority status in most societies. Jews have reached the highest levels of politics, business, education, and other fields in the United States and other advanced societies. These theories postulate that despite their elevated status, the Jewish experience of persecution prevents them from taking their security for granted. Memories of historical traumas involving forced dislocations, banishment, and genocide were too recent and intense to be overlooked or forgotten. The case of Germany was instructive. Throughout the nineteenth century, many Jews had perceived Germany as the European society most open to Jews and even spoken of a Jewish-German synthesis. Yet Germany quickly turned on them in the 1930s, embracing a genocidal movement that destroyed the German Jewish community. This experience profoundly reinforced the sense that Jewish security was always at risk and they needed to be ever watchful for threats to it.

Despite their successes in the United States, scholars have noted, Jews have been prone to exhibit social *in*security, perceiving themselves not as a powerful group but as a beleaguered minority, subject to discrimination

---

[5] In a 2000 survey on "Jews in the Public Square," a third of Jewish respondents indicated that they thought most or many conservatives were anti-Semitic. Only seven percent held the same view of liberals. With regard to the Republican Party, a quarter of Jews considered most or many of its members anti-Semitic but only 5% held the same view of Democrats. Recall that these data were collected after years of conflict between blacks and Jews involving affirmative action, Jesse Jackson, and other flashpoints and following decades of efforts by the GOP to promote its support for Israel. See Cohen (2000b), 13–14.

and lacking safeguards against external attack. Studies of American Jews' perceptions of anti-Semitism reveal high levels of concern given the reality of Jewish success and integration since the 1960s. In the American Jewish Committee's annual survey of Jewish opinion between 2010 and 2017, more than 80% of respondents typically described anti-Semitism as a problem in the United States. On average, a quarter of participants deemed it a serious or very serious problem. Data such as these seemed to confirm the quip attributed to Abba Eban, Israel's foreign minister, that American Jews are a group "that can't take yes for an answer."

Given this perception, American Jews thus were prone to make common cause with other minority groups that bore the same burden, finding common interests in policies that prevented discrimination and aimed to ensure equal treatment. For at least the last third of the twentieth century onward, such theories suggest, Jews have found a strong commitment to maintaining an inclusive, pluralist society in the policies of the Democratic Party.

Kaufman Kohler, an influential Reform rabbi of congregations in Chicago and New York, perfectly captured the venerable idea that Jewish liberalism grows out of the rigors and tragedies of Jewish life. In a 1908 sermon, he puzzled over why American Jews seemed so politically progressive, so ready to enlist in every cause to ameliorate the condition of the masses. In the end, he argued,

It required all the grinding powers of Egyptian bondage, of Canaanite subjection, of Assyrian and Babylonian tyranny, of Syrian and Roman oppression, of mediaeval persecution and Church fanaticism, of barbarism and cruelty in all the lands of Christendom to make the Jew the bold and persistent champion of truth and of righteousness, the lover of liberty and the advocate of true Humanity.

Through these experiences, Jews could "feel what inhumanity means" and were thus prompted to be "broad-minded and large-hearted" when they encountered intolerance toward others (Kohler 1908).

This framework has been widely used to explain cooperation between Jews and African Americans during the civil rights era in the United States (Greenberg 2006). Of all white ethnoreligious groups, Jews were the most consistent allies in the drive to secure constitutional rights for black Americans. Jewish elites were actively involved along with blacks in founding the NAACP, the primary civil rights organization at the national level, and Jews were also among the Rev. Martin Luther King's closest advisers in the Southern Christian Leadership Conference. Young Jews were massively overrepresented among the white college students who went south for the Mississippi Freedom Summer in 1964 and two became martyrs to the cause (Schultz 2001). Jews could also be found active in many local campaigns to abolish discriminatory practices based on race (Moore 1994, chapters 6 and 7). Whether attempting to pass national civil rights legislation or defend black rights through lawsuits and direct action, the civil rights movement rarely lacked for Jewish participation.

Jews commonly explained their attraction to the movement for black liberation in terms of their own history as a persecuted people and their feeling of obligation to help another community in distress. Naturally, the real world was more complex than this: Some southern Jews did not speak out against segregation for fear of endangering themselves while Jews elsewhere were known to have discriminated against blacks in housing, employment, and other fields. As we will see in Chapter 8, bitter conflicts later broke out between blacks and Jews over jobs in public education in New York City and then over the program known as affirmative action. Jews also had an instrumental interest in expanding legal protection against discrimination for their own benefit. When the civil rights movement entered its black power phase in the late 1960s, many Jews were made to feel unwelcome and left the movement. Nonetheless, they maintained a belief that the fates of Jews and blacks were intertwined owing to their common minority status (Glaser 1997).

Such are the major Judaic explanations for the puzzle of American Jewish political liberalism. From the perspective of these theories, religious values, historical experience, and a sense of minority vulnerability appear to override narrow economic interests, disposing Jews to favor the more liberal of the two major political parties.

### CRITIQUING JUDAIC THEORIES

Each of these theories contains elements of truth but also suffers from weaknesses that undermine its capacity to explain American Jewish political behavior.

Critics of the *values theory* warn that drawing a "straight line" between Jewish religious tenets and liberal politics involves both "selective reading and considerable historical amnesia" (Barnett 2016, 246). Consider how advocates of what is called prophetic Judaism read the Hebrew Bible. They cite passages that give principal emphasis to (or foreground, in social science jargon) attacks on rulers and the wealthy who fail to promote social justice but tend to deemphasize (background) those strands of Jewish religious thought that uphold traditional sexual mores, complementary gender roles, and the idea that Jewish exile from the homeland resulted from sinful behavior.[6] By contrast, those who often describe themselves as advocates of traditional Judaism call attention to the conservative social norms they perceive in Judaism while interpreting social justice in a much more individualist manner.

The richness of Jewish scriptures and teachings, like other religious traditions, can support a wide range of political viewpoints on virtually any public issue. Given the tradition of argumentation and debate woven into Jewish theology over two millennia and the lack of political sovereignty among Jews for centuries, it may be impossible altogether to discern *any* clear and unambiguous political norms embedded in Judaism (Leibowitz 1992; Susser 1981). In the case of ideology, Jews creatively construct religious laws that reinforce their preferred social-political values.

The *historical argument* that Jews approach American politics based on their experiences of emancipation in Europe is harder to sustain as time passes. The scholarly literature on partisan alignments demonstrates convincingly that long-established party cleavages erode over time unless they are reinforced by new political developments (Beck 1979). In the post–New Deal era, such strongly Democratic constituencies as Roman Catholics, evangelical Protestants, and trade unionists moved away from the Democratic Party and mainline Protestants, once the core of the Republican coalition, shifted toward a more centrist position. African Americans shifted their partisan loyalty to the Democrats in response to changes in their circumstances and in the cues transmitted by political parties during the civil rights struggle. They largely abandoned the party of Lincoln for the party of Kennedy and Johnson. Advocates of the historical argument cannot explain convincingly why Jews alone remained Democratic in their political orientations.

Even if the Jewish experience of persecution left them unsure of their social standing, as *minority theories* posit, there is no guarantee that Jews would respond to social insecurity by joining other out-groups. They might have followed the example of many Roman Catholics, long a persecuted community in the United States, who reacted to aspersions on their national loyalty by embracing right-wing causes to establish their American bona fides. Rather than joining other beleaguered groups in

---

[6] This process is not unique to American Jews. Jews in India similarly emphasized certain aspects of Judaism that would make it seem more compatible with Hindu norms and gave less emphasis to other aspects of the tradition (Katz 1996).

a coalition of outcasts, they tried to claim common interests with Protestants by displaying patriotic exuberance. During the era of the Vietnam War, Jews largely opposed the American military effort while Catholics supported it for most of the period.

These examples call into question whether the various theories of American Jewish liberalism do indeed address the central puzzle they purport to solve, why Jews tend to liberalism when their social traits should incline them to conservatism. Apart from these theory-specific criticisms, I have a more fundamental criticism that applies to all three types of explanation. The Judaic theories share an implicit assumption that generates additional puzzles about Jewish political behavior.

The causal factors identified by the major Judaic theories – religious values, historical experience, and minority status – are the common property of most Jews around the world, not the exclusive property of American Jewry. Jews elsewhere share a common religious tradition; draw on memories of communal discrimination, repression, and violence; and, Israel excepted, live as a small minority amidst a larger population. *If those traits promoted a liberal political outlook, as Judaic theories argue, we should see no major difference between Jewish politics in different countries nor any volatility in the Jewish embrace of liberalism.* But we do. Theories that are static in terms of time and place can explain neither why American Jews have varied in the consistency of their liberalism and partisan attachment over time nor why the American Jewish community (but no other national Jewish community) is found today on the left side of its nation's political spectrum.

Concerning the problem of time, Figure 2.4 revealed significant oscillations in the degree to which American Jews embraced the Democratic Party in the post–World War II era. Jewish support for the Democratic Party was overwhelming in the 1940s and 1950s, dipped down to a two-to-one ratio in the late 1960s, and returned to a three-to-one ratio of Democrats to Republicans in 1990 and thereafter. Even in just the exit poll era from 1972 to 1908, Figure 2.4 confirms, there were notable differences in support for the Democrats across elections.[7] During the first five elections from 1972 to 1988, the Democratic share of the two-party vote varied around an average of 65%. That same indicator shot up to an average of 81% from 1992 to 2008 when the lowest share of Jewish

---

[7] Mellman, Strauss, and Wald (2012, 27–28) corrected the exit poll data on Jewish voting by weighting Jewish respondents based on their geographic distribution. The averages reported in this paragraph use those corrected figures.

vote for the Democrats was significantly higher than its best showing in the earlier period. Jewish religious values, historical experience, and minority status were essentially constant over these years so they cannot account for the observed political volatility.

The puzzle of place, the divergence in political attitudes between Jews in the United States and elsewhere, also complicates Judaic theories. French Jews remain in the center of their political spectrum, supporting moderate parties of the right, center, and left (Greilsammer 1978; Schnapper, Bordes-Benayoun, and Raphaël 2010) while Canadian Jews, who once tended toward center-left preferences (Laponce 1988), moved decisively to the right for a time but appear to have moved back toward the center in the most recent general election.[8] Even with the movement toward the left in the most recent Canadian election, the Jewish community remains more identified with the conservative party. South African Jews are largely center-right while Jews in Britain, who once tended to divide their votes in a manner comparable to the general population (Kotler-Berkowitz 2002), have now swung decisively against the Labor Party. In the 2017 parliamentary election, when the Labor Party was accused of harboring anti-Semites who belittled the Holocaust and denounced Israel as a genocidal state, exit polls indicated Jewish voters were two and a half times more likely to vote for the Conservative party than for Labour (Clements 2017). Australian Jews have been disproportionately on the right for several decades (Rubinstein 1982). In none of these countries do we find anything comparable to the American Jewish pattern of a largely left-wing political orientation yet the Jewish populations in these polities inherited similar religious values, historical experience, and minority status as American Jews.

In distinguishing American Jews politically from their counterparts in other countries, I recognize that to be on the left or right in the United States does not necessarily mean holding the same issue preferences as left- or right-wing voters in other countries. Each nation has its own political spectrum where terms like "left" and "right" denote different issues and concerns. For example, viewing provision of health insurance as a right

---

[8] An exit survey of Canadian voters by IPSOS-Reid found that Jewish voters were virtually tied in their support for the Conservative and Liberal parties in 2015. The roughly two-to-one margin favoring the Conservatives over the Liberals in 2011 disappeared as the gap between the parties shriveled in 2015. Across the three general elections from 2008 to 2015, the Conservative–Liberal percentage gap went from −14% in 2008 to +21% in 2011 and then to barely 3% in 2015. I analyzed the data from the Ipsos Canada Election Surveys Dataverse at https://dataverse.scholarsportal.info/dataverse/Ipsos_elections.

rather than a privilege does not divide parties elsewhere to the same degree that it polarizes Democrats and Republicans in the United States. Perhaps a French Jew voting for a centrist party might be politically like an American Jew who supports the Democratic Party.

Such a criticism might have gained traction in the past when scholars emphasized the nonideological nature of American political life. That claim no longer holds much water with the heightened ideological polarization now displayed in the United States. Owing to elite and mass polarization and the apparent "partisan sorting" of citizens based on ideology, scholars now stress the growing ideological distance apparent in both Congressional and presidential voting behavior since 1980 (Wood and Jordan 2017, 263–299). Based on cross-national analysis of party platforms, American parties are now ideologically polarized to the same degree as parties in most European countries (Jansen, Evans, and De Graaf 2013, 380–382). In any case, people can respond only to the partisan spectrum available to them and the relative placement of an individual on the party/ideological spectrum remains an important statement about political choice.

We thus have two new puzzles to join the core anomaly of American Jews voting Democratic despite their Republican traits: Why are American Jews politically different from their counterparts in other countries? And why have American Jews exhibited short-term volatility in their preference for the Democratic Party and liberal policies?

These ancillary puzzles have arisen, I suggest, because scholars have framed the question inappropriately. Rather than asking why American Jews are politically liberal and then invoking static theories that take account neither of space nor time, we should try to identify factors unique to the United States that make Jews so politically different from comparable Americans *and* from Jews in other countries. Chapter 3 begins that task by offering the theoretical approaches that will be further developed in subsequent chapters.

# 3

# How Is America Different?

It is that influence of environment that nationalizes the Jew everywhere, and nowhere in so marked a degree as in the United States.
– Jacob Voorsanger, "Influence of Americanism," 1906 (p. 187)

The law of adaptation which lends every part of the globe with its mineral and plant, beast and man, its distinctive local coloring, works in a most eminent degree also upon the Jew.
– Kaufmann Kohler, "The Three Elements of American Judaism," 1888 (p. 315)

We must understand American Jewry in terms of its difference from other, and specifically from Continental, Jewries.
– Ben Halpern, *The American Jew*, 1956 (p. 44)

Judaism is not an independent variable; it is subject to the pressure of national stimuli.
– Stephen Whitfield, "Paradoxes of Jewish Survival," 1993 (p. 92)

Judaic theories do not account for the central puzzle of American Jewish liberalism nor explain why American Jews are politically different from Jews elsewhere or why their attachment to liberalism fluctuates from time to time. The theoretically anomalous link between American Jews and the Democratic Party and liberalism thus requires a new or revised theory. To begin to address those issues, I offer a model that explains this behavior in terms of the social and political conditions that Jews have faced in the United States. I argue that American Jews are politically different from Jews in other societies because they are *American* Jews.

My approach emphasizes how contextual factors shaped the meaning of citizenship in the Jewish experience and contributed to the way Jews in the United States perceived their political interests. There is no doubt that American Jews did bring with them to the United States important values, historical memories, and dispositions because of their experiences living as a besieged minority in other lands. But those factors cohered into a durable liberal political ethic only because they interacted with specific features of the American political system.

I am certainly not alone in arguing that Jews in the United States have experienced a unique environment, qualitatively different both from the places Jews lived in the past and even from most other democratic societies today. The epigraphs at the beginning of the chapter show us that Jews have said as much, repeatedly, over the centuries. So, too, have scholars of American Judaism, producing what one scholar referred to an "enduring cult" of American Jewish exceptionalism (Loeffler 2015a, 372).[1] For the purposes of this inquiry about political behavior, the perceptions of American Jews matter more than the accuracy of their assumptions. Whether the United States was a "post-emancipation" society or not – an open question (Sorkin 2010) – Jews certainly acted as if that was the case.

We thus need to investigate how this (perceived) environment matters politically for American Jews. That means asking about how the American environment (as Jews have understood it) makes American Jews different politically and different from whom. Answering those questions requires not just acknowledging that American Jews are different, where most scholars have ended their analysis, but adopting a comparative approach to explain it. To do so, I draw on three bodies of social scientific theory: contextual analysis, the political process model, and social identity theory (which will be more fully explained in subsequent chapters). Each of these theories will help us understand the attraction of liberalism – and, in time, Democratic partisanship – to the American Jewish community and how they produced a political culture that has sustained Jewish political distinctiveness.

---

[1] For a critique of American Jewish exceptionalism, see Michels (2010). There has been a broader challenge to the very notion of exceptionalism. Invoking what is known as "critical theory," some scholars have portrayed American exceptionalism not as an observation that may be true or false but as a doctrine that has been used to justify and/ or rationalize the actions of the state (Pease 2009). Perhaps so, but social scientists have long recognized that people will act on their beliefs whether those beliefs are true or not.

## POLITICAL CONTEXT

In studying the influence of the social environment on political attitudes and behavior, political scientists embrace a key assumption: Politics is strongly influenced by context (Eagles 1995; Zuckerman 2005). Much as biologists have determined that environmental conditions may switch genes on or off, political scientists have discovered that political tendencies may be amplified or muted by the conditions in which individuals live, work, and pray. If we narrow this down to the kinds of places that matter for politics, the operative social context for an individual may be family, school, workplace, social network, secondary organization, or a geographic area such as a neighborhood, city, county, state, region, or nation. These various social environments have the capacity to shape individuals' political and social behavior in diverse domains even when personal traits are accounted for in the analysis.

The contextual approach rejects the notion that people are atomized units whose behavior is determined solely by their individual traits; rather, it argues that human beings are enmeshed in social environments that leave a strong imprint on their values and actions (Barton 1968). Although contextual theory has a link to the German sociologist George Simmel's work on the "web of affiliations" that surround individuals in society, the approach is more commonly associated with French sociologist Emile Durkheim. In his famous 1897 book, *Suicide*, Durkheim contended that the act of taking one's own life was not simply a consequence of individual volition but a reflection of the influence of social groups on the self.

Durkheim compared the suicide rates of three religious groups in the nineteenth century based mostly on European social statistics. Looking within and across societies, he found that suicide rates were lowest for Jews, higher among Roman Catholics, and highest of all for Protestants. Because all three religions treated suicide as sinful behavior that carried divine sanctions, the content of religious belief could not explain the group differences. Rather, he argued, the variations reflected the level of social integration that characterized each religious community (see also White 1968).

Owing in large part to a history of discrimination that forced Jews to rely on one another, European Jewish communities were tightly bound social systems with extremely high levels of solidarity. Leaving that community by choice – whether by conversion, apostasy, or suicide – violated the communal norm to an extreme degree and amounted to desertion. At the other extreme, Durkheim viewed Protestantism as a religion that granted individuals a very high level of free inquiry and structural independence from the group. Giving individuals the power to read Scripture first-hand encouraged a tradition of schism that greatly undermined the role of religious authority. In Durkheim's words (2005 [1897] 114), "the greater concessions a confessional group makes to individual judgment, the less it dominates lives, the less its cohesion and vitality." With low levels of religious integration, individuals felt freer to engage in nonnormative behavior such as self-termination. Roman Catholicism stood midway between the two extremes. Compared to Protestantism, Catholicism developed a more centralized system of religious authority that restrained theological deviations and tried to surround individuals with Catholic culture and institutions. Hence Catholicism was more central to the lives of its adherents than Protestantism but could not match the degree to which Jewish communities regulated behavior via comprehensive religious law and strong communal institutions.

Political scientists are not much interested in suicide, yet they found Durkheim's logic helped explain individual differences in political attitudes and behavior. Early contextual studies showed, for example, that industrial workers who lived in homogeneous working-class neighborhoods were much more likely to support socialist parties than their peers who lived in mixed-class areas (Tingsten 1937). The author assumed that the residents of single-class areas were more integrated into working-class norms than the latter and hence were more likely to support workers parties committed to socialism. V. O. Key famously discovered that whites who lived near African Americans in the Southern "Black Belt" were more responsive to political candidates making racist appeals than whites who lived elsewhere (Key 1949). By the logic of contextual theory, the norm of white supremacy would be stronger among whites who faced proximate "threats" (as they saw it) in their immediate environment than among whites insulated by distance from minority populations. The former would exhibit more racial solidarity than the latter.

At its core, then, contextual theory asserts that place matters (McDaniel 2014; Therborn 2006). "Place" can refer to a specific, delineated piece of land or to a social environment saturated with distinctive ideas, cultural values, and history (Goodin and Tilly 2006). Using "place" in both the narrow (geographic locale) and broad (climate of ideas) sense, I compare and contrast the political behavior of (1) Jews in the United States and elsewhere and (2) Jews and non-Jews in the United States. In the first or "external" comparison, I study national differences rooted in geography.[2] We should not be surprised, then, if American Jews are responsive to the cues, values, and appeals they hear in their environment, the United States, nor that they have differed politically from their coreligionists in other places and times.[3] Although the two groups being assessed in the second or "internal" comparison seemingly inhabit the same physical space, they differ in the culture that defines their understanding of the American political system. Conceptually, they occupy different "containers" that structure political reactions. Both sets of distinctions will help us understand the peculiar way American Jews act in the political realm.

Accordingly, I emphasize the importance of the American context in the evolution of Jewish politics in the United States. The gist of the argument is that American Jews found in the United States an environment that, having broken the link between religion and citizenship, gave Jews not just religious freedom but also full access to public life. Their inclusion as citizens with rights enforced by law provided the foundation on which Jews could achieve success and social integration to an extent unparalleled in the Jewish experience of diaspora. The political system itself provides the foundation of American Jewish liberalism. It has pushed American Jews in different political directions than Jews in other countries *and* their fellow citizens in the United States. Occasionally, it has even driven American Jews apart from one another.

Although many scholars of American Jewry have acknowledged the power of context in the abstract, few have examined the mechanisms that contributed to and sustained American Jewish political culture. Rather than speaking generically about their attraction to liberalism, I will dig deeply into the way Jews have understood their place in the United States through the concept of citizenship and the meaning of a secular state. How did liberalism manifest itself when American Jews confronted specific issues on the political agenda? Did it have the same meaning in domestic and international affairs? How did they manage to maintain their political culture when it was confronted by growing demands for Jewish peoplehood that seemed to emphasize illiberal policies? By examining such questions, I will be able to offer a revised take on the anomalous political behavior of American Jewry.

---

[2] I flip the definition of these two types of comparison from Endelman (1997, 1) because they make more intuitive sense to me that way.

[3] For earlier (implicit) contextual approaches to Judaism, see Diner (1994), Hyman (1992), and Mendelsohn (1993). The most explicit model is Endelman (1997).

## POLITICAL OPPORTUNITY STRUCTURE

What made the United States different for Jews, I argue, was a governmental structure and set of political arrangements that created an opening for Jews to assert and defend their interests in the political system. Even as a small minority, Jews could contend realistically for political influence owing to a favorable political context. To better understand that environment, I employ a central concept from a scholarly approach known as political process theory (see McAdam [1982] for an early statement of the theory and McAdams and Lance [2013] for application to another religious tradition).[4]

Associated with social movements, the concept of political opportunity structure refers to arrangements that either facilitate or retard effective political mobilization by groups that aspire to improve their treatment by society. Groups may have grievances, those grievances may be understood to require political action, and groups may possess resources that can be devoted to efforts to ameliorate their circumstances through collective action. But this does not matter much if the political system is not open to penetration by groups and movements on their behalf. The problem is especially acute for small groups that are socially disfavored and face obstacles to achieving their political ambitions.

By opportunity structure, I refer formally to the "constraints, possibilities, and threats" that confront any group attempting to improve its status (Koopmans 1999, 96). These opportunities are "political" in the sense that they depend on the institutional arrangements of the state and the disposition of potential allies or enemies toward the group's ambitions. As I will show in more detail in Chapter 4, the structure of national government and citizen attitudes in the late eighteenth century aligned in a way that favored Jewish efforts to achieve recognition as full citizens of the Republic. Through Article VI and Amendment I, Jews believed the US Constitution granted them both citizenship status (political rights) and legal protections. It did so, they argued, by establishing the principle of a secular state that disclaimed religious identity and forbid legal privileges or special restrictions for any religious group. When faced with perceived threats to their community, Jews capitalized on the structure of

---

[4] Some scholars perceive political process theory and the concept of political opportunity structure as competitive explanations for the success or failure of social movements. I see them rather as essentially identical approaches.

government to defend zealously their equality under the law as individuals in a secular state.

Research on successful social movements has also demonstrated the importance of access to political elites and others who have influence that can be wielded on behalf of groups seeking redress of grievances. Anne Costain (1992) showed how modern-day feminists were "invited" into the political process by policy entrepreneurs in the executive and legislative branches, enabling them to promote their priorities from within the political system. At a much earlier period, Jews too also depended on sympathetic partners to secure full implementation of their rights. They enjoyed alliances with other groups also committed to maintaining the liberal regime of religion and state.

The original constitutional provisions regarding religion passed by virtue of cooperation between individuals influenced by the Enlightenment and those Protestant sects (as they were called) who feared that other religious groups, especially other Protestants, would use state power against them (Lambert 2003). When threats to the liberal system arose, Jews could and did find allies and advocates outside their own community, religious and secular alike, who assisted their fight against these dangers (Hanson 2013). Elected and appointed Jewish officials within the federal government also played important roles in promoting communal interests. These openings existed owing in part to a tradition of balanced competition between largely nonideological "catch-all" political parties that appealed to virtually all constituencies without regard to religion (Diner 2017, 364). Hence Jewish concerns could be expressed and addressed regardless of which party was in power at the time.

Beyond structural aspects of the state and the availability of allies, the favorable political opportunity structure encountered by American Jews also rested on specific policies and historical developments that enhanced Jewish integration. In a thoughtful essay about the development of the American Jewish community, Hasia Diner (2017) mentions some external factors that aided the Jewish quest for inclusion (see also Dollinger 2000). As one "foreign" group among many during the great surge of immigration from the Civil War to 1924, Jews were not specially targeted for ethnic harassment and often managed to secure exemptions from restrictions that kept out other groups.[5] In a society obsessed with race, Jews

---

[5] Jews, especially women who were denied access to schooling in Russia, might otherwise have been excluded from entry for illiteracy had Congress not accepted Jewish requests to include Yiddish as one of the acceptable languages. Jews also fought against barring

escaped further restrictions on naturalization and citizenship by being considered as whites rather than people of color. Although social discrimination continued, it was generally well below the levels Jews encountered outside the United States and was mainly the province of individuals rather than the state. As David Smith (2015, 178) observed, anti-Semitism "succeeded as prejudice but failed as politics." Diner goes on to mention the coincidence of mass Jewish immigration with periods of chronic labor shortages and the respectability of Judaism, especially when contrasted with Protestant animus toward Catholics. These circumstances further facilitated Jewish political inclusion.

## POLITICAL CULTURE AND PARTISANSHIP

As I turn to the historical evidence about the development of the American Jewish political culture in Part II, it is important to clarify something about American Jewish political development: *American Jews developed a liberal political culture well before they acquired a clear partisan identification.* Prior to the 1930s, American Jews did not exhibit stable attachment to any political party. The historical evidence suggests that Jews were frequently divided among themselves about which political party best pursued policies consistent with their liberal political leanings.

In the five major electoral eras prior to the 1930s, Jews "floated" among and between parties. During the colonial period, where scholars lack systematic data about the small Jewish population, we can say only that Jews were divided over the conflict between the colonies and the mother country. Ira Forman (2001) has described the Jewish population during the early national period (1789–1828) as largely aligned with Jefferson and Madison's Democratic-Republicans rather than the Federalists. In the political system between 1828 and 1860, when the Federalists had disappeared, the major line of competition ran between two factions that emerged from the Democratic-Republicans. The Democrats were identified with Andrew Jackson and Martin Van Buren, the Republicans (soon to become the Whigs) with John Quincy Adams and Henry Clay.[6] Jews were more attracted to the Democrats who

---

immigrants convicted of revolutionary activity by stressing that the Czarist regime often prosecuted innocent Jews who advocated reform.

[6] To this day, many local and state Democratic parties host a "Jefferson–Jackson Day" to celebrate their two founders.

were, they felt, "the more egalitarian and radical of the two parties" (Forman 2001, 146).

Jewish partisan patterns inherited from a previous age were not immune to the fallout that reshaped the party system from 1860 to 1896. The Civil War scrambled party allegiances in the United States, as the Democrats became a sectionalized party anchored in the South and the Republicans, successors to the Whigs, were the party of the victorious North. Yet Jews did not simply vote for the dominant party in their region. The German Jews from the early part of the second great immigration wave held steadfast to the Republican Party. On the other hand, the Yiddish-speaking Eastern Europeans were more inclined to the Democrats. Both the regional and class divisions of the Jewish vote were reflected in election outcomes as the sixty Jewish political elites that Forman identified in the period were split equally between Democrats and Republicans.

The dominant party alignment in the era from 1896 to 1932, the fourth party system, defies easy description despite the continuity in the names of the leading contenders. Rather than vote as a bloc, there is strong evidence that Jews, like other immigrants, often accommodated to the political movements they encountered on the ground, becoming Democrats or Republicans depending on local geography. In places like New York City, home to the largest number of Jews in the country, various parties competed for the political affections of Jews, and their votes might well divide among the contestants and swing between parties from one election to the next. Jews were prone to ticket splitting and voting for third-party candidates throughout the period. In elections below the presidential level, Socialists carried some Jewish districts that were predominantly working class. In the presidential elections of 1912 and 1916, one might have expected overwhelming support for Woodrow Wilson, the Democratic governor of New Jersey who was considerably more progressive than his GOP opponents. Yet Jewish attitudes were ambivalent when Wilson led the United States into World War I. The Jews of German heritage were supposed to have been sympathetic to the Axis powers until the United States joined the conflict against them. The much more numerous Eastern Europeans who despised Russia found reason to favor the Central Powers from the outset.

Looking at the electoral data from multiple cities in the first third of the twentieth century, scholars have reached two conclusions. First, there was considerable vote shifting from one election to the next. Offering the most careful estimates, Weisberg reports that the Jewish vote for Democratic

presidential candidates dropped from 50% to 17% between 1916 and
1920 and careened from 34% to 63% in the elections of 1924 and 1928.
Third-party presidential candidates representing the Socialists and
Progressives took around a fifth of the Jewish vote in 1920 and 1924
but collapsed just four years later. Moreover, Jews tended to vote their
economic interests during most of the period, with the more affluent
favoring the Republicans and the working class disposed to vote for
Democrats (Gamm 1989, 55–59). Given this complexity, we can speak
of political tendencies but must not portray the Jewish vote as monolithic
or stable until the rise of the Roosevelt coalition in the 1930s.

To reiterate, the liberal political culture that American Jews developed
from the eighteenth through the twentieth centuries, was not permanently
affixed to any single political party until much later. Even then, I argue, the
attachment to the Democrats that emerged in the 1930s had less to do
with the Jewish political culture than immediate concerns about economic
issues. I thus focus in Part II on the formation and maintenance of the
American Jewish political worldview, not its partisan component, which
is covered in Part III. I now turn to founding period when American Jews
first experienced and embraced a liberal regime of religion and state.

PART II

# DEVELOPMENT OF THE AMERICAN JEWISH
# POLITICAL CULTURE

# 4

# How Jews Fell in Love with the American Regime

... the Israelite in all countries differs from his compatriots proportionately to his ill-treatment.
— Henry Cohen, *National Loyalty*, 1893 (p. 8)

In trying to understand American Jewish liberalism as an *American* phenomenon, I've identified shortcomings in the three principal theoretical approaches developed by scholars. Yet there is one strand in the literature that helps us comprehend the puzzling politics of American Jews. Trying to explain shifts in Jewish political attitudes in the 1970s, Peter Medding (1977, 1989, 1992) offered a "general theory of Jewish political interests" that he subsequently elaborated in other publications. The theory asserts that Jews react to political forces by determining the direction "from which the greatest perceived threat to Jewish micro-political interests is seen to come" and acting accordingly (Levey 1996, 380).

On the face of it, this theory is attractive because it offers *political* causes for political behavior. Although Medding does not put it this way, his approach suggests that Jews follow the principle known in game theory as minimax regret. Rather than trying to optimize, choosing the political alternative that is best among all the options, Jews seek at all costs to *avoid* selecting the path that leads to the worst imaginable outcome – the kind of marginal existence they experienced in Europe for much of their history. Asking if something is "good for the Jews," the conventional yardstick, is really a way to screen out the least desirable consequences. Perhaps because the political interests theory was developed in political science, a discipline neither well represented in Jewish Studies (Zuckerman 1999) nor, until recently, much interested in religion as a political variable (Wald and Wilcox 2006), it has not been widely utilized.

Drawing on Medding, I attempt to account for the three empirical puzzles associated with American Jewish political behavior. In doing so, I also exploit a disparate collection of scholarship: Leonard Fein's (1988) observation about how Jews calculate political self-interest, Paula Hyman's (1992) discussion of geographic context in Jewish politics, Liebman and Cohen's (1990) instructive comparison of American and Israeli Jews, and Isaac Kramnick and R. Laurence Moore's (1996) insistence on the importance of the constitution's Article VI. Weaving these strands together, I suggest, improves our understanding of the three puzzles about Jewish political behavior that animate this inquiry. This chapter sets out the theory that is applied in subsequent chapters to the political activity of American Jews over time.

### FOUNDATIONS

To put the argument in broad terms, American Jews found themselves in the late eighteenth century as residents of a nation-state that embraced an inclusive understanding of citizenship. Rather than limiting access to the polity based on blood and soil, as in Romantic regimes, the founders extended the boundaries of citizenship to encompass individuals who demonstrated basic competence to participate in society.[1] In particular, the United States disclaimed a religious identity and defined the criteria for membership on grounds other than ethnic or religious ancestry. The idea of citizenship after the Revolution required only "volitional allegiance" (Kettner 1974) in a system based on civic (rather than religious or ethnic) nationalism. This produced a political opportunity structure favorable to Jewish efforts to ensure their own status as equal citizens.

Although they had very little to do with creating the American nation-state along liberal lines and were not the intended beneficiaries of the liberal principles, Jews faced a novel situation in the United States, an opportunity to participate fully in society without having to renounce

---

[1] During much of American history, the benefits of citizenship did not extend to African Americans; Native Americans; Asian immigrants; or, to the extent that citizenship requires access to the franchise, to women. That said and acknowledged, the franchise and citizenship more generally were much more widely available in the United States than in most other countries at the time. Eventually, the United States came to a broader understanding of citizenship. The marchers shouting "blood and soil" in the Charlottesville, Virginia alt-right rally in 2017 would beg to disagree.

their religious affiliation. The chance to become part of the citizenry was not a common experience for European (or North African) Jews and even in France, which emancipated its Jewry late in the eighteenth century, citizenship carried a significant price in the form of demands by the state to relegate Judaism to the narrow confines of the private sphere. In America, to the contrary, citizenship did not preclude the Jews from asserting their values in the public square or creating Jewish institutions outside the state provided they did not cross broad constitutional lines.

The United States became one of the first nations to create a secular state that was friendly to religion, an ideal environment for the growth and prospering of American Judaism. In contemporary American political discourse, critics charge, the idea of a secular state has become associated with hostility rather than neutrality to religion. Given that American Jews celebrated their religious freedom as a precious inheritance early in the nation's history, none more so than their rabbis, it is unlikely they would have developed a view of the state that treated religion negatively. Rather, they used the concept of a secular state not to attack religion or religions, but rather to argue that civil government had no responsibility over matters of faith and belief. They understood the concept properly, according to Lupu and Tuttle (2008, 5), as calling for "a government that receives its authority from the people, not from revealed or transcendent sources, and that recognizes the limited scope of its authority over the people."[2] As Chapter 5 will document, the implications they drew from this premise of classical liberalism determined the framework of the liberal political culture to which American Jews have adhered.

Jews found this new openness enticing, quickly insisting on the privileges of membership in the polity as citizens rather than resident aliens. They approached the political system not as supplicants seeking special benefits but as people with the same "ownership" stake in America as other citizens. In relatively short order, they became political actors who penetrated the state (via the judiciary and other modes) to reinforce the norms that had led to their equality under the Constitution (Forbath 2014). As such, they worked to shape the understanding of law so that the secular character of the government, what I call the liberal regime of religion and state, was fortified and extended. While painting their efforts as campaigns for the public good rather than sectarian initiatives and pledging their fidelity to the American founders, they clearly emphasized

---

[2] This definition leaves ample room for disagreement over what kinds of government actions are permissible under the Constitution.

an interpretation of the legal and constitutional framework that legitimized political opportunities for Jews in the United States. They became anything but passive in these endeavors.

To unpack this dynamic, I start with the experience of European Jews in the Middle Ages after their expulsion by the Romans from the territory they considered the homeland. This reveals the contrast between how Jews had traditionally related to government and their very different approach to politics in the American context.

## THE EUROPEAN CONTEXT

As late as 1170 CE, more than a thousand years after their expulsion from their homeland (called Palestine by the Romans but Judea or Jerusalem by the Jewish diaspora), about four-fifths of the world's Jews still lived in the Middle East. By around 1500, the Jewish population was divided roughly in half between Europe and the Middle East/North Africa. Two centuries later, two-thirds of Jews lived in Europe, with the vast majority settled in the eastern part of the continent (Dellapergola 2001).

The situation of the Jews in Europe, who were to be the principal source of the American Jewish community, varied enormously over both time and space. Although the historian Salo Baron warned against the "lachrymose" view of Jewish history as one long pogrom, one can still say that European Jews were insecure (at best) in most places where they lived.

A subject people for most of their history, lacking sovereignty and agency, Jews were unusually dependent on the goodwill of rulers (Yerushalmi 2005). During the Middle Ages, beneficent rulers could provide guarantees of residence, shield Jews against religiously inspired violence, provide opportunities for their welfare, and even allow them some limited degree of communal self-government. Individual Jews were often treated better if they could fill essential state functions debarred to others (such as tax farming or money lending), offer access to global credit through international family connections, or supply court physicians or other expertise not readily available to rulers. The Jewish community developed a habit of relying on well-placed intercessors to plead their case and secure their interests. Some of the advocates were rewarded by the rulers they served with the grant of privileges that raised doubts about their loyalty to their brethren congregated in ghettos and *shtetls* (Zenner 1990).

But rulers who needed scapegoats could and did expel Jews, promote physical attacks on their communities, tax Jews at rates that effectively impoverished them, and deny them many forms of autonomy. The Jewish intercessors could lose their access to rulers, privileged status, and even their lives should they fall out of favor at court. Even under the most benign leaders, Jews experienced a precarious existence because favors bestowed on a whim by a monarch could equally suddenly be withdrawn. In fact, during the medieval period, entire Jewish communities were evicted from England, France, Spain, Portugal, Italy, the German states and principalities, and Hungary, sometimes more than once. By the mid-sixteenth century, Europe was largely devoid of professing Jews.

The situation of Jews was not uncommon during the Middle Ages (Biale 1987, chapter 3). Like other groups in the corporatist system of the feudal order, Jews accepted protection provided by political authorities in exchange for the obligations to support the rulers. This "exchange relationship" was typical of feudalism if not its very definition. But the Jewish case was arguably different and had lasting consequences for Jewish political culture because of the religious basis of their persecution.

Keeping Jews powerless and in abject poverty powerfully reinforced the message that those who rejected Jesus would pay a price, helping to cement social order. This became particularly salient in late medieval Europe, as Kenneth Stow (1992) observed, when rulers increasingly conceived of themselves as Christian sovereigns. As monarchs consolidated centralized rule, they vested their legitimacy in a mystical bond sanctified by divine will.

Fusing religion with nationalism provided France with "the vision of itself and its people as constituting an unblemished *corpus mysticum*, propaganda [that] was destined eventually to become accepted as fact ..." (Stow 1992, 296). Jews, the eternal alienated people who rejected Jesus Christ, could not be a permanent fixture in such a society. Even when they returned to the continent in the eighteenth and nineteenth centuries, Jews were still not considered equals. In the words of Benjamin Nones (quoted in Schappes 1971, 95), "Among the nations of Europe we are inhabitants everywhere – but Citizens no where [*sic*] *unless in Republics*" [emphasis in original]. Jews came to recognize the link between church and state as an omen that foretold their persecution. Only secular republics held out the hope of civic equality.

This background helps explain why Jews were drawn to the European colonies in North America which operated on very different principles than the mother countries. When he called the United States the "first new nation," Seymour Martin Lipset (1967) highlighted the importance of equality as a founding principle. His choice of title emphasizes the contrast between the United States, a post-feudal society, and the European nations that inherited a medieval political and social system. The idea that the United States had skipped the feudal stage of history, that it was "born free" and did not have to fight to achieve a democratic revolution, was the premise of Louis Hartz's influential book, *The Liberal Tradition in America* (1955). Like Hartz, who was astonished that historians did not ground their accounts of the United States in its origins as a "fragment" society," I am surprised that scholars of Jewish politics have not made the post-feudal American founding central to their interpretation of American Jewish politics.

### THE AMERICAN CASE

Jews in most of the American colonies enjoyed religious freedom in the narrow sense of the right to practice their religious rituals in private. Yet these freedoms did not extend to the political realm even in arguably the most permissive of the colonies, Roger Williams' Rhode Island. In 1684, the General Assembly promised that Jews would enjoy "protection" in the colony but, "being not of our nation," would retain the status of a "stranger" (quoted in Sachar 1927, 96). By 1740, Jews in the American colonies were also empowered with economic freedom on a par with other British colonists (Marcus 1967, 8). An Act of Parliament passed that same year entitled colonists to apply for British citizenship after seven years' residence. The law even permitted Jews to omit the phrase "upon the true faith of a Christian" in swearing an oath of naturalization. In 1777, New York was the first of the newly independent American states to pass a constitution that boldly enforced full civic equality for all its citizens.

Their coreligionists elsewhere might well have envied American Jews for their liberties but the latter, while grateful for their freedom, thought their status was incomplete. Although some of the colonies had granted Jews political rights, these varied significantly from one colony to the next. Rather than such "partial liberty," Jacob Rader Marcus wrote of the American Jew, "he wanted it whole" (quoted in Chyet 1958, 20). According to Jaher's (2010, 33) account of the post-Revolutionary period, "Jews faced two impediments to full citizenship, sectarian establishments and hindrances to political activity." To achieve these ends required a new understanding of citizenship and the nature of the state. By adopting the Constitution in 1787, Jews believed, both goals were achieved in the United States. How did this happen?

The intellectual foundations for this development go back to the spread of classical liberalism among the American founders. The philosophers who taught them to prize what some call the Enlightenment project believed that human reason deserved a broad scope. Hence, "the state must permit private as well as public pursuits of individual happiness and must therefore be limited to enforcing personal rights" (Smith 1988, 70). As such, they concluded, the formal-legal link between religion and state perverted freedom and put the state in a role it should not occupy. They felt equally hostile to other acts and practices by which the state promoted "unearned privilege" (Gitlin 2015) in the economy, law, social behavior, or other domains. Hence, the idea of separating religion and state was part of a larger complex of ideas that constituted classical liberalism.

As we will see later, the liberalism described in this account is *not* identical to the contemporary political philosophy of the same name. The term "liberalism" today encompasses (at least) two different types, one that stresses "economic equality or differentiation among people" and another that emphasizes "individual rights and freedom" (Barnea and Schwartz 1998, 20). A person could in principle adopt both forms of liberalism as an end but they are in tension concerning means. Economic egalitarianism usually requires state actions – income redistribution, market intervention, progressive taxation – that often strike advocates of classical liberalism as destructive of individual rights and freedoms. For the purposes of studying the American Jewish political culture, I reserve "liberalism" as a term for the classical variant that insists governments refrain from limiting "individual autonomy and self-actualization" by promoting instead "openness, tolerance, and acceptance of people and life styles that are different or unusual" (Barnea and Schwartz 1998, 21).[3] Economic egalitarianism that required a substantial degree of state regulation did not become part of this equation until the mid-twentieth century.

Through English-speaking writers of the liberal persuasion, principally John Locke in his *Letter Concerning Toleration* of 1689, the Revolutionary generation learned to distinguish sharply the role of the church from the role of the state. While not all founders endorsed this path

---

[3] These values are phrased in a twenty-first-century context and the founders of classical liberalism would not have extended them to the degree that is now normative. The culture of the Enlightenment Age did not generally promote equality for atheists, homosexuals, women, people of color, or other minority groups. Had they been consistent in implementing an Enlightenment regime across the board, the founders would have taken such actions.

for the new nation nor were entirely consistent in its application, the idea infused such major contributors to American political culture as Jefferson, Madison, Franklin, and Washington.

The battle played out most dramatically in a conflict about taxes in Virginia, just three years before the Constitutional Convention. Late in 1784, Governor Patrick Henry proposed to assess Virginians to fund teachers of Christianity. Playing for time, Henry's opponents succeeded in postponing a vote until January 1785, ostensibly allowing legislators to consult their constituents' wishes on the subject. During the recess, the opponents led by James Madison and George Mason campaigned to mobilize opposition among the dissenting Protestant churches that rejected an alliance between church and state for sectarian reasons. James Madison wrote his famous *Memorial and Remonstrance* against the bill and it circulated widely (and anonymously) around the state. The campaign worked. By the time the legislature reconvened, the opponents had deluged it with petitions opposed to the assessment and the bill was abandoned. Seizing the opportunity, Madison reintroduced Thomas Jefferson's Statute for Religious Freedom that had previously been tabled. The Virginia legislature passed the bill by two-to-one on January 16, 1786.

Madison's *Memorial*, along with Jefferson's Statute for Religious Freedom, articulated the case against public taxation for the benefit of any religion. Echoing Enlightenment values, Madison insisted that the state should neither confer benefits nor impose costs based on religious affiliation. The state should resist such involvement because it had no competence in religious matters and such concerns were best left to individuals:

Before any man can be considered as a member of Civil Society, he must be considered as a subject of the Governour of the Universe: And if a member of Civil Society, do it with a saving of his allegiance to the Universal Sovereign. We maintain therefore that in matters of Religion, no man's right is abridged by the institution of Civil Society and that Religion is wholly exempt from its cognizance.

To establish religion by granting tax benefits, as in the Henry proposal, "degrades from the equal rank of Citizens all those whose opinions in Religion do not bend to those of the Legislative authority." A properly constituted state, following this logic, did not claim authority over religion or demand certain beliefs or behavior as a condition of admission to full citizenship. Nor did it prefer religion by providing the state's imprimatur or funding. Fundamentally, liberal theory adjudges the state incompetent in all matters of religion. Therefore, as Jefferson affirmed in the preamble to the Virginia Statute, "our civil rights have no dependence on our religious opinions any more than our opinions in physics or geometry."

## CONSTITUTIONAL ACTION

These beliefs would radically redefine the conception of citizenship in the new republic that Madison helped craft only a year later. Under liberal democratic theory, citizenship is conditional on "the abstraction of self from particularity" (Peled 1992, 433). That is, citizenship is a right to be conferred on individuals as individuals without regard to any "extraneous" trait other than the basic competence to participate in society. By contrast, Republican/ethnocultural approaches assume that societies require "ethnic homogeneity and common cultural backgrounds" as sources of social integration. These often take the form of Romantic regimes, sometimes called ethnic democracies, which define the nation in terms of "blood, religion and soil" (Jaher 2002, 40–41).

In such regimes, the dominant "nation" exhibits a pervasive sense of "owning" the polity (Brubaker 1996). Drawing on the Enlightenment, liberal regimes condition citizenship instead on acceptance of the polity's legitimacy and consent to core political values (Smith 1988, 227). In liberal democracies, the nation is based on a creed and citizenship is awarded, not on the basis of common ancestry, but by virtue of commitment to the creed. As Jaher (2002, 4) notes, these differing approaches reflect competing forms of nationalism, one (liberal) that is essentially territorial and civic, the other (nonliberal) "organic" and "*volkisch*" in character.

At the Constitutional Convention in 1787, as he had in the Virginia legislature, Madison steered delegates toward the liberal understanding of citizenship. He wanted to ensure that "no legitimate claims could be made by the state against the individual" regarding religious beliefs or requiring assent to any doctrine (Kloppenberg 1998, 45), hence his support for separating religion and state in fundamental law.

This goal was implemented by acts of both omission and commission. The Constitution was conspicuously free of religious language or sentiment. In the Declaration of Independence, Jefferson had appealed to "the Laws of Nature and of Nature's God" and man's Creator to sustain his claims. The Articles of Confederation, the governing document of the thirteen states formulated in 1777, had invoked the "great Governor of the world" in its thirteenth article. Even after the Revolutionary War, many states adopted constitutions that similarly invoked God, Jesus, or Christianity as the foundation of the new government.

The federal Constitution, however, did not mention God, directly or indirectly, by name or by phrase, explicitly or implicitly, nor in any way suggest that the new nation was to have a religious identity. (Less than a century later, the absence of such references would prompt an unsuccessful mass movement to amend the document.) Even the proceedings of the Philadelphia Convention in 1787 were conducted in a secular manner. At an apocryphal moment when the Convention had deadlocked and seemed destined for failure, Benjamin Franklin called on the delegates to hire a chaplain and begin their sessions with prayers for divine guidance. Tellingly, as the result of an absence of enthusiasm and fears that choosing a chaplain would be divisive in a religiously diverse group, the motion was not even voted upon (Sirico 2013). The Constitution was strikingly different from other governing charters at that time in its failure to assign the national government any positive religious responsibilities.

The one explicit reference to religion in the founders' Constitution was negative, consistent with the thrust of the document to limit and restrict the reach of government. The critical provision was buried in the third paragraph of Article VI, which collected several disparate provisions under one heading. The final sentence required all national and state officials to swear allegiance to the Constitution. That sentence ended with a modifying clause: "but no religious test shall ever be required as a qualification to any office or public trust under the United States," making clear that the oath or affirmation required of federal officials was not to be religious in character.[4]

Accordingly, the presidential oath prescribed in Article II ends with a promise that the newly sworn chief executive will "preserve, protect and defend the Constitution of the United States." Adding "So help me God," the practice of swearing the oath on a bible, and the role of clergy in giving invocations at the inauguration ceremony are all social customs with no legally binding status, observed by some presidents and not others. In like manner, the oaths of office developed at the time for members of both houses of Congress and the Supreme Court omitted any references to a deity.

---

[4] The Convention received a letter from a prominent Jewish resident of Philadelphia, urging the delegates *not* to imitate Pennsylvania, which imposed a religious test in its constitution. The letter apparently reached the delegates after the ban on religious tests had already been accepted.

Despite characterizations of the Constitution as "a daughter of the Enlightenment" (Lacorne 2011, 34–35), the "no religious test" provision was as much a tactical maneuver by practical politicians as a philosophical position (Bradley 1986). Many delegates to the Convention may not have objected on principle to religious tests, nor to prayers in legislative assemblies, or religious language in oaths of office. All were common practices in the states and might have inspired resistance to a federal constitution that banned them. But as political realists, the founders also worried that such practices at the federal level might generate controversy in a religious environment rife with fractious and competing Protestant religious denominations. Baptists, who led the opposition to the Virginia assessment, probably would have been fine with state-supported teachers of Christianity if *their* version of Christianity were to be taught. Absent such guarantees, it seemed better to prohibit religious tests, state-funded religious education, or legislative chaplains altogether. Such practices remained optional at the state level.

The first Congress under the Constitution (1789–1791) amended the founding charter in response to a public demand for an explicit bill of rights. As he had at the Constitutional convention, Madison again guided the process. The members of Congress produced the famous religion clauses that begin Amendment I: "Congress shall make no law respecting an establishment of religion, or prohibiting the free exercise thereof." (Although approved in 1789, these words were not formally incorporated until the amendments were ratified more than two years later.) Like the prohibition on religious tests in Article VI of the original Constitution, these clauses could be justified in terms of liberal values but were probably accepted on practical grounds to avoid religious competition among Protestants.

## JEWISH REACTIONS

The lack of religious sanction for the new nation and the explicit prohibition on religious oaths as a condition of public office paved the way for Jews' full inclusion in the national polity. How did the Jewish community during the founding and early national eras react to these provisions? In the absence of Jewish newspapers or much in the way of private correspondence to answer the question, the position of the Jews in America was best expressed in the greetings sent by major Jewish communities to George Washington on his election as president and through references to the Constitution in sermons and public addresses.[5] The messages of congratulations, written *before* the first amendment was added, share the assumption that the Constitution granted Jews full and unconditional citizenship.

Neither Article VI nor the religion clauses of the first Amendment owed anything to the Jews who resided in the United States at independence.[6] Nonetheless, Jews treated the document as their Magna Carta. A 1789 sermon in a New York synagogue noted that "we are ... made equal partners of the benefits of government by the constitution of these states" (quoted in Kramer 2003, 17). In a paean to George Washington, Savannah's Jews noted that the government he helped create had "enfranchised us with all the privileges and immunities of free citizens" (quoted in Rabinove 1990, 136). Their coreligionists in four cities told Washington in 1790 that the freedom won in the Revolution was not "perfectly secure, till your hand gave birth to the Federal Constitution." In the same year, New York's Shearith Israel, the first Jewish congregation in the United States, adopted a constitution acknowledging its location in a nation based on the principle of "equal liberty civil and religious" (Sarna 2004, 43).

The Jews of Rhode Island thanked the new president for making them "equal parts of the great governmental machine" (quoted in Kramer 2003, 18). The author of the tribute emphasized that the new document did more than accord them mere toleration, a flimsy guarantee at best, but rather assured them something rather more precious, "invaluable rights as free citizens." In a 1798 sermon, the influential religious leader Gershon Seixas asserted that God "established us in this country where we possess every advantage that other citizens of these states enjoy" (quoted in Schappes 1971, 92). Like their fellow citizens, he elaborated, Jews enjoyed "participating of equal rights and immunities." Judging by the words of Jewish leaders in the early Republic, passage of the First Amendment seems to have completed their emancipation.

What did they mean by using terms such as equality, rights, privileges, immunities, and citizenship? On a literal reading, it might appear that the

---

[5] As if to prove the old adage about two Jews, three opinions, the six major Jewish communities actually sent four different addresses to George Washington. See Adler (1932, 2).

[6] Scholars have suggested that the Biblical model of the ancient Hebrew kingdoms exerted considerable influence on the American founders (Shalev 2009; Straus 1885). However, this image was shaped by Christian understandings that did not have much to do with the relative handful of Jews then present in the colonies or the early nation.

language of Article VI applied narrowly to oaths for public office and nothing else. As a very small community composed mostly of immigrants, few Jews could have aspired to hold key positions in national government. However, the power of the ban on religious tests for national office symbolized something much greater, the elevation of Jews from second-class citizens to the exalted rank of "freemen" who could participate fully in public life.[7]

Thinking back to the Revolution, a prominent Jewish physician said that Jews enlisted in the Patriot's cause because it "entitled them to a participancy of equal privileges, of equal franchise, and of being placed on the same eminence with all mankind" (De la Motta 1820, 12). In addition to respect for their sacrifices, they were repaid, he noted, with "the equal participation of public functions" and "the enjoyment of equal rights and franchise" (De la Motta 1820, 15). Referring specifically to Article VI, the Jews of Richmond, VA defended the young nation in the War of 1812 "for the country, too, was theirs – they were part of the legislative power, alike in the eye of the law, not distinguished by any disqualifications because of their belief or religious conduct" (Foner 1946, 41–42). When the governor of South Carolina called for Thanksgiving prayers in language that excluded all but Christians in 1844, when he then reaffirmed that request on behalf of a Christian nation, he was admonished by the editor of the *Occident* for ignoring the Constitution:

If, therefore, the other inhabitants have a right to the consideration and the liberties which they enjoy, the Jews have it equally so; especially as they come not to ask any exclusive privileges, but to be left in possession of the immunities which the constitution guarantees to all, and to be allowed to join in the joys, the sufferings, and aspirations of their fellow-citizens.

Jews were not alone in drawing such a conclusion. Whereas Jews on the Continent might be tolerated or protected, Hannah Adams wrote (1817, 132), the United States had gone further by vesting them with "all the rights of citizens." In their communications with Jews, the first four presidents did not challenge the interpretation of the Constitution as a source of equal rights (Abraham 1895). Echoing the sentiment of the letter sent him by the Jewish community in Newport, Rhode Island, George Washington expressed satisfaction that "All possess alike liberty of con-science and immunities of citizenship" in the new Republic. Thomas

---

[7] As late as 1914, S. M. Stroock (1917, 131) defined citizenship as a status conferred on members of a nation who possessed "all of the rights, franchises and privileges of a freeman."

Jefferson told a Jewish correspondent that American law protected "our religious, as they do our civil rights, by putting all on an equal footing." Replying to the same correspondent, John Adams emphasized his pride that the United States had granted equal status to Jews and offered a wish that "your nation may be admitted to all privileges of citizens in every country of the world." Given his leadership in drafting the Constitution and the Bill of Rights, little wonder that Madison celebrated the "perfect equality of rights" bestowed on the Jews, pointing to their "good citizenship" as proof that equality begets loyalty and patriotism (Hunt 1910, 29–30). John Quincy Adams boasted to James Hume about American leadership in "admission of the Jews to civil rights" (quoted in Borden 1984, 109). No wonder Jews of the late eighteenth century believed the US Constitution granted them political equality at the federal level "as of right together with all other citizens" (Marcus 1989, 83).

In describing the philosophy of the Constitution to various audiences, the founders frequently deployed stylistic variations of the word "liberal." Washington, for example, described the new US government as a reflection of the "spirit of liberality" sweeping the world, pointing specifically to the "large and liberal policy" underlying the philosophy of rights and elsewhere to the "liberality of sentiment" evident in interreligious relations in the new nation. Scholars have argued at great length and with considerable passion about just what liberalism meant at the founding, distinguishing between a liberal individualism that prizes individual freedom above all and a republican liberalism that emphasizes the state's responsibility to promote "virtue" among its citizens. Or perhaps even "liberal" was used, then as now, simply to connote broad-mindedness and generosity of spirit.

In the case at hand, the question of what role religion should play in a liberal state, I think the evidence supports the claim that the founders conceptualized the new American state as essentially secular. They would have avoided using that adjective to describe their handiwork at a time when "secular" was often equated with antireligiousness. At its inception, as noted earlier in this chapter, classical liberalism as a doctrine aimed to remove what it saw as the principal obstacles to human freedom, the pillars of feudalism such as "social customs, ties of feudal dependence, and religious conformity" (Ball, Dagger, and O'Neill 2014, 45). That meant confining the state so that it could not organize, regulate, or draw on religion as a source of legitimacy.

Political secularism, the best term for this orientation, need not connote hostility to religion nor the hope or belief that it will inevitably decay.

Some ideological secularists may hold such views but the concept itself does not depend on those assumptions (Fox 2015, 26–38). Rather, as Bhargava (2009, 88) argues, secular states follow the bedrock principle of nonestablishment that translates into certain practices:

... in a secular state, a formal or legal union or alliance between state and religion is impermissible. Official status is not given to religion. No religious community in such a state can say that the state belongs exclusively to it. Nor can all of them together say that it belongs collectively to them and them alone.

These practices are intended to promote several virtues – the maintenance of *social peace* by avoiding conflicts between irreconcilable difference in ultimate values, *toleration* by refusing to persecute individuals based on religion, and *religious liberty*. The latter goal is served by allowing individuals the scope to criticize and challenge all religious doctrines and empowering them to freely choose, change, or reject any religious identity (Bhargava 2009, 90).

That sentiment was plain in Madison's thought when he wrote in 1822 that "religion and government will both exist in greater purity the less they are mixed together." Washington had earlier endorsed a similar position in his response to a letter of congratulation from the Presbyterians of Massachusetts and New Hampshire in 1789 (Twohig 1993, 274–275). Their letter had noted with some hint of exasperation that while they accepted the ban on test oaths, they had expected in the Constitution at least "some explicit acknowledgement of the only true God and Jesus Christ whom he has sent ..." As Washington replied gently, "the path of true piety is so plain as to require but little political direction" and that instilling such piety in the masses was the responsibility of ministers of the gospel, not the state. That alone explained "the absence of any regulation respecting religion" in the Constitution. In a less guarded moment during the conflict over the religious assessment proposed by Patrick Henry in 1785, Washington had told George Mason bluntly that religious groups should pay for their religious instruction rather than draw on public funds (cited in Cousins 1958, 64–65).

Jews were not alone in affirming the founders' approach to questions of religion and state. Major political leaders voiced similar interpretations in the early nineteenth century. Senator Richard Johnson of Kentucky, who would later serve as vice president under Martin Van Buren, drafted the report of a congressional committee in response to a proposed law to curtail Sunday mail delivery, a practice begun twenty years earlier. The attempt to end the practice was spurred by petitions from Protestant religious groups, seeking to protect Sunday as the sabbath (Verhoeven 2013). As an active Baptist, a denomination that had allied with Madison in resisting the Virginia religious assessment, Johnson reminded the advocates that the constitution "regards the conscience of the Jew as sacred as that of the Christian." As a civil rather than a religious institution, the state had no authority to confer legal recognition to the Christian sabbath and such efforts represented a slippery slope leading to further incursions:

The conclusion is inevitable, that the line cannot be too strongly drawn between Church and State. If a solemn act of legislation shall, in one point, define the law of God, or point out to the citizen one religious duty, it may, with equal propriety, proceed to define every part of divine revelation; and enforce every religious obligation, even to the forms and ceremonies of worship, the endowment of the church, and the support of the clergy. (Committee on Post Offices and Post Roads 1830, 1)

Jews were thus in good company when they read the Constitution as creating a republic with a secular state.

It's not entirely clear which specific Constitutional provisions (or provisions not included) the authors of the Jewish tributes to George Washington had in mind when they emphasized citizenship or the secular character of the state. As noted, their praise issued forth *before* the First Amendment was ratified so it must have been something about the original constitution that excited their enthusiasm. But the document passed in Philadelphia said remarkably little about citizenship which was, for the most part, left to the discretion of the states (Smith 1997, chapter 5). The language of the Jewish tributes suggests that they were referring to Article IV, which declared that "citizens of each state shall be entitled to all privileges and immunities of citizens in the several states." This assurance was not new, having already been guaranteed in the Articles of Confederation, and some observers believed it did not bestow any fundamental rights but simply indicated that any rights granted by a state to its own citizens must be extended to visitors from other states.[8] Yet Jews may not have read too much into Article IV because most judges subsequently found "a core of fundamental rights" as part of the "privileges and immunities" that were part and parcel of citizenship (Kettner 1978,

---

[8] The Fourteenth Amendment, passed after the Civil War, clarified that the "privileges and immunities" referred to the laws of the United States, not just state statutes, and required both due process and the equal protection of the laws. This amendment would later become the basis for expanding the religious rights of minorities. See Chapter 9 for its impact on Jewish partisanship.

260). Even if states could retain their own religious establishments and exclude Jews from full political rights, as they did for another half century, Jews could still describe themselves as citizens of the United States.

Given the timing and precedents, it's more likely that the Jewish communities were celebrating the absence of any religious declarations in the Constitution and emphasizing the Article VI prohibition on religious tests. Religious oaths were the concern of the sole letter sent by an identifiable Jew to the Convention. Moreover, the idea that full citizenship required the right to hold office was embedded in colonial practice and extended back to British laws that defined "freemen" as individuals who were eligible to seek public office. By usage at the time, citizenship seemingly implied the possession of political privileges. In the words of a disciple of Jefferson writing in 1789, "Citizenship confers a right of voting at elections, and many other privileges not enjoyed by those who are no more than inhabitants" (Ramsay 1789, 3). Jews who had lost their British citizenship when the colonies broke their ties to the mother country regained that status with the adoption of the Constitution.

Though they were not alone in venerating the Constitution (Kammen 1986), Jews do seem to have developed a veritable cult around it. For the future of Jewish politics in the United States, it does not matter if the Jewish community correctly interpreted the will of the founders, if that is even possible. It matters more that Jews *believed* the Constitution granted them equal status and enabled them to live in a secular state at the national level. They subsequently embarked on a campaign to promote that interpretation, clashing with others who read the Constitution in different ways. That campaign remains active to the present day.

## ADDRESSING THE THREE PUZZLES

By the late eighteenth century, American Jews perceived their new nation as having developed a regime of religion and state that treated the latter as essentially secular. In so doing, the system empowered them with the full rights of citizenship, something they had never experienced elsewhere in the diaspora. That, Jews further believed, provided the foundation for their success in the American Republic. As we will see in Chapter 5, preserving the secular character of the state preoccupied them in the early national period. The following chapters illustrate continuity in the core political priority of American Jewry through the centuries.

How does this contextual approach potentially help resolve the three puzzles about the political behavior of Jews in the United States? Does it improve on the Judaic theories that I criticized by helping us better understand why American Jews are clustered on the Democratic/liberal side of the political spectrum, why no other diaspora community today is similarly situated, and why the American Jewish attachment to the left rises and falls in the short term?

As I argued in Chapter 2, the predisposition of American Jews to favor the Democratic Party and support liberal political causes more than other Americans is puzzling because Jews possess traits that usually incline voters to favor conservatism. Compared to those non-Jews who share the same background traits, we saw in Chapter 2, Jews stand out even more. The argument in favor of a contextual solution to this puzzle is fairly straightforward: American Jews have become so Democratic/liberal in modern times because they perceive Democrats and liberals as a bulwark against the fusion of church and state. Having such allies allays somewhat Jewish fears/concerns that the United States will move toward a regime based on blood and soil. History has taught American Jews that classical liberalism's approach to religion safeguards their full inclusion in the society and political system. Particularly in the era after World War II, when challenges to political secularity became more common, they have supported the party that is associated with that perspective.

Why is such a position unusual among Jewish communities worldwide? That is the second puzzle we confront. Simply, there are virtually no other Jewish diaspora communities today in secular states that are friendly to religion. Even though many of the surviving religious establishments in democratic states are tolerant of religious differences, they much more closely intermingle religion and state than does the United States (Fox 2007). Britain has become very open to Jews but it is still a country with a state church and a law that requires the monarch and any potential heirs to the throne to remain in the Church of England. It is a tolerant society but not one with a liberal regime of religion and state. At the beginning of the twentieth century, Canada was distinguished from the United States by the absence of any legal-constitutional barriers between religion and state – "no formal rejection of establishment, no benchmark value of separation of church and state, no strong idea of equality of religions, and no acceptance of the equal status of non-believers" (Weinrib 2003, 34). Hence when the Canadian Jewish Congress submitted to Parliament a request to excuse Jewish merchants from a Sunday closing law in 1906, it could not do so in the name of "rights" and had to make a plea for justice which was denied (Weinrib 2003, 39). Although passage of a new Constitution in 1982 brought Canada closer to a liberal regime, it still permitted the country's most populous province to restrict state funding for religious education to Roman Catholic schools alone. It is not clear that Canadian Jews aspire to a secular state nor that the issue divides the major parties along a left–right axis as in the United States.

In most societies, religious minorities such as Jews typically mobilize to obtain the same benefits and privileges accorded under law to larger and more powerful religious communities. The strategy makes sense given the heritage of state establishment and the tradition of imposing costs and benefits based on religious affiliation. Jewish communities elsewhere may well appreciate their status and the freedoms that accompany it but have little or no hope of changing the religious character of the state. Hence, their political goals do not encompass the objective of removing all vestiges of religious identity from national identity. They thus define their political interests quite differently from their American coreligionists who prioritize protecting the liberal church–state regime by vigilant opposition to incursions that threaten their civic equality.

If the contextual approach accounts for why American Jews are politically liberal unlike their coreligionists elsewhere, does it help us understand the short-term oscillations in American Jewish behavior? Scholars have observed a V-shaped pattern in American Jewish support for the Democratic Party – high levels of Democratic voting in the 1950s and 1960s, a significant drop off in Democratic support in the 1970s and 1980s, and then a rebound to a much stronger Jewish-Democratic electoral connection since the 1990s (see Figure 2.4). While Jews always gave more support to Democratic presidential and congressional candidates after World War II, the gap separating them from the entire electorate was not constant across elections. It compressed in the 1970s and '80s and expanded from the '90s onward. Judaic theories simply do not speak to this puzzle.

Medding's theory of Jewish political interests alerts us to the importance of threats that American Jews perceive when they monitor the political situation. The downturn in Jewish support for the left after the 1960s is often explained, perhaps overexplained, by pointing to social disruptions that shifted political alliances. The factors cited include growing conflict between blacks and Jews over the direction of the civil rights movement, community control of schools, affirmative action, and other policies; concerns about the attacks on Israel and disagreements about Israeli policies; support for Jewish dissidents in the Soviet Union; and a host of other issues. Jews were not the only component of the old

Democratic coalition to grow estranged from liberalism during this period. Catholics, white Evangelical Protestants, and labor unionists recoiled from some of the social movements that found a degree of welcome in the Democratic Party – feminism, gay rights, opposition to the Vietnam War, and other causes associated with the political left.

It is not so easy to explain why Jews alone turned back in large numbers to the Democrats in the 1990s. Some of the issues that precipitated Jewish unhappiness with the left may have been settled and removed from the Jewish political agenda. But if all the issues that contributed to the split had been settled, why didn't Catholics and members of labor unions also reconcile with the Democratic Party rather than becoming blocs that subsequently swung between the two parties? Some underlying force, absent among Catholics and other constituencies that deserted the Democrats during the 1970s and 1980s, seems to have brought Jews back into the Democratic fold.

From Medding's perspective, the rebounding Jewish-Democratic alliance since the early 1990s must have arisen from the perception that Jewish interests were now under threat from a new source. Chapter 9 will demonstrate that Jews did indeed become persuaded in the late 1980s and 1990s that the danger to their core priority emanated from a group that became closely tied to the Republican Party and that the Democratic Party resisted – the social movement known as the Christian Right. The movement's prominence in Republican ranks renewed Jewish fears that the United States was going to be defined in religious terms and that Christian values were going to be implemented in public policy. Judaic theories offer no other basis to account for this development, the third puzzle of American Jewish political behavior.

In Chapter 5, I turn to the period from the adoption of the Constitution in the late eighteenth century through the American Civil War of the 1860s. During this time, Jews developed a more systematic perspective on the Constitution and amassed institutional resources that enabled them better to promote the secular state. They were transformed from essentially passive recipients of a liberal regime of religion and state into a constituency capable of mobilizing in defense of that regime. Although it is common to think of the secular state as a factor in domestic political controversy, many of the issues that first engaged the organized Jewish community involved events outside the United States. During these early controversies, Jews learned to understand the impact of political developments on their interests and to articulate their concerns in the language of classical liberalism.

# 5

# Jewish Political Culture in the Early National Period

... a good Jew is an equivalent for a good citizen.
Julius Bien, "Past and Future of the Order," 1898 (p. 232)

By the end of the eighteenth century, Jews in the United States had already achieved levels of political inclusion unmatched in Jewish history. As Chapter 4 recounted, they did so less by their own labors than by the efforts of American political leaders to construct a liberal state based on Enlightenment principles. That classic regime of religion and state was facilitated by propitious conditions in North America – the absence of a feudal tradition, religious diversity, strong individualism, and, most importantly, structural rules that collectively constituted the political opportunity structure. As beneficiaries of the new order, Jews could in principle take advantage of their rights by engaging in public life on behalf of their own interests. This chapter traces how they did so during the early and middle periods of the nineteenth century.

When the liberal regime was established by the Constitution, Jews were a tiny share of the American population, numbering at most 1,500 out of nearly 4 million inhabitants counted by the census of 1790 (Rosenswaike 1960) and comprising mostly foreign-born immigrants. Over the course of the nineteenth century, aided by massive inflows from Europe during the Age of Immigration, the Jewish community grew in both size and influence. Even after it was augmented by the two great waves of central and then eastern European migration, the Jewish population of the United States remained small by relative standards and geographically concentrated, conditions that limited its national political reach. Nonetheless,

Jews proved willing to enter the political arena when their status as citizens or the concept of political secularism appeared to be threatened.

The religion and state regime that benefited Jews faced several social and political challenges during the first full century of American nationhood. In responding to these crises, Jews developed a set of institutions and a style of political action that persisted well into the twentieth century. This chapter discusses the evolution of Jewish political practice during the first half of the nineteenth century by focusing on the strategy and tactics of political elites within the community. I look first at the *forms* of political action, the organizational and tactical repertoire used by Jews to defend their interests. Then I look more carefully at the *discourse* of communal leaders, the language, concepts, and ideas they deployed in making the case when they felt Jewish rights were threatened or abridged. Both would become standard practices as the American Jewish political culture developed during the period.

This overview may be read to imply that there was a top-down, hierarchical nature to Jewish political action, that elites dictated the community's priorities and preferences to a supportive constituency that then implemented the directives faithfully. Nothing could be further from the truth, then or now.[1] The organizations created by Jewish elites were self-selected, constituting loose social networks rather than well-developed structures with defined roles and operating principles. These organizations often rose or fell based on the funding they could raise from the wealthier members of the community, making them hardly representative of the Jewish population. Most Jewish organizational life occurred at the grass roots as local communities built synagogues, schools, social service agencies, and other institutions without central direction or coordination. Individuals in various cities and states frequently appointed themselves as Jewish spokespersons, undertaking political action on their own initiative without coordinating with national bodies.

Nonetheless, the elites in the large cities like New York acted as if they commanded authority among Jews nationwide and often spoke in the name of American Jewry. The organizations they created undertook activities addressed to communal needs and developed a language that continues to undergird collective action by Jews in the United States. Never as coordinated or influential as outsiders may have assumed, the

---

[1] A student once asked me if there was a leadership principle among American Jews. Somewhat flippantly, I told him that Jews had a very simple leadership principle: We don't have any.

elites still mattered in the construction of an American Jewish political worldview.

## CHALLENGES TO JEWISH EQUALITY

To understand the foundations of American Jewish liberalism, this chapter focuses on the core issues that raised Jewish concerns about the liberal regime of religion and state, their prize inheritance from the Revolution and Constitutional Convention. In the first half of the nineteenth century, Jews were particularly agitated over two controversies. They protested in 1816 when the first Jewish consul appointed to represent the United States abroad, Mordecai Manuel Noah, was summarily fired by Secretary of State James Monroe. During this period, they also mounted a campaign against a treaty negotiated with Switzerland in 1850, an agreement that appeared to exclude them from its coverage. Although ostensibly foreign policy issues, the Noah affair and the prolonged Swiss Treaty controversy agitated American Jews because both called into question their inclusion as equal citizens in the body politic. The failure to secure redress, particularly in the latter case, prompted the formation of the first communal defense organization by American Jews.

The new organizational weapon forged by mid-century was soon drawn into action. Jews mobilized at mid-century in response to three crises associated with the Civil War – a law that restricted military chaplains to Christians alone (1861), an order issued by the Union Army expelling Jews from Army-occupied Tennessee (1862), and a proposal in Congress to amend the Constitution by adding language that explicitly identified the nation as Christian (1863). There were other questions of significance – Sunday-closing laws that seemed to punish Jewish merchants, proposals to add religious instruction to the public school curriculum, the use of sectarian language in government proclamations – but these were localized in nature.[2] The same was true for campaigns by local Jewish notables and their allies to remove from state constitutions the remaining religious disabilities and Christian test oaths for public office.

---

[2] I've been unable to find evidence that Jews were involved in fighting the campaign against Sunday mail delivery discussed in Chapter 4. Although Jews were no doubt happy that Congress refused to act, citing the First Amendment, there was no discernible Jewish political activity around the issue.

## Noah

A flamboyant native-born American, Mordecai Manual Noah, was named consul to the Kingdom of Tunis in 1813. Noah had applied for the job by emphasizing that his Jewish heritage equipped him to represent US interests in the Barbary states where Jewish families were deeply involved in the trans-Atlantic trade (Sarna 1981, 15). Barely a year after his arrival, Noah was fired by Secretary of State James Monroe. Although the real reason for his dismissal was exceeding orders and incurring major unauthorized expenses in ransoming captives kidnapped at sea, the letter of dismissal reported instead that Noah's religion had produced "a very unfavorable effect" and he was thus terminated. The inaccurate statement of cause was meant to shield US involvement in freeing the captured seamen.

Despite having invoked his Judaism as a factor that warranted his appointment, Noah now acted as if any consideration of religion was thoroughly contrary to American values. He responded to Monroe's letter with apparent incredulity: ". . . my religion an object of hostility? I thought I was a citizen of the United States" (quoted in Marcus 1996, 110–111). As such, his dismissal "violated one of the most sacred and delicate rights of a citizen." Noah chided President James Madison for violating his own declaration that "the religion of a citizen is not a legitimate object of official notice from government."

Noah did nothing to discourage his coreligionists from attributing his dismissal to anti-Semitism rather than his diplomatic misdeeds. Believing Noah's claim that he had been fired due to anti-Semitism, the pushback by his coreligionists was very much anchored in Constitutional values and rhetoric. One of Noah's defenders, Isaac Harby of Charleston, reminded Secretary Monroe that the Constitution forbade imposing disabilities based on religion:

It is upon the principle, not of *toleration* . . . but upon the principle of equal inalienable, *constitutional Rights*, that we see Jews appointed to offices, that we see them elected in our State Representation . . . They are by no means to be considered as a Religious sect, tolerated by the government; they constitute a portion of the People. They are, in every respect, woven in and compacted with the citizens of the Republic. Quakers and Catholics, Episcopalians and Presbyterians, Baptist and Jews, all constitute one great political family. (quoted in Blau and Baron 1963, Vol. 2, 320–321, emphasis in original)

The language in these protests conveys the sense that Noah's dismissal violated the prohibition on religious tests in Article VI. (Monroe's language in attributing the decision to terminate Noah to the host nation's religious sensibilities does seem very much like a religious test for holding public office.) Noah took the principle of Article VI and extended it by claiming that the Constitution forbade government from taking *any* notice of a citizen's religion. Harby took a parallel track, claiming that Jews as citizens were not to be treated any differently than other Americans based on religious grounds. That was central to the idea of a secular state. Thus, the state should not treat a Jewish consul differently than a diplomat from any other religious tradition.

Even as his own appeal was denied, Noah raised an important question: Did the Constitution apply only to US officials or could foreign governments impose their own religious tests on American citizens abroad? That issue lay at the heart of the subsequent dispute over the Swiss Treaty thirty-some years later, a watershed event in American Jewish political mobilization.

### Swiss Treaty

In 1850, the United States negotiated a commercial treaty with Switzerland that provided for "reciprocal equality" of treatment for Swiss and US citizens in the other country. But the grant of equality pointedly reserved these rights to Christians alone. Several Swiss cantons prohibited Jews from visiting or living temporarily or permanently in their territory, meaning they were effectively debarred by treaty from its benefits. On submission to the Senate, President Millard Fillmore, Secretary of State Daniel Webster, and Senator Henry Clay all objected to these provisions. The treaty was subsequently renegotiated, replacing the explicit Christian-only language with somewhat opaque text that promised equality of treatment where and when it did not conflict with the constitution and laws of the contracting parties. Because Swiss law at the state and local level restricted Jewish rights, the new language made a distinction without a difference. Nevertheless, responding to State Department assurances that the Swiss had privately committed to equal treatment of American Jews in their land, the Senate passed the revised treaty in 1855. Several American Jews who tested the provisions were in fact denied entry or expelled from Swiss cantons, underlining the hollowness of the guarantees.

When they learned of these discriminatory practices, some Jewish leaders urged mass mobilization against the treaty. The *Israelite*, a Cincinnati newspaper with national circulation, exhorted Jews to resist:

> Agitate!
> Call meetings!
> Engage the press in your favor!!!!
> Israelites, freemen and citizens!
> Hold public meetings; give vent to your sentiments,
>     resolve upon a proper course of action against the
>     mean and illegitimate instrument made in violation of
>     the Constitution of the United States.
>
> *(quoted in Stroock 1903, 26)*

Jewish communities responded. Following local assemblies in major cities, a national convention of Jews meeting in Washington, DC, in 1857 petitioned President James Buchanan to provide them with that remedy "to which they deem themselves entitled as citizens of the United States" (*Israelite*, "This Memorial," November 6, 1857). Surprisingly, they did not ask for outright repeal or amendment of the treaty but rather urged Buchanan to insist on the priority of the American constitutional prohibition against religious discrimination in both countries, effectively nullifying the Swiss cantonal laws restricting Jewish rights.

As they would later do later when protesting such domestic policies as the Christian-only military chaplaincy or the Christian amendment to the Constitution, American Jews framed their opposition to the Swiss treaty in terms of both Article VI and Amendment I. They reminded American officials that the nation's founding documents created a government "disclaiming all religious distinction as to the political rights of its citizens," a proviso that they argued applied "without distinction" at home and abroad. Whether or not the Constitution allowed the US government to make treaties that resulted in unequal treatment of US citizens based on religion, Jewish advocates insisted that such distinctions violated the principle of equal citizenship under the law.

Local protest meetings hewed to the same line (*Israelite*, "This Memorial," October 2, 1857). At Charleston, the petitioners called the treaty "a stain upon our National Constitution." They decried that "citizens of this Republic, professing the Jewish Faith, have been deprived of the greatest and noblest boon of political rights, that of equality before the law without distinction of religious profession, as contained in, and granted by the First Amendment ..." A local conclave in Washington described the Swiss treaty as "worthy of the dark middle ages," calling it "averse to the laws of Nature, which knows no Jew or Gentile; averse to the law of the land; and averse to the age of progress in which we live" (*Israelite*, "This Memorial," October 2, 1857). At Indianapolis, protesters endorsed a resolution claiming that a treaty "to protect one class of citizens more than another" was both tyrannical and unbecoming to a republican government. Characteristically, they asserted a claim to their "full and unimpaired rights as citizens of the United States." As in the domestic sphere, they avoided particularistic language and expressed their protest in the universalist discourse of citizenship and constitutional values.

Despite the unwillingness of the Swiss to address the concerns of American Jews, the American government neither amended nor abrogated the treaty.[3] Pondering the failure of the effort, some Jewish leaders saw a striking contrast between the intense mobilization of American Jews aroused by the Damascus and Mortara affairs, earlier episodes when Jews in other countries were mistreated and denied human rights, and the "indifference and apathy" that greeted calls for action on other issues such as the Swiss treaty where American Jews were directly affected. Using the challenges of the Swiss Treaty as an example, they called on Jews to give their "closest attention and fullest consideration" to the community's "home interests," which were "swelling into greater magnitude" with each passing year. Failure to act zealously on behalf of the "principle of civil and religious equality," they contended, provided "a precedent for further executive or legislative acts prejudicial to our rights and privileges" (*Jewish Messenger,* "Address: Plan," November 4, 1859).

These critics called for a national organization rather than ad hoc and uncoordinated action by individual communities. They thus proposed a plan that became the organizational blueprint for the Board of Delegates of American Israelites, a coalition among Jewish congregations that in its twenty years of existence would attend to various civil rights issues affecting the American Jewish community (Tarshish 1959). The new machinery would be tested shortly during the War Between the States.

## Civil War Issues

Jewish leaders were alarmed by three developments associated with the Civil War. At the outbreak of the war, Congress established a system of military chaplains to minister to the needs of soldiers in the Union Army. When a New York regiment elected a Jewish officer to fill the post, he was

---

[3] Almost twenty years later, largely owing to French efforts, the Swiss eventually yielded and passed national legislation that prohibited discrimination on religious grounds (Isser 1993). This removed the formal-legal obstacles to Jewish residence in the confederation.

ordered to refuse it because the statute expressly limited the position to "regular ordained ministers of some Christian denomination." (The officer was neither.) Jews were expelled from Union-occupied Tennessee when the commanding general of the region, Ulysses S. Grant, accepted dubious claims that Jewish dealers had traded Southern cotton illicitly, thus helping to fund the Confederate war effort. The order was particularly brutal because it gave Jews in the area, including long-time residents who had no connection to the illicit trade, a mere twenty-four hours to vacate the region and instructed Army officials to refuse to issue passes that would enable Jews to appeal the decisions at military headquarters. The order, issued for "Jews as a class," hearkened back to the corporate expulsions Jews had experienced throughout Europe during the Middle Ages.

The third challenge was symbolically connected to the prosecution of the Civil War although it persisted thereafter. In his second inaugural address, Abraham Lincoln famously portrayed the Civil War as God's simultaneous punishment of Southerners for practicing slavery and Northerners for acceding to the practice. Taking a different tack, influential Christian churchmen thought the war represented God's judgment on the nation for its failure to acknowledge God in the Constitution. The National Reform Association argued that the nation could return to the Lord's good graces by amending the Preamble, adding the words in italic:

We the people of the United States, *humbly acknowledging Almighty God as the source of all authority and power in civil government, the Lord Jesus Christ as the Ruler among the nations, His revealed will as the supreme law of the land, in order to constitute a Christian government,* and in order to form a more perfect union, establish justice, insure domestic tranquility, provide for the common defense, promote the general welfare, and secure the inalienable rights and the blessings of life, liberty, and the pursuit of happiness to ourselves and our posterity, and all the people, do ordain and establish this Constitution for the United States of America. (*New York Times,* "Amending the Constitution," February 2, 1864)

The proposal was duly introduced in the US Congress in 1864 and repeatedly thereafter but never became law.

In responding to the perceived threats posed by the chaplain bill, the expulsion order, and the Christian Amendment, Jews, like other small groups seeking a redress of grievances, faced a choice between outsider and insider tactics. Outsider tactics such as protests, demonstrations, petitions, and such are relatively inexpensive to undertake in terms of resources and thus appeal to groups lacking capital and access to political elites. Insider tactics – lobbying campaigns in particular – require financial resources to hire representatives and political connections that allow the group's representatives to penetrate the political system. In the Diaspora communities of Europe and the Middle East when mass politics did not exist, Jews had relied almost entirely on intercessors either chosen by the community or so-called "Court Jews" imposed on the Jewish community by the rulers whose favor was sought.

In contesting the three initiatives associated with the Civil War, Jews pursued a hybrid political style that combined lobbying political elites and launching mass appeals designed to move public opinion in a favorable direction, a strategy that made sense in a nation with a democratic political system. Although Jews with connections to political elites might be asked to plead the communal case, the representatives were more often chosen for their expertise and persuasive skills.

For the chaplaincy controversy, the Board of Delegates chose Arnold Fischel, a rabbi who had been serving as religious leader at Congregation Shearith Israel and was, in fact, also denied a chaplaincy despite his status as a minister. As part of his campaign against the Christian-only provision regarding the chaplaincy, Fischel obtained an interview with President Lincoln, who assured him the bill would be amended to include all religious communities. The New York rabbi remained in Washington to lobby members of Congress until the revised Militia Act was passed in 1862. Lincoln also responded to pleas about Grant's expulsion order by cancelling it immediately.

## THE DISCOURSE OF COMMUNAL DEFENSE

Jewish advocates approached these challenges to their political standing through the medium of "rights talk" (Glendon 1991), a mode of discourse emphasizing individual claims to fair treatment based on law. Unsurprisingly, the claims drew most heavily on the legal documents that created and sustained the liberal order of religion and state, Article VI and Amendment I of the Constitution, and the intentions of the founders as understood by the advocates of a secular state. Each of the challenges was portrayed as an attack on the foundational norms of the nation. Jewish leaders insisted that they did not seek either group privileges or sectarian advantages precisely because they objected to any government practices that conferred unique (and in their view, unconstitutional) benefits on certain groups at the expense of others. Jews, the activists insisted, simply wanted what the liberal regime of religion and state had promised, nothing more and nothing less.

I've no doubt that the choice of concepts and terms of argument put forward by Jewish advocates were selected in part for instrumental reasons. As a rhetorical strategy, nesting one's rights within the equality of law under the Constitution was likely to appeal broadly to other Americans who could see it as extending benefits to all rather than privileging one group over another. Similarly, invoking the will of the Founders was a powerful signal that the interests of the group were patriotic in nature. But the close correspondence between the tenor of the public and private communication suggests that the Jewish organizational elites said in public what they believed in private.

The passage of the discriminatory chaplaincy bill also drew protests based on Article VI. In its formal statement on the matter, the Board of Delegates called the exclusion of Jews from this public office a form of religious test in violation of Article VI (1862, 5–6). Their emissary to Congress saw the prohibition on Jewish chaplains as a sinister step on a slippery slope that could end with "further restrictions on further occasions" and, ultimately, to "oppressive laws as will deprive them of the full privileges enjoyed by other citizens" (*Jewish Messenger*, "Display Ad #4," December 27, 1861). Thinking the stakes were even higher, the *Israelite* demanded action against the law "if we mean to be and remain freemen under the constitution and laws of the United States" (*Israelite*, "That Chaplain Law," November 29, 1861).

Private correspondence among the activists emphasized the need to avoid language calling for tolerance and instead emphasized equality of citizenship under the Constitution. Rabbi Fischel, the coordinator of the lobbying campaign against the chaplaincy restriction, told his patron:

The great principle the Jews have to contend for is, [*sic*] that the Constitution takes no cognizance of religious sects and that consequently we do not want special legislation for the Jews, as is the case in England, but all legislation must be general for all American citizens without any regard to their faith. (quoted in Zola 2014, 87)

The message of the Constitution, that such matters were rights rather than indulgences, was conveyed by an outraged journalist (*Israelite*, "Breakers Ahead," March 28, 1862): "The Jews, Sir, do not appeal to your kindness, they seek not the mercy of man; justice is the thing we claim and especially that justice which the constitution and laws of the U.S., the declaration of independence and the progressive enlightenment grant us as men and citizens. We want no more and will take no less, not an inch less."

The editors of the *Jewish Messenger* framed the campaign against Grant's expulsion order as essential to "maintain our rights as American citizens" (*Jewish Messenger*, "Grant's Order" January 16, 1863). The cancellation of the order by President Lincoln removed the immediate threat but the issue persisted into the election of 1868. Whether they favored or opposed Grant's election to the presidency, many Jewish leaders would have endorsed the claim of one influential rabbi that on casting a ballot, "I am not a Jew, but I feel and act as a citizen of the republic" (quoted in Sarna 2012, 73). Chastened by the severe reaction to his order, Grant himself later recognized implicitly that it violated the norms of a nation which knew "no distinction of her own citizens on account of religion or nativity ..." (quoted in Marcus 1996, 202). The comment was all the more striking because it came in then president Grant's letter of introduction for a new American consul to Romania, a Jew who was appointed in part because of his role in fighting against the repression of Jews in eastern Europe.

To an even greater degree, the proposed Christian Amendment to the Constitution was perceived by American Jews as virtual revocation of their citizenship status. In the eyes of a prominent New York financier, the amendment's sinister purpose was "to disfranchise [*sic*] the Jewish community" (Nathan 1864). It would lead Jews to be "deprived of the rights of full citizenship" (*Jewish Messenger*, "The Constitutional Amendment," December 16, 1864). In the *Occident and American Jewish Advocate*, Isaac Leeser warned his readers that the attempt to "engraft Christianity onto the Constitution" meant that non-Christians "may well be excluded from every participation in the government of the country" (quoted in Zola 2014, 127). The Amendment, a stalking horse for stronger Sunday closing laws, religious oaths, Christian education in public schools and other projects, threatened Jews and other non-Christians alike with a "loss of their political and religious equality" (128). Its passage, he argued, would demote American Jews from full members of the polity to mere "aliens in a land where we had hoped for permanent freedom and equality" (134). In the eyes of the *Jewish Messenger*, the Amendment violated the core assumption of political secularism that "religious discipline is essentially distinct from civil authority." According to a correspondent writing to the same paper in 1864, its passage would likely "ultimately end in a series of persecutions and torture such as characterized the priest-ridden era of Europe" (Cohen 1864).

Memorializing Congress, the Board of Deputies of American Israelites said the Jewish community considered the revised preamble nothing less than the "total withdrawal of their precious rights as citizens equal with any others" (quoted in Zola 2014, 136). The campaign for a Christian Amendment, as it was called by the press, persisted into the 1890s and beyond; the proposal lost any realistic chance of passage and never advanced to even a Congressional hearing after 1874. That did not stop Jewish elites from monitoring closely efforts to pass the Amendment. Their opposition was not only about a loss of religious freedom but rather a campaign against devaluing the fundamental status of American Jews as citizens entitled to equality with their fellow Americans.

To a degree that was not manifest in either the chaplaincy or expulsion controversies, the proposed revisions to the Preamble prompted a visceral reaction that expressed itself in extreme language toward the Amendment and its supporters. Even as it languished in Congress over the decades, the Christian Amendment was portrayed as nothing less than:

> "a usurpation of all right and reason, a wild and frantic chase aiming at the immediate destruction of this glorious government"
> a "bigoted, anti-American proposition"
> "aggression upon the rights of our common citizenship"
> "an anti-Republican and monstrous idea"
> "the Sectarian Proposal to Adulterate our Glorious Constitution"
> "one of the most dangerous and vicious propositions ever entertained by sane minds"
> "the proposition to deface the Constitution"
> "the proposition to deform the Constitution"
> "an invasion of our right to liberty of conscience, presignifying [*sic*] legalized disabilities"
> "a prison fortress of religious tyranny"

and its supporters were denigrated as

> "a few raving zealots"
> "a self constituted body of fanatical men."
> "sundry laymen and clericals for the destruction of the Constitution"
> "pioneers in the work of digging the grave of religious liberty and social equality"
> "zealots and fanatics"
> "fanatical tricksters"
> "blind fanatics, hypocrites, crafty priests, and dissemblers"
> "a parcel of plotting fanatics and self-righteous hypocrites."

It is likely that Jewish elites framed the various outrages as betrayals of the Constitution because they believed their good fortune in the United States depended in the last analysis on its legal protection.

Such sentiments became more urgent as Jewish elites confronted the potential unravelling of the Union in the period leading up to the Civil War. Whatever their thoughts about slavery (and Jews were divided) or secession as a strategy, notwithstanding the various controversies in which Jews saw their rights at risk, many put the highest priority on maintaining a system that empowered them as citizens. Noting that the government of the United States "was the first to recognize our claims to absolute equality, with men of whatever religious denomination," a New York newspaper (*Jewish Messenger*, "A Day of Prayer." December 28, 1860, 196) praised the Union as "the source of happiness for our ancestors and ourselves." The Constitution that created it, the writer further declared, enabled Jews to live "in the enjoyment of full and perfect equality with our fellow-citizens." Apart from freedom of religion (and in what might have been a reference to Article VI), the article further attributed to the Constitution the ability of American Jews to "maintain the position to which our abilities entitle us, without our religious opinions being an impediment to advancement."

Rabbi Arnold Fischel (1860), whom we met earlier in the chapter as the advocate (lobbyist) challenging the exclusion of Jews from the chaplaincy, explained his embrace of the Union in these terms. In the waning days of 1860, he warned his congregants that their liberties as Jews "may be endangered by a change in the government of this country." Dissolution of the United States, he averred, might produce "disastrous changes" on the favorable political conditions they enjoyed. He contrasted the status of European Jews as "a distinct body, for whom distinct laws are to be framed" with the situation of American Jews under a constitution that "did not recognize any creed" nor permit any legal distinctions based on religious affiliation. Noting the "enlightened and comprehensive freedom" bestowed on Jews by the Union, he asked and then answered his own question about whether change would improve their status: "Can our rights be more secure, or our political position more favorable under any other government? No rational being could entertain such a delusion." He called upon members of the congregation "to hope, and to pray for the preservation of the Union."

Barely a month later, an unsigned editorial in the *Occident* almost certainly written by Isaac Leeser reached a similar conclusion from a different premise. Leeser (1861) condemned the pietistic spirit that sought to "to save people against their will" as a source of the current "raging against Southern slavery" that had swept the North. If the war produced sectional governments, he believed firmly, "the absolute guarantee of religious liberty" for Jews "would be struck down by the hands of fanatics." In the first Thanksgiving after the war, Jews in a New York congregation may have breathed a sigh of relief on hearing from a respected lawyer that the successful prosecution of the war spared them a "dark future as Israelites and as Americans" (Isaacs 1865).

By the end of the nineteenth century, most formal-legal constraints based on religious identity had been nullified in the United States. No state maintained a formal religious establishment after 1833 and the religious tests that survived were largely neutered by disuse. This did not mean that Jews lacked for grievances nor ceased watching for infringements of their citizenship. Indeed, during the twentieth century, the Jewish community mobilized as never before to resist other initiatives that threatened their interests. But these were in the main issues that affected Jews incidentally rather than frontal assaults in the manner of the Civil War challenges or the diplomatic issues discussed earlier in the chapter. We will now turn to the content of the Jewish political tradition and the means by which it was consolidated.

# 6

## Consolidating Jewish Political Culture

Religious liberty is a right; toleration is a concession.
– Oscar Straus, *Religious Liberty in America*, 1887 (p. 39)

Nineteenth-century banquets sponsored by service organizations typically began with a lengthy round of toasts. At the dinner of the Hebrew Education Society of Philadelphia in the 1850s, attendees raised their glasses to "Civil and Religious Liberty" (Hebrew Education Society 1899, 39–40). When Jewish leaders in Baltimore celebrated the launch of a fund-raising organization for the Jewish poor in 1885, they offered tributes to "Religious freedom, the greatest blessing to mankind" and "The United States of America" (Steinhart 1855). Six years later, responding to the toast, "Civil and Religious Liberty: The National Pride of our Country" at the same organization's anniversary banquet, a rabbi complimented America's founders for creating a nation "upon the basis of civil liberty, religious freedom, and perfect equality in the rights and representation of all its citizens" (Illowy 1861). In 1917, Simon Wolf, a national leader in Jewish circles, replied to a banquet toast to "America" by recalling his emotions on first reading the Declaration of Independence and Constitution in his native Germany: Even before landing in New York, Wolf declared, these documents had made him "to all intents and purposes an American" (Wolf 1926).

Like other symbols of national identification, these toasts reflect American Jewry's homage to the political architecture of the United States. As Chapter 4 demonstrated, American Jews were strong supporters of the US Constitution at its inception. From the founding through the late nineteenth century (as recounted in Chapter 5), they gradually developed a rhetorical framework to support their strong commitment to the classical liberal regime of religion and state. The discourse routinely deployed in various political battles gives a flavor of the communal political culture that emerged as Jewish advocates asserted their political legitimacy during the twentieth century.

This chapter looks systematically at the content of American Jewish political worldview by the time it was consolidated in the early twentieth century. Although it would be modified from time to time as new issues and developments arose on the communal agenda, this political culture reveals how Jews understood politics generally and defined their own role in the political community. I've drawn from a wide array of sources: rabbinic sermons preached on American holidays, tributes to the nation on ceremonial occasions, and remarks by notable Jewish leaders at centennial and other anniversaries. In facing new challenges in the early twentieth century, they championed their Constitutional perspective against competing interpretations at every opportunity.

Worldviews are the product of experience but must be sustained over the long haul by institutions that form, transmit, and reinforce cultural norms. At the outset of the twentieth century, the American Jewish community was undergoing significant change: The German-born and educated elites who spoke for the community during the nineteenth century were gradually supplanted by the Russian and eastern European Jews who arrived in large numbers from the mid-nineteenth century through World War I. Given a large cohort of eastern Europeans unfamiliar with democratic practices, the "veterans" believed, it became especially important to transmit the liberal political culture to them and their children. They worked to instill their respect for the Constitution and their reverence for citizenship in the emerging community.

## THE CONTEXT OF JEWISH POLITICAL CULTURE

While the elites in the Jewish community seem to have agreed on essentials – most especially their status as equal citizens in a secular state – they did not set out to articulate a fully formed community position that would be accepted by all. Rather, the liberal tradition in Jewish political culture emerged gradually, largely in response to battles fought against perceived threats to their full inclusion in the American political system. Some of those threats were recounted in Chapter 5. I begin here by summarizing the perspectives *against which* American Jews contended in their various campaigns. The positions that Jews developed can be understood only against the backdrop of forces that challenged their full membership in the political community.

In a nation of immigrants and a society without inherited rank, Jews encountered less anti-Semitism and milder varieties of it than were commonplace in the Old World (Pencak 2011). Yet even in this relatively benign environment, some stereotypes died hard. "Old Stock" Americans who traced their heritage to Britain entertained nativist prejudices against newcomers like Jews, Catholics, and other ethnic and religious minorities (some home-grown like Mormons) and directed much more virulent hostility to imported Asian laborers and freed African slaves (Higham 2002).

As trans-Atlantic ships disgorged tens of thousands of (mostly non-Jewish) newcomers from southern and eastern Europe onto American shores in the decades after the Civil War, those who claimed aristocratic ancestry reacted with furious defensive activity. In the nineteenth century, this sentiment periodically congealed into social movements that took the form of political parties (the Know-Nothings) and other mass-based organizations such as the American Protective Association (APA). These organizations undertook campaigns to defend social practices they saw as under threat from the alien hordes (as contemporary literature often designated the immigrants). Although couched in the language of American nationalism, the common thread underlying APA initiatives was defending white, Anglo Protestant hegemony through legislation and other projects such as the proposed Christian Amendment to the Constitution discussed in Chapter 5.

The Americanism movement was aimed principally at the dangers posed by Catholics, who, it was charged, put their loyalty to Rome above American patriotism. Even if they weren't the principal target of nativism, Jews were still wary of efforts to define the United States based on ethnic and religious identity. They were particularly alarmed by rhetoric designating the United States a Christian nation.

Jews had long assailed public officials who used such terminology. They objected not merely that the language was sectarian nor that it promoted intolerance but that it violated their rights under the law. Reviewing gubernatorial proclamations that framed the Thanksgiving holiday as a Christian celebration in 1854, an *Israelite* author declared with some hyperbole that nothing else was so "utterly repugnant to American constituted law, so violently opposed to the spirit of our constitution and more dangerous to our free institutions than this promulgation by the officers of the State of their private religious opinions under the seal of their office ..." (*Israelite*, "Thanks Giving," December 15, 1854).

When California's speaker of the House told Jews they should accept Sunday closing laws as a tolerated minority in a Christian nation, the *American Israelite* lampooned him as "His Holiness King Stowe" (*Israelite*, "Sunday Trading Bill," May 11, 1855). The newspaper described him harshly as a traitor who "endeavors to undermine the rights of the citizens" and, for good measure, "a perjurer ... who has taken the oath, to support the constitution of his State and of the United States, and then attempts to violate the first and most essential principle of these constitutions, the equality of rights to all." In a Thanksgiving Day sermon, a rabbi indicted Pennsylvania's governor who had issued a holiday proclamation addressed explicitly only to Christians. By conflating his religious beliefs with state business, the rabbi charged, the official had ignored "the character of the Constitution of the United States" (Jastrow 1868, 5).

From the perspective of Christian Nation advocates, Jews were incapable of true membership in the political community because they were under the sway of a tribal faith that put the interests of the Jewish community above that of the nation. This was not a new claim against the Jews, having been used centuries earlier by opponents of Jewish emancipation, and even Napoleon, who conferred citizenship on French Jews, had first to be assured that they were French rather than Jewish nationalists.

Some people who otherwise held liberal views, such as the Cornell historian Goldwin Smith (1891), saw Jews as an alien presence unfit for democracy. "Detached from their own country," he wrote (137), "they insert themselves for the purpose of gain into the homes of other nations, while they retain a marked and repellent nationality of their own. They are not the only parasitic race, though they are incomparably the most important and formidable." To become patriotic citizens, Jews had to be "derabbinized and denationalized" (141), giving up circumcision, a sense of chosenness, their Sabbath, dietary laws, a commitment to in-group marriage, the Hebrew Bible, and virtually all other markers of group identity.[1]

---

[1] Even though he had satisfied all the criteria on Goldwin Smith's checklist, British Prime Minister Benjamin Disraeli still drew anti-Semitic barbs from Smith when the historian taught at Oxford.

Because American Jews *had* been emancipated – admitted to the privilege of citizenship by the Constitution – Smith was not calling on the state to withdraw the formal-legal citizenship that Jews enjoyed by birthright or naturalization. Rather, he was arguing that Jews could not be good citizens and were destined to remain an estranged people who were not truly part of the American nation. The idea that Jews were a nation within a nation, and hence untrustworthy, was commonly deployed against them by advocates of Christian America.

As an intellectual construct, the claim that Jews could not be true patriots was repellant but not threatening. Jews worried much more when Christian America sentiments entered legal discourse. For Jews, any such assertion about the religious identity of the United States was a direct challenge to their own status as equal citizens. As historian Naomi Cohen (1989, 17) observed, "By its very definition, a Christian nation precluded full equality" which is why Jews fought so vigorously against any linkage between religion and state.

The issue was joined in 1892 when Associate US Supreme Court Justice David J. Brewer asserted in *Church of the Holy Trinity vs. United States* that "this is a Christian nation" (143 U.S. 457), a doctrine he later expounded in magazine articles, public lectures, and a book. Although Brewer's claim was highly disputed and seldom cited as a legal precedent, the idea of the United States as a Christian Nation was not his alone. According to the legal scholar Linda Przybyszewski (2000), Brewer's dictum was widely accepted by other Protestant judges who took for granted that the "civic order of the Republic rested on the Christian faith of its citizens."

The Jewish press repeatedly denounced Christian leaders who justified the primacy of Christian values in public policy merely because Christians constituted a majority of the population. Such rhetoric was captured by the remarks of an unnamed minister at an 1867 public meeting in Pittsburgh. While insisting that the proposed Christian Amendment to the Constitution did not violate the prohibition on religious tests for public office, he opined that it was better "to infringe the rights of men than the rights of God" (*Israelite*, "Bigots at Work," April 26, 1867). A Baptist preacher was quoted in another context offering Jews what he must have thought was friendly advice:

Let the Jews go peaceably about their own affairs, accepting the fact that they are citizens of a Christian nation and they will continue to enjoy the prosperity and respect which has been accorded them by the Christian citizens of America in the past (Friedman 1908).

To Jewish ears, this sounded at best patronizing, at worst like a veiled threat to the equal citizenship they cherished.

Although most scholars dismissed Brewer's statement as a mere *obiter dictum*, an observation that does not interpret the law in question nor stand as a precedent, Jews found it and similar statements a fundamental danger to their own legal status. The same vitriolic rhetoric that Jews employed in their fight against the Christian amendment (see Chapter 5) reappeared in their reaction to Brewer's contention about the religious character of the American state. They dismissed his argument, recognizing the danger inherent in awarding to Christianity "a legal and a civic status not properly found in our fundamental State papers" (Hassler 1907, June 7). Indeed, the very idea of imposing a religious identity on the state struck them as contrary to the letter and spirit of the Constitution and the will of the founders.

## HOW JEWS UNDERSTOOD THE REGIME OF CHURCH AND STATE

As I noted in Chapter 4, Jews celebrated passage of the Constitution in the late eighteenth century as their fundamental charter of rights and liberties. They emphasized those aspects of the document that most closely adhered to classical liberalism's notion of religion as essentially a private matter beyond the purview of the state and barely relevant to its functions. They were confident that their interpretation accurately and completely channeled the intentions of the founders, laying out a legal framework that granted them the same equal rights and legal protections enjoyed by other citizens. The Jewish political culture was also an implicit (and sometimes explicit) rebuke to those who treated them as at best a tolerated minority or as a population incapable of patriotism.

By the early twentieth century, we can discern several propositions that had become commonplace among American Jews and provided the foundation for the political culture that survives in large part more than a century later. Although some of these beliefs have been mentioned earlier, they bear repeating as a part of a comprehensive system of interlocking assumptions. They can best be stated in the form of propositions with supporting commentary.

**Secularity:** The Constitution was intended to govern civil life and leave religious matters to society. The source of political authority in the United States was the People, not any religious system or group. Hence, it was inappropriate for religious groups or individuals to seek civil sanction for their sectarian religious values. Religious associations of all types were essentially private corporations entitled to basic protections under the law but not part of the state apparatus (McGarvie 2004).

By 1879, the *American Israelite* declared that "the very fundamental principle" underlying the Constitution was that equal "rights, privileges, and duties" were entirely independent of religious creed (Straus 1879). Concluding his sermon celebrating the centennial of the Constitutional Convention in 1887, the rabbi of a large Philadelphia congregation described the founders' document succinctly: "No creed, no sect should be distinguished. The State shall favor none" (*Jewish Exponent*, "Sermons," September 23, 1887). Even more concisely, his colleague in another pulpit reduced the philosophy of the Constitution further: "The civil law had to do with relation of men to each other, and not with the relations of men to God" (Mueller 1899).

The concept of a secular state was articulated much more fully by two influential American Jewish leaders, one religious, one secular. A German immigrant and the principal organizer of Reform Jewry in the United States, Rabbi Isaac Mayer Wise argued that the framers of the constitution had drawn their principles of statecraft from the Hebraic political tradition (Wise 1872). He concluded that the purpose in drafting the document was a secular state: "All these things are done, not for the sake of God, but for the sake of man. They are not done directly by God, but directly by man, and for his benefit exclusively." Hence, there was no basis for either favoring or discriminating against citizens based on religion. Where such values reigned, the idea of a Christian nation was an "offspring of fantasy."

Louis Marshall, the key figure in the twentieth century leadership of American Jewry and himself the child of German immigrants, made the case for the secular state as a lawyer. He acknowledged that most American colonies had extended rights based on religious criteria, favoring some residents and penalizing others. But during the struggle for independence, the colonists united across colonial boundaries and forged a bond based on common national interests. Steeped in the ideas of the Enlightenment, they drew on that sentiment to found a republic based firmly on the equality of men. These developments led to "the entire elimination of every religious conception from our scheme of civil government" (Marshall 1908b). So firmly did Marshall insist on this point that he even objected to language in a 1908 government pamphlet that presented a carefully hedged and qualified assertion that the United States was a Christian county "in the sense that the largest number of people here believe in the religion of Christ" (US Department of Commerce and Labor 1908a, 4–5). He argued that including such language in an official document violated the Constitution and traditions of the United States by stimulating a theological discussion (Marshall 1908a).[2]

This expansive definition of secularity extended the penumbra of the Constitution beyond believers to encompass as well "the agnostic, the infidel, the nonbeliever of every stripe and every shade" (Marshall 1908c). By the mid-nineteenth century, as the ideas in the federal constitution permeated the states, the "divorce" between religion and civil government became "absolute and complete." As Nina Morais put it (1881, 267), Americans came to agree that "the state is a social expedient, not a divine organism." *Der Tog*, a New York Yiddish newspaper, affirmed that sentiment on Independence Day in 1924, noting that the holiday really celebrated independence "from the idea that a Government is an ethnic instrument, that political institutions are the reflex of racial instincts, that to be a member of a certain country one had to have a certain ancestry" (Marcus 1996, 312). The foremost church–state authority in the Jewish community took for granted that the peculiarly American understanding of religious liberty extended beyond concern with infringement of conscience. The Constitution, he averred, forbade any and all consideration of religion "with respect to anything that the state may grant or regulate" (Kohler 1930, 670). As such, blood and soil nationalism had no legitimacy in the United States.

**Christian Nation:** Lacking a religious identity or state church, the United States could not accurately be described as a Christian Nation. While the term might be accurate descriptively in a country with a Christian majority, it had no legal status. Jews should resist efforts by any group based on particularistic claims.

As noted earlier in this chapter, Jews battled against the idea of the United States as a Christian Nation, deeming it a "a perversion of historical and legal truth" to claim that majority status had any implication for civil status (Hassler 1907, June 7). They could not ignore traditions such as swearing oaths on the Bible, the national motto on American coins,

---

[2] Marshall urged Oscar Straus, the secretary of commerce who had written a biography of Roger Williams and other publications that emphasized the separation of religion and state, to drop all references to religion in the pamphlet. Marshall also noted that the offending statement was incorrect because the "religion of Christ" was Judaism and most Americans thus practiced the religion of Paul. It's unlikely Marshall would have made this point to any government official but a fellow Jew.

congressional and military chaplaincies, or the use of "Anno Domini" (in the year of our Lord) in legal documents but dismissed these examples of ceremonial deism as "pious boot-legging" with no substantive meaning (Jacobson 1913, 5). In time, these "survivals from our political evolution" would be cut out of the political body. Those who thought that majority status granted Christian privilege had forgotten the elemental truth that "constitutions are framed largely for the purpose of restricting the brutal exercise of its power by a majority" (Hassler 1907, May 31).

**Citizenship:** Jews, as such, were not a bloc or party deserving toleration. Neither were they a "nation" in the sense of a people that "sees itself as distinct from all others, deserves self-determination, and can be secure and fulfill its national destiny only if it has its own national state" (Barnett 2016, 36).[3] Rather, Jews were individuals who shared a religious heritage. Their religious views were entitled to respect to the same degree enjoyed by other religious associations, but not to political power. Jews belonged to the United States on the same terms as everyone else and had the same "ownership" rights as their countrymen based on the principle of equal citizenship.

Considering the positive associations engendered by the concept of tolerance in the contemporary world, it is jarring to encounter its bitter denunciation by Jews in the nineteenth and early twentieth centuries. Strangely, this negative connotation originates with George Washington's famous response to the letter of welcome sent to him by the Jews of Newport, Rhode Island, in 1789. Although much of the letter involved Washington quoting back the text sent by the Jewish community, he added to the original by denouncing tolerance as the "indulgence of one class of people that another enjoyed the exercise of their inherent natural

---

[3] James Loeffler (2015a) has offered a powerful counterargument to the claim that American Jews rejected Jewish nationalism. He sees nationalism as less about creating an independent nation or achieving some form of recognized autonomy within an existing state and more about identifying with threatened communities abroad (372). In that sense, American Jews simply "outsourced their Jewish nationhood to the State of Israel" (375), making their nationalism invisible. This approach amounts to transforming politicized ethnic consciousness, a variable quality among Jews, into bona fide nationalism (Wald 2008b; Wald and Williams 2006). Further, as Barnett has argued (2016, 147), it is not surprising that American Jews would rally in support of their coreligionists abroad when the latter were threatened. They had done so in the nineteenth and early twentieth centuries over the Damascus Blood Libel (1840), the various outbreaks of anti-Jewish pogroms in Russia (especially Kishinev in 1903), and other outrages that put Jewish lives at risk. These actions should not be equated with nationalism.

rights." Jewish leaders could not quote this phrase often enough. In their discourse, the modifier "mere" so often preceded "tolerance" that the two words seemed permanently conjoined.

Like Washington, Jews argued that they warranted equality by right, not as a concession or privilege. As early as 1845, an editorial in the *Occident* opined that "the Jew is not tolerated in this country; he belongs to the constitution ..." (*Occident*, "Israelites," January 1, 1845, 498). Proclaiming the word tolerance "odious" to Jews, a Chicago rabbi (Schanfarber 1906) insisted that the Jew opposed religious legislation on the principle that "this country has nothing to do with religion." A sermon preached in 1911 nicely distinguished between "the pale, sickly plant of religious tolerance" and "the rich, ripe fruit of absolute religious equality" (*Jewish Messenger*, "Thanksgiving Day," November 24, 1911). A distinguished jurist pushed the metaphor one step further by likening toleration to a "noxious week" that had finally been "extirpated" and denied nourishment on American soil (Sulzberger 1904, 1). In the United States, Jews insisted, "there is neither tolerator nor tolerated" (Hassler 1907, May 31).

The tone of the assertions became increasingly pugnacious in the early twentieth century as Jews became increasingly comfortable asserting their place in the American political order. The celebration of the 250th anniversary of the arrival of Jews in America in 1905 called forth reflections on their status in the United States. Referring to Jewish sacrifices in the cause of American independence and subsequent wars, Rabbi David Philipson of Cincinnati asserted in 1906 that Jews "need not crawl before any man in America" because they had purchased equality "by the blood of our ancestors" (*Two Hundred and Fiftieth Anniversary* 1906,145). The committee that arranged a Carnegie Hall celebration of the anniversary assured its audience that the Jew appreciated the Constitutional freedoms he enjoyed but "does not regard those blessings as a mere gift from others, but as of right his ..." (243). A prominent Boston layman, celebrating the same anniversary at Faneuil Hall, confidently described American Jews as "part and parcel of the great American body politic" rather than "adopted children in an alien land" (63). Jews do not, said another speaker in New York, cringe and fawn when seeking liberty and equality but demand it as a birthright (145).

Escalating the tone around the time of World War I, the *American Israelite* proclaimed in 1916 that American Jews "resent the pretention that we are permitted to live in our country as a privilege or that we owe gratitude to anyone therefore, except to the fathers who so wisely planned this commonwealth" (*Israelite*, "Right, not Toleration," October 12, 1916). Cyrus Adler echoed the sentiment in a private letter to a fellow Jewish activist. Acknowledging that he had worked tirelessly to achieve equal rights for Jews, he added somewhat peevishly that these rights "in no way call for a special gratitude" (quoted in Robinson 1985, 229).

Jews also denied forcefully that their patriotism was tainted because they owed their loyalty first to the Jewish "nation" and only then to the United States. One of the core tenets of the numerically dominant Reform Jewish movement was precisely that Jews no longer constituted a "nation." They consistently distinguished between their status as Jews in the synagogue but Americans in the street, reducing Judaism from an all-encompassing tribal identity to a religious preference. To suggest that Jews formed a nation apart from other Americans, it was claimed by an influential layman, violated the norms of American government:

America is not the place for the national Jew, because the very principles upon which this American Government was founded and the very reason we are here, is because there is no distinction between one man and another and all men are brothers... The Jew must not be the one to destroy that idea in America. (quoted in "As to a Jewish Congress" 1906, 89–90)

At the 250th anniversary celebration, a distinguished jurist declaimed of his coreligionists "that we are Jews in our religion, that we are Jews in caring for our own, but that in all else we are American citizens . . ." (Mack quoted in *Two Hundred and Fiftieth Anniversary*, 1906, 144). We will see in Chapter 7 how this mantra, a staple of Jewish discourse, made so many American Jews ambivalent (at best) about the prospect of diaspora nationalism at the Versailles Peace Treaty following World War I and the prospect of reconstituting a Jewish state in Palestine. Yet it was essential if Jews were to insist that they were indissolubly linked to their fellow Americans by the bond of citizenship and had no other national loyalty.

**Responsibility:** Jews had a special obligation to the United States for it was the first nation to grant them equal citizenship as a matter of law. Indeed, they perceived the adoption of the Constitution was one of the most important developments in the history of Judaism. For the first time since their exile from the Judaic kingdoms of the Biblical period, Jews enjoyed the same sovereignty as other citizens. As such, Jews had a responsibility to ensure that the Constitution was respected and its provisions enforced. This obligation should be discharged by responding vigorously to violations of the liberal regime and avoiding sectarian language or action in their own advocacy.

Jews heeded (and then some) James Madison's famous admonition to take alarm at the first sign of attempts to infringe Constitutional rights. As Jews, freemen, and republicans, an Orthodox rabbi instructed his congregation in 1855 that they must "watch that liberty be not injured by the men we raise to power" (*Israelite*, "Thanksgiving at the Greene Street Congregation," December 14, 1855). When in 1858 Congress passed a treaty with China guaranteeing the rights of American Christian missionaries but not Jews, a rabbi acknowledged that though the impact would be trivial, the *theoretical* wrong "is an infringement on our rights, and ought to be resisted" (quoted in Borden 1984, 80). Ten years later, a rabbi still felt compelled to urge "ye sons of Israel" to "raise your loudest voice, whenever the slightest attack is attempted on your freedom and equal rights" (Jastrow 1868, 7). The mobilization of Jews throughout the eighteenth and nineteenth centuries is proof of how much they took that responsibility to heart.

But Jews did not limit such scrutiny to Christians alone and policed themselves aggressively to ensure that they did not provide unwelcome models of religious advocacy even in the private sphere. When faced with attacks on their rights as American citizens, Isaac Leeser told the readers of his newspaper in 1855, Jews must resist the tendency to form a Jewish party or section within a political party (*Occident*, "Politics," February 1, 1855). Even when facing dire threats from "traitors to justice and freedom" bent on overthrowing Article VI and Amendment I, he counselled, Jews should coalesce with "the friends of the constitution, of equal rights, of freedom, not as Jews, however, but as true citizens of America" (30). For strategic reasons, they must learn to "separate the Jew from the citizen."

Mayer Sulzberger, an associate of Leeser and editor of his *Occident* for a time, complained that his coreligionists tended wrongly to "rush forward to claim civil rights for Jews as Jews, instead of as citizens" (quoted in Whiteman 1987, 17). That never happened when the Board of Delegates on Civil and Religious Rights (successor to the Board of Delegates of American Israelites after 1878) engaged in advocacy. The reports presented annually by Simon Wolf routinely included strong declarations that the Board had always framed its appeals based on the rights accorded American citizens and refused to claim special privileges for American Jews beyond that legal status.[4]

The depth of commitment to privilege American citizenship over Jewish particularism was revealed even more clearly by three instructive episodes from the late nineteenth and early twentieth centuries.

As the US centennial approached in 1876, the B'nai B'rith fraternal order commissioned a statue celebrating religious liberty to be donated to the US government. An internationally known sculptor was retained to produce a monument dedicated specifically to the Constitutional prohibitions against "disfranchisement or political discrimination on account of religion" (Abraham 1875). The proposal garnered objections because it seemed to suggest Jews had a special obligation to celebrate what were, after all, fundamental rights due all Americans as equal citizens under the Constitution (Sanger 1876). It would be, the critics argued, "undignified and a debasing and unworthy exhibition of great want of self-respect" if Jews were to suggest they owed gratitude for special favors.

When the statue was finally dedicated in late November, long past the scheduled date, the speaker emphasized that it should not be interpreted in a sectarian manner. "We do not conceive that it is strictly as Jews that we enjoy Religious Liberty," he declared, "nor do we profess any distinctive character as members of a great community" (Sanger 1876).[5] Jews enjoyed exactly the same liberty as others and the statue was meant "to disclaim the idea that we are exercising our powers by mere sufferance or toleration."[6]

In 1909, the Central Conference of American Rabbis (CCAR) of the Reform movement debated a proposal to ask Congress to appoint paid, full-time Jewish chaplains in the armed forces (Central Conference of American Rabbis 1909, 137–143). The motion arose after the discovery that the military then employed not a single Jewish chaplain to minister to

---

[4] The ten reports presented to the UAHC from 1892 through 1901 contained a total of seventeen explicit statements disavowing any claims of special rights for Jews.

[5] The statue now stands outside the National Museum of Jewish History in Philadelphia, a short walk from Constitution Hall. The entrepreneur responsible for the statue of Haym Solomon in Chicago followed the same strategy by proposing the monument as a tribute to American diversity (Young 2011).

[6] When a group of Sephardic Jews proposed in 1889 that a similar statue be commissioned to commemorate the expulsion of Jews from Spain and the voyage of Columbus, both events of 1492, the *American Israelite* responded archly that it refused to make a "Jewish" demonstration of an event that should be celebrated by all humanity. "We cannot and will not single ourselves out as a special political community, and erect for ourselves a modern Ghetto," the article insisted (*Israelite*, "Jewish Demonstration," June 27, 1889).

Jewish enlistees. Perhaps remembering their own agitation over the chaplaincy during the Civil War, a CCAR committee urged the organization to tread gently. Instead of seeking government support for chaplains, they recommended that congregational rabbis in towns with military installations should volunteer to fill the need for Jews in the armed services. When a delegate instead pushed his brethren to petition the government for the appointment of Jewish chaplains, several rabbis objected vociferously. Declared one: "It is the very foundation of our republic, that State and Religion be entirely separate. Are we going now to endorse the idea of appointing these officials in our name, to officiate in the army and navy?" Acknowledging that he expected to hear "the Eagle scream" because his resolution suggested "fusion of Church and State," Rabbi Calisch chided his colleagues who seemed to have no problem intermingling church–state finances by receiving tax exemptions for their synagogues. Unmoved, the motion was rejected.

The relation of American Jews to the United States also faced serious challenges from the emergence of Zionism among eastern European immigrants in the late nineteenth century. Like other forms of Jewish nationalism, the movement for a homeland rested on an assumption that Jews formed a distinct "nation" with interests that differed from those of other groups in their current country of residence. To most of the German Jews who still dominated American Jewish organizational life at the beginning of the twentieth century, such movements challenged Jews' claim to belong fully and exclusively to the American nation. Organizing Jews on political grounds, they cautioned, violated the constitutional principle separating religion and state that forbade them to form a Jewish community "for any other than strictly religious purposes." (Kohler 1915). As subsequent chapters demonstrate, this issue continued to challenge Jewish claims that their sole political commitment was to the preservation of the United States.

**Religion and Politics:** Religion is dangerous to politics because it stirs up latent hostility and encourages fanaticism that threatens the Constitution. For their part, Jews should avoid religious language in the public sphere and defend their rights as American citizens without "God talk." When challenging practices that seemed unconstitutional, they should form alliances with other groups so that Jews are not perceived as seeking selfish goals. So the Jewish political culture counselled.

Jewish writers took for granted that any linkage of religion and state invariably undermined both. They ascribed the founders' aversion to a Christian state to their awareness that fusing church and state had ignited "more persecution, more bloodshed, more wars, more misery during the so-called Christian centuries, than any other single thing" (David Phillipson quoted in *The Two Hundred and Fiftieth Anniversary* 1906, 139). From his experience of trying to remove Christian religious teaching from the Denver public schools, Rabbi William Friedman (1908) testified to the toxic nature of political conflicts based on religion. "Confessional" political conflicts tended to arouse "the poisonous serpents of venom and ill will" because rational consideration was "consumed by the fires of impulsive passion and inherited prejudice." Louis Marshall advised American Jews to stamp out the "virus of religious controversy" whenever it threatened to impinge on the political system (Marshall, 1908c).

**Mission:** Jews should be reminded constantly of the virtues of the American political system and the way it enabled Jews from around the globe to obtain refuge from religious persecution and state-sanctioned inequality. Like the commandment in Deuteronomy recited at Sabbath worship, Jews should "teach diligently unto to their children" the text of the Constitution's religious provisions, emphasizing the meaning of equal citizenship. Apart from policing the boundary between religion and state, monitoring potential violations, Jews had an obligation to act in ways that brought credit to their faith and they should be seen to honor their obligations as American citizens. In his peroration to a Thanksgiving sermon in 1912, Rabbi Max Klein reminded his congregants of their responsibility as Jews and citizens to "consider America the instrument in the hand of God, teaching the world Justice and Humanity" (Klein 1912). Such expressions were so common that Jonathan Sarna (1998) identifies a veritable "cult of synthesis" melding American and Jewish precepts and Sylvia Barack Fishman (2000) describes a similar "coalescence" of American and Judaic themes in contemporary Jewish culture.[7]

To distill these six principles into a short credo, I turn to an unsigned editorial in a New York newspaper (*Jewish Messenger*, "Thanksgiving Day," November 24, 1911). The unknown author wove the six propositional strands into a single braid that articulated the core political interests recognized by American Jewry in the early twentieth century.

---

[7] In the polemical *Rabbis and Lawyers*, Auerbach (1990) argues that this synthesis was a historical fiction that did enormous damage to the integrity of American Judaism.

... the rights of all citizens must be determined in the light of their citizenship regardless of their religious affiliations. The humblest citizen must be protected and safeguarded without reference to his church connection ... The maintenance of this principle, as a principle, is a sacred obligation upon us, not alone merely as Jews, for the preservation of our rights as such, but as Americans that we may hand it down to posterity unimpaired in sanctity and undimmed in lustre ... *there will be no quasi-political object which will associate our energy more vigorously than the preservation of this principle* [my emphasis] ...

Virtually a mission statement, the editorial captures the underlying assumptions, the rhetorical style, and the operative strategy employed by American Jews since the founding of the Republic. In a nation with a secular regime like the United States, Jewish rights were a function of citizenship on which religion had no bearing. Rather than assume that this arrangement would perpetuate itself, Jews must organize and advocate on behalf of these values. If Jews were not a political party, they nonetheless had a program to guide their actions. But because programs are not self-executing, Jews needed to act to defend the equality promised by the Constitution.

### RABBIS AS SOCIALIZING AGENTS

The leaders of the Jewish community understood that political cultures must be reaffirmed until they became communal norms (Brumberg 1986, 217). The political culture of American Judaism at the outset of the twentieth century was no exception. The journalists, professional advocates, lawyers, and others who developed its content also transmitted it to the Jewish masses. To encourage ordinary Jews to take ownership of its assumptions, elites worked through the pulpit and educational institutions. While many rank-and-file Jews remained outside the sphere of Jewish newspapers and national organizations, most who connected with the community probably did so through their local congregations. Hence rabbis became critical nodes in communicating Jewish thought to local networks and sustaining commitment to the classical liberal regime. They were joined by the educational institutions that developed to address the needs of the eastern European immigrants, adults, and children alike.

Although one might imagine rabbis tending only to the spiritual and educational needs of their flocks, leaving politics to others, the assumption would be quite wrong. As we have already seen in this chapter, rabbis in the late nineteenth/early twentieth centuries participated in constructing the Jewish political culture and ranked among its most ardent publicists.

Rather than stand aloof from political controversies, many clergy waded in full stream to help their congregants navigate the political waters. Enough did to provide us with a good sense of how they communicated with their congregants.

The rabbis brought a distinctive worldview about American politics to the Jews sitting in the pews. To a remarkable degree, their sermons treated the American constitutional system as divinely created and ordained. They virtually deified the founders and their work, treating the United States as the truest expression of Jewish religious values and the creation of the federal constitution as a world-historical event. They used special occasions – national holidays, anniversaries, and other public celebrations – to propound this message. These clerics shared the commitment of secular elites to promoting the liberal regime of religion and state.

I focus here on three leading Jewish religious leaders of the nineteenth century whose words have been preserved in sufficient quantity to reconstruct their political thinking. Though no three individuals can be said to represent fully the variegated Judaism that developed in America, these leaders differed sufficiently in ethnic background and approach to Judaism to encompass the variety of the American Jewish community prior to the massive immigration of eastern Europeans in the late nineteenth century. Each has been recognized as an influential spokesperson for Jews of his time.

Isaac Leeser (1806–1868), born in Germany, migrated to the United States in 1824 and assumed religious leadership of Congregation Mikveh Israel in Philadelphia five years later. Though not an ordained rabbi despite his prestigious pulpit, he was described by his biographer (Sussman 1995, 12) as "the outstanding Jewish religious leader in America prior to the Civil War." He helped shape Jewish orthodoxy as it was first manifest in the United States.

Leeser was succeeded in the Mikveh Israel pulpit by Sabato Morais, an Italian-born religious scholar born in 1823 who arrived in the United States in 1851. Described in the *New York Times* as "the most eminent rabbi in this country" at his death in 1897 (Kiron 1996, 157), Morais was closer than his predecessor to Sephardi Judaism and thus reflects the views of that stream of Jewish immigrants. Although an important defender of Orthodox Judaism, Morais also contributed to the emergence of the Conservative movement, a more centrist type of Judaism, by helping create the Jewish Theological Seminary.

Considered the first ordained rabbi in the United States, Max Lilienthal was a German born (1815) immigrant who arrived in the

United States in 1845. Although he arrived as a modern Orthodox rabbi, he gradually moved toward the emerging Reform movement and found a pulpit in Cincinnati in 1855. Prior to his death in 1882, he spent decades as rabbi of Bene Israel congregation and helped shape what was called moderate Reform Judaism during the second half of the nineteenth century. More broadly, he is remembered as a "seminal rabbinic leader whose experiences over more than thirty years shaped the American rabbinate" (Ruben 2011, 1).

His religious traditionalism notwithstanding, Isaac Leeser became a strong advocate of the rights of American Jews, launching jeremiads in his many writings and in the pages of his monthly newspaper, the *Occident*. Leeser accepted that life for Jews in the United States was qualitatively different owing to the equal rights provided by the Constitution; under its beneficence, he preached in 1844, "the spirit of Judaism can shine forth ... without let or hindrance from the malign influence of political disqualifications" (1867, 532). He ended the sermon beseeching God to "preserve the constitution which secures equal rights to all." Jews should not leave the task of defending the Constitution solely to God. Rather, they should use their vote to elect public officials who defend civil and religious liberty, the two objects, he asserted "Jews should prize, next to our religion, as the best gift of God to man" (*Occident*, "Rishuth III," March, 1865, 531).

Leeser offered a fundamentalist interpretation of equality under the law. Any law that restricted the rights of individuals for religious purposes, whether making Sunday a day of rest for the Union Army or mandating closing businesses on Sunday, was beyond the legitimate purview of the state articulated in "our beloved constitution" (*Occident*, "Are We Equals?" January 1, 1863). Echoing Thomas Jefferson, he insisted that the state had no interest in restraining individuals based on religion unless their behavior did manifest harm to their fellow citizens. His belief in the equality owed to Jews by the Constitution extended even to their mourning the death of President William Henry Harrison in 1841. Jews should mingle their tears with those of their countrymen, he advised because "as the equals in the eyes of the law," Jews had suffered a loss "which is no less ours than theirs" (1868, Vol. 4, 31–32).

Leeser was especially sensitive to what he saw as violations of the principles enumerated in the Constitution. He insisted that Jews had equal rights *in principle* but frequently stressed that the numerical dominance of Christians often undermined the *practice* of equality. His language was sometimes apocalyptic. When Congress approved the Swiss treaty in 1854 (see Chapter 5), Leeser glumly noted that notwithstanding Jews "theoretical rights," they remained in exile (*galuth*) in the United States. As Jews, his brethren could "make all the noise in the world, and brag aloud after our heart's content, *we are yet strangers* in stranger lands" (quoted in Borden 1984, 91, emphasis in original).

Although Leeser believed that God had directed the Chosen People to this land and bestowed religious and civil liberty on them, he did not accept that the New World had supplanted Messianic longing. While affirming his pride in bearing the title of "American," he nevertheless admitted a preference for a Jewish homeland. As an Israelite, he confessed, he would welcome a reconstituted Jewish state where "the Israelite would be free, not because the stranger grants it, but because his laws, his religion, his faith, constitute him a part and parcel of the state itself" (1868, Vol. 6, 131). Even so, he constantly advised his readers to value, celebrate, and pray for the United States, where Jews had found equality and the means to preserve it – the franchise and citizenship.

Sabato Morais, who left a voluminous record of sermons and other public addresses, was no less voluble than Leeser in praising the United States, "this land of equal rights, where the religious tenets of a majority can claim no higher privileges than those revered by a minority ..." Even during the trying days of the Civil War, his Thanksgiving Day text referred to the "terrestrial lustre of the American Constitution" (Morais 1862) and characterized it as the "palladium of our liberties (1861). Some years later, he expanded on those phrases by depicting the Constitution as a document "which discards any religious test, and favors no dogma" (Morais 1876b, 6). As a Philadelphian, he could not resist identifying Independence Hall where the Constitution was written as "the spot which the grandest of all incidents in modern history has hallowed" (Morais 1876b, 2)

Not unlike Leeser, Morais' sermons were replete with prayers of gratitude to God for founding and sustaining the Republic from its enemies. On Thanksgiving of 1876, he urged the congregation to pray "for the permanence and undiminished lustre of the Northern Republic," which was "the seat of political and religious liberty" (Morais 1876b, "Thanksgiving"). In Morais' view, God's embrace of the nation was not unconditional: Only if the nation adhered to the Constitution would it eventually assume its rightful place as "a Divine-appointed mistress of a new world, and the tutor of the old" (Morais 1876b, 7).

Morais' patriotic language about American institutions and leaders used a tone that might be classified as "political sanctification" (Bennett

1975) if not outright blasphemy. During the Civil War, when it appeared that the American experiment might come to an end, he likened himself to Moses beholding the Promised Land from a distance (Morais 1863, 2):

> I have (without irreverence let it be said) stood with my mind on the Summit of Pisgah to survey this land of promise, which has beckoned to her hospitable shores the weary of all nations and climes. More fortunate than the immortal Seer of old, I have been permitted to enter this new Canaan, every spot of which is sanctified by the footsteps of revolutionary heroes.

Such Biblical analogies were not unusual in nineteenth-century preaching but Morais went well beyond that practice in a fourth of July sermon that granted universal historical significance to the American founding (Morais undated).[8] He portrayed the United States in messianic terms as "the harbinger of the world's deliverance" which had thrown off "absolutism and priest-craft." The day of deliverance was nearer because God had sent the American colonies George Washington, "the great Sower of righteousness." Together with Abraham Lincoln, Washington was "predestined to level the way for the approach of salvation" and thus should be recognized by Jews as God's minister to their small community. Once all the world adopted the American liberal model of religion and state, he foresaw that Jews worldwide would forever cease their weeping, transforming their traditional three weeks of mourning for the destruction of Jerusalem and loss of political sovereignty "into a period of festivity."

Morais further insisted that God's protection of the United States depended not only on the personal righteousness of Americans in their private conduct but equally on their loyalty to the secularity of the state. He joined his fellow Jewish leaders in denouncing the attempt to import Christianity into the Constitution, warning that the nation's prosperity would persist only so long as "that invaluable heirloom is left unimpaired" (Morais 1862). He called on divine aid to "thwart the intentions of those who aim to do us evil" by forging an alliance between religion and state.

---

[8]  In an 1872 sermon in Cleveland, a rabbi asserted that the Declaration of Independence was nothing less than "the redemption of the world" (*Israelite*, "Declaration," July 26, 1872). Rabbi Israel Goldstein of B'nai Jeshurun congregation in New York City reached the outer limits of deification when he reformulated the Ten Commandments for American Jews (1926). The revised first commandment recognized God for bringing Jews out of oppression and into "this land of freedom." He also added a new fifth commandment, "Honor America thy fatherland" and followed it up with three additional injunctions against adulterating its standards, stealing its good name, or failing to honor one's oath of allegiance to the United States (Goldstein 1926).

Max Lilienthal, the German-born proponent of Reform Judaism, echoed his colleagues' praise of the United States for its liberal political character but extended the implications beyond the limits they maintained. Almost from the moment of his arrival on American soil in 1845, he became intoxicated with the freedom that Jews enjoyed under the Constitutional regime. To a friend back in Europe, he sent "greetings from New York, from the blessed land of freedom, the beautiful soil of civic equality!" (quoted in Philipson 1919, 166). After shaking off the dust of Old Europe, after breathing the "free air of Columbia," he declared, he could finally say "I am a man like every other." How deeply this attitude penetrated even his religious thinking is apparent from his decision, early in his rabbinic career in the United States, to replace a traditional Jewish prayer for the head of state with an alternative he composed for sovereign citizens of a republic (Ruben 2003, 6).

Continuing what amounted to a love affair with the United States, he joined his fellow rabbis in emphasizing how the American political system treated Jews as they had not been treated elsewhere. In an imaginary dialogue with America, he spoke for his fellow Jews (Lilienthal 1865):

You received us here, not asking from what country art thou coming? From what race art thou descending? To what creed and denomination art thou belonging? No, the only question was and is: Art thou a man, well then go forth and enjoy the innate rights of man! Here, on this sacred soil of virgin liberty, there was no discussion about religious toleration or political emancipation; there was no bargaining about the self-evident truth and right of man ...

Jews accepted the invitation, rejecting their own tradition of tribal nationalism so they could be full-fledged participants in the American project, simultaneously "good sons of our sacred covenant" and "faithful and loyal citizens of our country."

Lilienthal emphasized the importance of Jews acting as citizens of the republic rather than as self-interested partisans with special interests apart from those of their fellow countrymen. His own oratory heeded that advice. He began a Thanksgiving Day sermon by reminding his congregants of their responsibility to support the government of the land where they lived. This extended to the celebration of the public holiday that had brought them together. Under the Talmudic maxim that "the law of the land is the law," he declared that an official holiday took precedence over "sectarian rejoicing" and Jews must therefore withhold their "gladness as Israelites" until the assembly had first acknowledged their "pride and our glory as Americans." That priority was implicit in his definition of the

American Jew: "In creed a monotheist, in descent a Hebrew, Israelite or Jew, in all other public or private relations, an American Citizen" (quoted in Phillipson 1919, 179).

Lilienthal might well have been speaking of himself when he declared that Jews in the United States treated the "sublime" Constitution "almost like a new divine revelation" (quoted in *Occident*, "Cincinnati," July 1, 1868). In a single sentence from an 1867 sermon, he likened Independence Hall in Philadelphia to Mt. Sinai, Jerusalem and Mecca (quoted in *Occident*, "Religious Liberality," May 1, 1867, 11). As someone who perceived the Constitution as a sacred document, he considered deviations from it as akin to heresy. From his perspective, the proponents of adding Christian language to it were attempting to "defile" what he called "the noble covenant" of the founders. This belief in a secular state underpinned his crusade against religious teachings in public schools.

Despite their agreement on the virtues of the American political system for Jews. Lilienthal parted company with Leeser and Morais over the implications of this reality. Lilienthal felt that Jews who lived in the United States no longer needed to seek redemption through restoration of the Jewish commonwealth in the Holy Land. Rather, as Lilienthal repeatedly affirmed, America *was* their Promised Land. By shearing nationalism away from religion, leaving the latter as something private and beyond the purview of the state, the United States had effectively cleansed Judaism of any national ambitions. Judaism was now a religion rather than the basis for national identity and there was simply no need for any new homeland. To a traditionalist like Leeser, this was the same heresy advocated by the philosopher Baruch Spinoza, who was excommunicated by the Jewish community in the Netherlands in 1656.

Despite their considerable differences in adherence to traditional Jewish religious norms, the three clergymen, among the most influential religious leaders of nineteenth-century Jewry, shared views on the nature of the American political system and its positive impact on the American Jewish community. They disseminated those views from the pulpit, in their writings, and as leaders/founders of important Jewish institutions. They were not the only agents transmitting the American Jewish political culture regarding religion and state.

## EDUCATING THE COMMUNITY, YOUNG AND OLD

Apart from the pulpit, other Jewish organizations also worked to inculcate communal respect for the liberal regime of religion and state. Given their role as socializing agents, it is not surprising that Jewish schools and other educational centers were active in promoting respect for the Constitution as the foundation of Jewish success in the United States. Like today's cultural warriors, Jewish leaders understood that educational institutions are "meaning makers" that socialize students into cultural norms (Sewell 1999).

There was a missionary tone to discussions among community leaders about the urgency of transmitting Jewish political culture to the recently arrived eastern European immigrants. Unlike many Germans who arrived in the United States with strong educational and professional credentials in the mid-nineteenth century, most Russian immigrants had acquired only rudimentary schooling in the Pale of Settlement. Hence the German-born leaders of Jewish organizations, together with the acculturated Russians, targeted the eastern Europeans for intensive educational outreach. There was also an ideological agenda: Jewish leaders worried that untutored eastern Europeans might be attracted to "dangerous" political movements, such as socialism, communism, or anarchism, or even Zionism. Isaac Mayer Wise (1907) called it criminal to teach the immigrants "that there is another land somewhere, or that there will be another land somewhere, that is or will be 'better than this.'" For all these reasons, community leaders prioritized educating the newcomers about their equal status in the eyes of the Constitution.

The leaders worried that succeeding generations raised in the United States might not appreciate how good they had it, politically speaking, or how easily it could go awry. After reminding the young men of B'nai B'rith about their inheritance, one Jewish leader challenged them to assume responsibility for preserving it:

Israelitish youth of America, thus you find this new promised land! Are you ready to guard and watch over the liberties of your people and bequeath the liberties you enjoy to your posterity? Are you prepared to defend the right and to scorn the wrong? Have you prepared yourself to discharge to the fullest extent the duties of citizenship? (Wolf 1870)

To ensure that the youth were indeed capable of defending the regime, another prominent leader urged the community to accept as a "sacred duty" the responsibility to "educate our children in the liberal and republican spirit of our institutions" (Cohen 1857). For most observers, this meant sending Jewish children to secular public schools. Hence the claim in a Columbus Day oration that the common school system was "the broadest, safest, surest foundation upon which to erect the superstructure of our liberties, civil and religious" (*Jewish Messenger*, "Model Celebration," October 21, 1892).[9] To keep the schools secular spaces where students would absorb "the great ideal truth of the absolute equality of rights and the brotherhood of all men," local leaders pushed hard against such "Christianizing" practices as Bible reading, Christian hymns, religious subjects for essays, decoration of school rooms, celebration of religious holidays, and the access of missionaries and tract societies to the students (Berkowitz 1889).

Immigration historians have learned much about the institutions that educated newcomers during the massive post–Civil War immigration wave (Klapper 2007). By contrast, there is remarkably little information about the *content* of the curriculum, the nuts and bolts of what was taught about civic education in the schools and institutes where the immigrants and adult learners studied. The evidence I've found, though hardly comprehensive, does broadly indicate that the core ideas embedded in Jewish political culture about political secularism and equal citizenship were reinforced through both public and private education for children and adults alike. In this effort, Jews were the agents of change, not its passive beneficiaries.

What material was used to teach civic education? There were numerous civics textbooks to choose from. In New York, home to the largest Jewish community, Jewish students may have been exposed to *America for Coming Citizens*, a textbook written by a local teacher and fellow Jew. Henry Goldberger (1922) devoted the third chapter to the development of religious freedom. Going beyond the usual Pilgrim story, he emphasized the absence of a state church in the United States and included two study questions inviting the reader to comment on this feature. The appendix contained an essay by Theodore Roosevelt calling for complete separation of church and state and arguing that no public money be devoted to religious education. The essay, too, was followed by a study question in which the student was asked to indicate how the principle of church–state separation was implemented in the United States.

The message in Goldberger's text was repeated and reinforced in a Yiddish–English textbook also aimed at Jewish newcomers. Readers were instructed that Jewish well-being in the United States rested in large part on "the secularity of the Government" (Wiernik 1912, 428–429),

---

[9] The schools could fulfill that potential only if they remained non-sectarian, one of the major issues that Jewish communities fought for throughout the nineteenth and twentieth centuries (Central Conference of American Rabbis 1906).

a foundation that protected Jews from the "unfavorable conditions" faced by their coreligionists everywhere else. Any attempt to incorporate Christianity into the law was resisted because it threatened the equal status of Jews and their full citizenship in the Republic granted by virtue of Article VI.

Apart from public schools, there was a call to ensure that young people educated in Jewish private schools – whether religious or secular – were also made aware of their rights as American citizens. In a book about private Jewish education in New York, Alexander Dushkin (1918) encouraged educators not to neglect the teaching of civic responsibility. But rather than simply repeat what was taught in public schools, he urged a supplementary curriculum in which questions of American civics "were interpreted from a Jewish viewpoint" (310). That is, he wanted issues such as immigration, separation of state and church, and Sunday closing laws to be discussed "with regard to their effect upon the Jews." His model curriculum set aside twenty minutes per week for the discussion of American history and civics in these terms.

Other Jewish organization targeted immigrant adults beyond school age. Among other goals in its credo, the *Jewish Advocate*, founded in 1902, aimed to interpret "the highest ideals of Americanism" for those who came from abroad (*Jewish Advocate* undated). The principal private institution addressing their needs in New York, the Educational Alliance, was established in the late nineteenth century as a settlement house. Under the leadership of Paul Abelson, the Civics Department set out "to reach the immigrant immediately after his arrival and familiarise him with American life, customs and manners and its civil and political institutions" (Civics Department 1905, 1). This mission was implemented by offering a broad range of courses on American history and government, taught in both English and Yiddish. During the 1903–1904 academic year, working with the New York City Board of Education, the Alliance offered almost twenty lectures on topics related to civic education with an instructional staff of nine (Brumberg 1986, 168). Annual reports suggest these lectures, especially those in Yiddish, were extremely well attended.

Although the full text of these lectures is not available and many doubtless were oriented to the practical steps required to obtain citizenship, Abelson's notes and course outlines make clear that the curriculum gave attention to the religious provisions of the US Constitution dear to American Jews (Abelson, "Religious Liberty" and "Meaning of

America").[10] The syllabi for history and civics classes listed four major characteristics of American freedom: equal rights, civil liberty, religious liberty, and universal education (Department of Civics 1905). These four components were described elsewhere as "the essentials of American Political Life" and further praised as "America's contribution to civilization." A teacher's guide advised instructors to emphasize certain sections of the Constitution above all others, including the amendments embodying the guarantees of civil and religious liberty. These components, teachers were advised, constituted "the most significant" elements of the Constitution and warranted the most class time.

To show how this might be done, a model lesson plan guided the instructor through the Establishment Clause of the First Amendment (Board of Education 1922, 26–27). The lesson began with the teacher asking pupils if national, state, or local government could force individuals to attend church. After three less than satisfactory answers, the question was repeated. When that did not elicit the correct answer, the teacher was to distribute the text of the Constitution and ask a pupil to read the Establishment and free exercise clauses of the first Amendment. One of the students who had earlier given the wrong answer was then asked again if government could legitimately require religious attendance and told to provide a reason for his answer. The lesson ended when the student responded that the state could not do so because it was forbidden by the first amendment to the Constitution. If the pedagogy was less than inspired, the message about the Constitutional basis of religious freedom was nonetheless conveyed.

His own class notes show that Abelson framed his lectures to emphasize the perspectives found in the dominant political culture of American Jewry. The topic was introduced under the heading "Religious Liberty" which was underlined in triplicate, an emphasis given no other heading. The first point indicated that the United States was the only nation that separated church and state. Again, the operative phrase was underlined and the sentence ended with an exclamation point. The second point, "the significance to the Jew," suggests that the instructor emphasized the benefits to Jewry of the secular state.

Many local communities established their own version of the Educational Alliance so the ideas and classes taught in New York probably spread beyond the City. One additional agent, the Jewish Chautauqua Society in Philadelphia, also took on the task of educating

---

[10] I am grateful to Stephan Brumberg for bringing this material to my attention.

adult American Jews about their place in the United States. An offshoot of the original Chautauqua Institution, the Jewish variant offered its summer session in Atlantic City rather than the bucolic main campus in upstate New York. Among its activities, the Society developed a syllabus for a course in American Jewish history that included a module on Jewish civil rights (Berkowitz 1905). While the Educational Alliance concentrated on adults from New York City, the Jewish Chautauqua Society aimed at a more middle-class constituency organized in study circles around the country.

Knowing what was taught does not guarantee that the information was learned. The saga of Mary Antin shows how even a self-described Russian immigrant living in the Boston slums managed to absorb the implications of America's regime of religion and state. Whereas in Russia Jews loathed state institutions as engines of repression, Antin fully embraced the American system and its most revered figure, George Washington (Antin 1916, 58). Her lengthy poem about Washington, declaimed before her class, credited him with writing the Constitution. In a stanza on behalf of "the luckless sons of Abraham," she drew a straight line between the Constitution and her happiness as an American:

> Then we weary Hebrew children at last found rest
> In the land where reigned Freedom, and like a nest
> To homeless birds your land proved to us, and therefore
> Will we gratefully sing your praise evermore.

She also showed her awareness of the Constitution's religious protections when she ignited a "toy riot" on the school grounds by declaring her religious unbelief. Surrounded by a group of angry pupils – "enemies of liberty" as she called them – she insisted that "this persecution was contrary to the Constitution of the United States" and that George Washington would have defended her right to declare her unbelief without penalty (Antin 1912b, 213). Alarmed by the assault on her freedom, she later realized that she had in fact trespassed on an important norm that religious arguments do not belong on public school territory. Thanks to her teacher's "private initiation in the doctrine of the Separation of Church and State," Antin reported that she no longer worried about the safety of the Constitution at the hands of her classmates. At the end of her memoir, after recounting her ascent from the slums to a respected position in society, she concluded that the path she trod had first been "surveyed by the Pilgrim Fathers, who transcribed their field notes on a very fine parchment, and called it the Constitution of the United States" (Antin 1912c, 525).

As I noted earlier, political cultures are important because they contain values that constrain political behavior. Once consolidated, the culture described in this chapter provided both an agenda – defense of the classical liberal regime by preserving the secular American state – and a road-map about how it was to be secured for posterity. The next chapter recounts the operation of the culture as American Jews confronted a new round of challenges in the early twentieth century.

# 7

# Early-Twentieth-Century Challenges to Jewish Political Culture

Chapter 6 presented the political culture of American Jewry as it was consolidated by the late nineteenth/early twentieth centuries. Applying the term "consolidated" does not mean the American Jewish political worldview was frozen. Rather, as the Jewish community evolved, the culture encountered challenges driven by new circumstances. Given this fluidity, the dominant political culture of American Jewry operated mostly as a source of cohesion but sometimes as the cause of political division during the first half of the twentieth century.

I present three case studies from that period: the campaign to repeal the Russian Treaty, the "nationalities problem" during and after World War I, and the spread of Zionism among American Jews. As we have seen before, controversies seemingly about foreign policy were permeated by concerns about their impact on the standing of Jews in the United States. So it was again. Despite challenges to the liberal political culture in two of the cases, all three were resolved in a way that ultimately reaffirmed the central political principles Jews had developed decades before.

## RUSSIAN TREATY

After the failure to repeal the Swiss Treaty in the mid-nineteenth century (see Chapter 5), American Jewish leaders discovered other international agreements that allowed the treaty partner to limit the entry and residence rights of American Jews. Finding a similar provision in an 1832 agreement with Russia prompted serious mobilization against that treaty decades after its passage. The provisions that allowed Russian consuls to deny visas to Americans of Russian descent or other American Jews were certainly less objectionable than the ongoing, often violent persecution of Jews in Russia, a perennial concern of Jewish advocates. Yet the treaty was given extraordinary attention by the Jewish press and, after its founding in 1905, by the American Jewish Committee (AJC). Precisely because so many American Jews had family ties and personal connections to the Jews who remained in the Pale of Settlement, the treaty was especially irksome and became salient. Compared to the efforts of its predecessor, the Board of Delegates of American Israelites, the AJC had more resources and better connections to public officials. Hence the campaign for repeal ultimately succeeded.

At first, American Jewish leaders pushed American diplomats to exert pressure on Russia to comply with the treaty guarantees. When Russian authorities failed to respond positively, the strategy shifted to securing outright repeal. Louis Marshall (1911c) announced the new approach in an address to the Union of American Hebrew Congregations (UAHC) in January 1911. A leading New York attorney and founding member of the AJC, Marshall emphasized how the Russian treaty particularly disadvantaged American Jews who had legitimate family or business reasons to visit Russia but were denied visas or otherwise hampered by Russian authorities.[1]

Despite the grievances of Jews who were his audience, he chose to frame the issue in terms of American citizenship. Marshall called the US government's willingness to accede to Russia's denial of visas to American Jews "a stain on the honor of our Nation and on the integrity of American citizenship" (Marshall 1911c, 5). But unlike the past, when the Jew might have accepted such ignominy without protest, he argued, the stakes had grown because the insult was not to the Jew alone but to the entire American people, most especially to the "priceless treasure" of American citizenship (6). His words conveyed a message that the passport issue was not a parochial concern of a distinct group of Americans but a matter of genuine national concern. After all, as the Reform Movement had itself declared just a few years earlier, the passport was nothing less than "the credential of American citizenship" (UAHC 1905, 5352). In Marshall's public advocacy, the Jewish dimension was incidental.

---

[1] Russian consuls in the United States were instructed to ask for the religious affiliation of Americans seeking visas. Even though Article VI of the Constitution probably didn't apply, the practice was roundly denounced as a religious test.

The leadership of the American Jewish Committee first sought to neuter the treaty by "going to headquarters." Exploiting the close ties of the German Jewish elite to the Republican Party, they secured a meeting with President William Howard Taft to press for repeal of the treaty ("Statement of the President" 1911). In a telegram sent after the meeting, a disappointed Jacob Schiff (1911), a financier who helped fund the AJC, reported that Taft had resolved to take no action. To Schiff, the decision meant that President Taft chose to overlook what was an "insult to the entire American people." In response, he recommended the AJC undertake "a serious and lengthy campaign of agitation and education of public opinion" to force the president's hand. As before, the campaign merged insider and outsider tactics.

In this campaign, as Marshall's comments reveal, the discourse remained consistent with the American Jewish political culture described in Chapter 6. Throughout the repeal process, it was understood that advocates should adopt Marshall's approach to the controversy by disclaiming narrow Jewish interests. That injunction certainly had instrumental value, given that the treaty was certain to be defended as good for American business interests, but it also aligned with the emphasis on universalism in Jewish political culture.

In a circular requesting support from leaders of American public opinion, the AJC described the stakes as "the integrity of American citizenship" and "Russia's attitude toward the American passport" (Sulzberger 1911). Per minutes of a conference held with New York State's two US senators, Marshall tried to broaden the pro-repeal constituency by reporting that Russia had also refused to recognize State Department travel documents issued to Catholic priests and Protestant missionaries, erecting a religious test "indefensible under our Constitution" (Marshall 1911b).

Marshall (1911a) made another effort to minimize the role of Jews in the agitation by asking a New York congressman to introduce a resolution of abrogation in the House of Representatives. Marshall told Rep. Francis B. Harrison he was suitable for the task because "you are not a Jew, and, therefore, the question is more apt to he considered an American question, which it should be, than a Jewish question, which it is not." Another New York congressional representative from the Lower East Side, William Sulzer, told the AJC chairman that he had introduced a resolution to terminate the treaty that framed it "on American and not Jewish grounds" (Sulzer 1911). As he then confided with what amounted to a written wink, "This was done at the request of our friends." Throughout the anti-treaty campaign, leading activists such as Julian Mack stressed the importance of using non-Jewish sources to press the attack in order to divert attention "that it was as a result of pressure from us" (Mack 1911).

The message was heeded. In letters to a Georgia senator, Jewish leaders in the state sought to correct his impression that the controversy hinged on Jewish rights. They reminded the senator that the Constitution forbade government to take religion into account when dealing with its citizens. Hence, Russia's behavior insulted American honor and "must not be treated as a Jewish question" (Kriegshaber, Marx and Cross 1911, emphasis in original).

The principal target of the repeal campaign did not buy Marshall's framing of the issue. In the White House memorandum on the February conference, Taft acknowledged that he empathized with the AJC's concern for its coreligionists abroad. "... if I had the same justifiable pride of race that you have," he confessed, "and the same sense of outrageous injustice that comes home to a man of that race much more than it can to a man who is not of the race, I should feel as you do." But, arguing directly contrary to the entire rhetorical thrust of the Jewish audience, Taft declared that as "President of the whole country" he had to balance their appeal for action against the national interest. The scale tipped toward inaction.

Six months later, amid the public campaign launched to overturn the treaty, Taft still saw the issue principally in religious-ethnic terms. Simon Wolf, then head of the UAHC civil rights committee and a Washington, DC, attorney, informed the AJC in July that the president believed that repeal would in fact harden Russian attitudes to its Jewish population and thus stimulate even more immigration of Russian Jews to the United States. That, in turn, would generate pressure for more restrictive immigration legislation, leaving Russian Jews even more exposed to repression and violence (Wolf 1911).

According to his letter to Marshall, Wolf privately encouraged Taft to consider the electoral implications of his actions. The president was expected to face a strong reelection challenge from the presumptive 1912 Democratic nominee, Woodrow Wilson. Wolf reminded the president that his reelection would depend on winning the vote in New York City, Chicago, Baltimore, Boston, Cincinnati, St. Louis, and San Francisco, cities with significant Jewish populations. Not that Jews voted as a bloc, he stressed, but community members were "aroused as they have never been before on a question, which is thoroughly American and not Jewish" and they would hold Taft responsible for inaction.[2]

The US House passage of Congressman Sulzer's resolution terminating the treaty forced Taft's hand and he informed the Russian government of his intent to abrogate the treaty. Apart from winning the conflict, Jewish leaders were no doubt pleased that the House resolution omitted any reference to Jews. Instead, it asserted the "fundamental principle" that the Government will not adhere to any agreement that permits the other party "to discriminate between American citizens on the ground of race or religion" (United States 1911, 1918). Even so, a worried Julius Rosenwald, the Sears and Roebuck magnate from Chicago, counselled the AJC against doing anything to celebrate the victory publicly (Rosenwald 1912). Fearing that a Jewish angle would antagonize other Americans and the Russian government, he advised that "the less evidence the Jews give of their satisfaction over the termination of the treaty, the better it will be for all concerned." In the synagogue, however, Jews would hear from their rabbis that the repeal of the treaty was "one of the grandest moral achievements of our century" (Klein 1912).

The tactics of the repeal campaign remained true to the American Jewish political culture by emphasizing that Jews were seeking rights as citizens of the United States, not as Jews. Not all Jewish leaders subscribed to the idea that Jews should downplay their identity by speaking in universalist rather than particularist language. One notable dissenter, David de Sola Pool (1912), an influential leader of Sephardi Orthodoxy, denied that repeal represented a significant victory for Jews. He doubted that Russia would enforce the travel rights of Jews even if the treaty was renegotiated.

The problem with the passport campaign, he declared, was precisely that it was fought not on Jewish grounds but on American principles. Because the battle was waged as an American campaign, by "Americans who happened to be Jews," the outcome would do nothing to strengthen the backbone of Jews in the United States or elsewhere (p. 24). For Jews to celebrate what he derided as "a trifling concession to justice" granted after nearly a century of effort was a sign of Jewish weakness, an undignified

---

[2] This tactic was used – in private – on other issues as well, even by Marshall. In trying to arouse New York's two US senators against a restrictive immigration bill introduced in 1907, Louis Marshall encouraged a Jewish Republican leader from New York to play the Jewish card. By reminding the senators that their large Jewish constituency was very much concerned about immigration legislation, Marshall hoped his fellow New Yorker could "move them by the sound of the Shofar" (Marshall 1907).

display of emotion that revealed the "fawning, bent-backed attitude of the Ghetto" (p. 23). He much preferred the forthright way Jews in England had insisted on their rights to serve in the British Parliament from 1831 through 1860 (Pool 1917). In asserting that claim, the English Jews "did so without the flabby tergiversation of claiming them solely as a citizen" but as Jews, plain and simple (128). Jews in the United States, he declared, ought similarly to fight on their behalf as Jews, first and foremost, rather than hiding their identity behind their status as American citizens.

Pool's attack on the American Jewish political culture seems to have been a minority perspective but it pointed to something that would become more important as American Jewry, the largest and most influential component of the Jewish diaspora, took a leading role on behalf of Jewish brethren elsewhere. The question of how Jews should fight and what they should advocate became central to two subsequent developments, the condition of Jews in post–World War I Europe and the growth of Zionism as a mass movement in the United States. These two cases would give the liberal political culture its sternest test to date.

## THE NATIONALITIES CONTROVERSY

Long before Jimmy Carter formulated the idea of religion as an international human right, Jewish advocates (among others) sought to apply the ideals of the American liberal regime to the outside world (Fink 2004). Although Jewish efforts to protect their coreligionists abroad dated from the nineteenth century, they became a major preoccupation in the aftermath of World War I. Jewish organizations lobbied the victorious Allied powers to impose a liberal definition of citizenship on the defeated Axis nations, pioneering what became known later as international religious freedom. Such a policy, they believed, would afford Jews and other eastern European minorities the same rights and opportunities as their American counterparts.

Concern for Jews outside the United States arose before the war as a result of continuing violence against Jews in Russia and Rumania, as well as threats to the security of Jewish residents in the Balkans. With the outbreak of World War I, the organized Jewish community mobilized to provide relief to Jews threatened by the conflict. As it had during earlier outbreaks of violence against Jews in the Pale, the American Jewish Committee led fundraising efforts to provide relief to the victims of the pogroms and the war. As it became clear that Russia's monarchy was decaying, questions arose about how these Jewish populations could best be protected once the violence abated. The choice between "emancipation and nationalism" (Silver 2013, 354) divided the American advocates of the liberal regime from the Zionists who claimed to represent the eastern European Jews who had migrated to America.[3]

The position of the AJC and its allies on the "nationalities" was a logical extension of its approach to ensuring the security of Jews in the United States. From the AJC perspective, the Jewish minorities across eastern Europe needed the same civil rights protections from their governments that the US Constitution provided American Jews. The AJC's ally, the Union of American Hebrew Congregations, tellingly signaled that its goal for the Jews in the east was "no more and no less than all the citizens of this country possess, equal rights and equal opportunity" (UAHC 1916, 8116).

This could best be accomplished, the AJC leadership believed, by treaties requiring states in eastern Europe to extend civil and religious rights to all residents. The liberal rights would be guaranteed by the victors and, it was hoped, enforced through international law by the nascent League of Nations. To secure this policy, AJC worked with the State Department and the Wilson administration, seeking formal recognition of a delegation of leading American Jews at the Paris peace negotiations following the war.

The Zionists, who were stronger in eastern Europe than among the diasporas of the United States and western Europe, had very different conceptions. To them, the Jews of the region should be recognized as nationalities and granted specific rights *as Jews*. Some of these rights might be claimed by other national minorities in the defeated countries but Jews would receive specific protections for practices unique to their situation. These could include guaranteed representation in national parliaments, virtual autonomy from central government rule, control over state funding of Jewish institutions, and other benefits based explicitly on religious/ethnic criteria.

The Zionist perspective seemed to strike directly at the heart of liberal norms by defining Jews as a nation, albeit without a state, but with distinct rights and privileges not available to other citizens. This contradicted directly and forcefully the American Jewish political culture that defined Jews as a people sharing a religious heritage but deserving equal rights

---

[3] For an exhaustive account of this conflict, see Frankel (1976). Pianko (2012) has discussed the continuing relevance of the conflict between liberal individualism and nationalism among Jewish public intellectuals.

based on citizenship alone. To do otherwise, defenders of the liberal political culture warned, would amount to treating Jews as a nation within a nation and justify anti-Semites who indicted Jews on grounds of dual loyalty.

Zionist views were represented organizationally in the United States by the Congress movement (later to be known as AJCongress to avoid confusion with the American Jewish Committee or AJC). The Congress organizing committee emphasized its differences with the elite-driven American Jewish Committee by planning a nation-wide referendum among Jewish communities to select delegates for what it called a Congress of American Jews. Its leaders stressed the importance of democracy in all Jewish deliberations. Yet while the two organizations differed in terms of representativeness and ethnic composition, the latter more German, the former more Russian, the key division was their different understandings of Jewish identity and how that played into the debate over the preferred strategy to assist Jewish communities in war-ravaged eastern Europe. As we will see later in the chapter, it would also divide them over the ultimate goal of political Zionism, a Jewish state in the ancestral homeland of the Middle East.

As early as 1914, the American Jewish Committee and the Congress movement leadership had tried to forge a common approach to the situation of eastern European Jews. In discussing an inaugural Congress, the two groups proved unable to resolve their differences over several points, all of which reflected radical differences in how the Congress was imagined. The Congress movement's Zionist organizers foresaw a standing organization that would operate as the central voice of a federation of Jewish local, state, and national organizations. Because this would seem too much like a parliament of the Jews, the AJC approached a Congress as a one-time gathering to help secure the physical well-being and long-term rights of Jews in states previously allied with the Axis powers. It was not to speak on or about American Jewish politics in the least or to have a permanent existence.

Not surprisingly, the negotiations broke down because the Congress movement was unwilling to accept the AJC's insistence that any Congress be held "for the sole purpose of considering the Jewish question as it affects our brethren in belligerent lands" (*Jewish Congress vs. AJC* 1915, 9). Consequently, the two groups held dueling conferences in 1916, the Congress movement at the end of March in Philadelphia, the AJC in mid-July at New York's Astor Hotel.

Recognizing that their approach was anathema to the AJC guardians of Jewish liberalism, delegates to the preliminary conference of the Congress movement sounded a great deal like their AJC counterparts. Almost the first words spoken at the preliminary pre-Congress meeting proclaimed that the delegates had assembled "as patriotic Americans and loyal Jews" expressly to secure for Jews elsewhere human rights "equal to those enjoyed by every other citizen in the lands in which they live" (Preliminary Conference 1916, 4).[4] Yet the gulf between the two organizations became apparent when the Congress adopted an agenda that called for equal rights for Jews where those were denied to them, something the AJC would have embraced, but followed it up with the phrase "as well as national rights in such lands in which national rights were recognized" (21). In his valedictory to the conference (38), Rabbi Stephen S. Wise closed with a bit of verse that encapsulated the Zionist world view: "We are a people yet/Though all the world forget." By asserting the peoplehood of Jews, admittedly an ambiguous term, Wise drew close to what liberal critics in the United States and western Europe considered forbidden territory, conceptualizing the Jews as a nation apart.

Months later, Wise sharpened his attack on the critics of Zionism for the "inflexibly conservative character of much of Jewish pseudo Liberalism" (Wise 1916, 125). The liberal Jews of the AJC decried Zionism as "race striving," he explained, which may have made sense in the nineteenth century when Jews were denied any chance of statehood. Under those conditions, it was not surprising that they embraced a cosmopolitan internationalism that he described less than charitably as a stew which "attenuated into colorlessness" every "racial, religious, national, and lingual" boundary (Wise 1916, 125). World War I gave the lie to this vision and made clear that the postwar world must be constructed with full awareness of the durability and inviolability of racial, religious, and national identities. Jews could not escape this reality "for the fact is that we are a race or the surviving members of a racial group" (126). In a rather confusing conclusion, he simultaneously took ownership of the liberal position but confused its meaning with a multicultural rhetorical flourish: "America means not the triumph of one race or faith or nationality. One becomes an American not by surrendering self but by spending self in a maximum of loyalty and service."

---

[4] I don't believe the wording was solely instrumental. In their public statements, American Zionist leaders insisted that a Jewish state would not in any way impair the citizenship status or public image of American Jewry.

The speakers at the rival New York meeting of the American Jewish Committee spoke in virtually identical language as the earlier conference of the Congress movement. They called for civil, religious, and political rights for Jews in all lands and national rights for Jews in countries that accorded such to other groups. Indeed, the leaders of the Congress movement, including Louis Brandeis, were given the AJC platform and made stirring calls for Jewish unity. But the unity was dissipated in the debate following Brandeis' remarks. The Philadelphia pre-Congress meeting had resolved that the initial Congress agenda must include "establishing the congress as a permanent institution" (Preliminary Conference 1916, 75). By contrast, the AJC meeting had passed a resolution limiting the Congress agenda solely to matters affecting eastern European Jewry. In firm but polite language, Brandeis rejected the proposal (Conference of the American Jewish Committee 1916). This was in fact the same issue that had divided the two groups during their fruitless negotiations from 1914 to 1915.

It is easy to treat this difference as a trivial matter of personal rivalry between the two organizations. No doubt there was competition for preeminence by the liberals and Zionists, to use Wise's characterization, or "uptown" (German) vs. "downtown" (eastern European) Jews. AJCongress sought to create a permanent, democratically elected assembly to speak for American Jewry while the American Jewish Committee thought it already played that role even though its leadership was largely self-selected. This was not a trivial point but a meaningful difference about changing the political organization of American Jewry.

At the AJC's Astor Hotel event, Nathan Strauss noted his uneasiness with the idea of an elected assembly deciding policy positions for American Jewry (Conference of the American Jewish Committee 1916). American Jews did not constitute a state within a state, he cautioned, but were merely "part of the population that have before us some special grievances that we want to redress and correct" (71). The objection was put much more forcefully by Cyrus Adler, who had previously tried to negotiate a joint meeting with Brandeis. In response to a query from the *American Hebrew* about the timing of the Congress, Adler said that holding a Congress was a bad idea and denounced the Congress movement as a blatant attempt "to consolidate the Jews of American into a separate nationalistic group" (Adler 1916). At base, this was a debate about the status of American Jews as citizens who advocated equal rights or as members of a putative "nation" or race who had interests distinct from those of other Americans.

By late December of 1918, the two rivals had resolved their differences sufficiently to convene the first American Jewish Congress in Philadelphia and agreed to send a joint delegation to the peace talks in Paris (*Report of Proceedings* 1918). The delegation was tasked principally to ensure that the new or enlarged states created by any peace treaty would confer citizenship on all inhabitants and to ensure that "all citizens, without distinction as to race, nationality, or creed, shall enjoy equal, civil, political, religious, and national rights and ... the equal protection of the laws" (quoted in Marcus 1996, 339).

As it often does, a strategy of ambiguity enabled the two contending forces to paper over their disagreement. While the language of this resolution invokes the American Constitution, the preferred formulation of the liberals associated with the AJC, the mention of "national rights" and another resolution calling on the Allies to effect "the development of Palestine into a Jewish commonwealth" suggests that both the Congress and Committee achieved their goals. Leaders of the AJC went along with "national rights," it was alleged, only to "avoid a riot" among the eastern European immigrants (Silver 2013, 347). And the references to Palestine were acceptable perhaps because the term "commonwealth" had multiple meanings that did not necessarily include the concept of a political unit. The American delegation did petition President Wilson to support national rights in March 1919.

In due time, the delegation sent to Paris returned triumphantly to the United States, claiming victory on the core items in the AJCongress agenda. But in his address to the next Congress in 1920, Louis Marshall, now president of the AJC and the most influential member among the Jewish delegations in Paris, acknowledged some shortcomings that would subsequently enrage major partisans of the Congress movement (American Jewish Congress 1920). Rather than refer to "national rights," the key hope of the Zionists, Marshall reported that the final documents submitted by a consortium of Jewish organizations substituted the phrase "rights of minorities differing from the majority in race, language or religion" (84). The Peace Conference further diluted the concept of national rights by refusing to grant full political autonomy to these minorities.

Linguistically, minority group members seeking legal recognition and unique benefits based on their ethnoreligious status were transformed into persons entitled to equal rights solely as citizens. The treaties with the new or enlarged states specified "full and complete civil and political rights to all *individuals* [emphasis in original] belonging to religious, racial, and linguistic minorities residing in the countries" and stipulated that citizenship was to be conferred automatically on residents when the agreements were signed (American Jewish Committee 1942, 27). There would be no multiethnic federations but rather centralized national states with subunits based only on geography (American Jewish Congress 1920, 29).[5] Furthermore, any reference to national or minority rights was confined to countries that actively inhibited Jewish rights and only then if the nation's governance and territory were already being considered by the Peace Conference (Robinson 1985, 375).

Although he apparently made good faith efforts to implement the AJC's vision in Paris, Marshall subsequently framed the entire effort in terms compatible with the liberal political culture.[6] Extending civil rights to Jews abroad amounted to a deliberate application of American constitutional norms to countries where Jews had not previously enjoyed the privileges of citizenship (Auerbach 1990, 116). Even more liberally, he interpreted the delegation's mandate from the AJCongress as seeking justice "not only for the Jews, but for all people who, like the Jews, are minority peoples" (American Jewish Congress 1920, 86). Marshall routinely celebrated the outcome for its universalism. Indeed, in language he would repeat in mass meetings and rallies across the United States, Marshall boasted that equal rights were not achieved "for Jews solely nor chiefly" but for "men of every race and language and of every faith who had never enjoyed the blessings of civic and religious liberty" (87). This was not the victory of a people or nation but, as the founders of the American Jewish culture would have found most palatable, a victory for all citizens. It was most especially a victory for those who embraced classical liberalism.

## PALESTINE

Considering the salience of the state of Israel to post–World War II American Jewry (Lipset and Raab 1995), it is challenging to think back

---

[5] Although he did not do so, some of Marshall's allies in the American Jewish Committee celebrated what they saw as a victory over the advocates of Jewish nationalism (Robinson 1985, 369). Marshall and Judge Julian Mack, another AJCongress delegate and a Zionist, insisted that they dropped the language for national rights and other goals only because of the determined opposition of other Jewish delegations and the indifference or hostility to the idea among the "Big Four" leaders of the Versailles conference (Mack, quoted in American Jewish Congress 1920, 28–29; Kohler 1933).

[6] Some critics doubted that Marshall did show good faith and believed that the call for national rights was intentionally undermined (Tenenbaum 1945).

to the era when Zionism was a minority movement looked upon with suspicion and even alarm by most Jewish elites. Yet that was the reality when Zionism first emerged as a mass political movement at the end of the nineteenth century.

Jewish liturgy has long preached the return of Jews to their Promised Land, ending centuries of exile after they were first exiled to Babylonia in the sixth century BCE and then expelled by the Romans following the Bar Kochba Revolt in 132–135 CE (AD in the Gregorian calendar). But the homecoming was a hope deferred to the messianic era until the 1890s when Theodore Herzl, a highly assimilated Hungarian-born Jewish journalist working in Austria, proposed what became known as "practical" or "political" Zionism. Herzl called on Jews to gather in Palestine, as the land of the ancient Jewish Kingdoms had become known, and to begin building a state. Jews should purchase land, create a Jewish society, build an economy, and develop alliances with powerful nations and empires to restore their rightful homeland. Herzl had concluded that Jews would never be accepted until, with a state to manage, they became "normal." Normality meant returning to the soil, taking on jobs and occupations that were productive, creating a modern economy that would bring respect to the Jewish people. Although a Jewish remnant had remained in Palestine, Herzl envisioned a mass return by Jews from around the globe.

The message, which was not entirely new, nevertheless struck a chord with the Jewish masses in the Russian Empire and soon led to a mass movement. As a commentator once reminded us, Zionism is a family name not a proper noun. Hence the Zionist movement fractured almost from the beginning into multiple streams that were divided on the nature of the Jewish state, the best ways to bring it about, and even where it should be located. In the Jewish religious world, the extreme wings – Orthodox Jews and those committed to the Enlightenment – were on balance the most negative about this idea.

Most Orthodox Jews saw Zionism as arrogating unto human beings what only God was meant to do – ingather the exiles in the Promised Land. They also worried that the state would be Jewish in name only (Luz 1988). Among the Reform Jews who predominated in the United States, Zionism was perceived as an outmoded Oriental philosophy that reflected narrow Jewish tribalism. The German Jews who led the Reform movement – and the laity who followed them – outdid one another in denouncing Zionism. Almost as a mantra, they repeated that America was their Zion, Washington (or Jefferson or Lincoln) their messiah, Washington, DC or New York their Jerusalem. Wedded to the idea that Judaism was a religion, not a nationality, they did not welcome the idea of a Jewish state that suggested otherwise. Indeed, they saw Zionism as a pernicious force that would reinforce the anti-Semitic stereotype of Jews as disloyal to their country, just as nativists impugned Catholic patriotism because of their ties to the pope and the Vatican.

Although most of the eastern European Jewish migrants from the 1880s onward voted with their feet, choosing the United States over the arduous life in Palestine then ruled by the Ottoman Empire, they were not immune to the appeals of Zionism and provided the mass base for American Zionist organizations. Zionism found a constituency on the Lower East Side of New York and wherever the Russians and eastern European Jews settled most thickly in the new world.

Just as Israel divides American Jewry today (Waxman 2016), Zionism reinforced differences between the more socialist, left-leaning Russian Jewish proletariat and the German Jewish elite. This was largely a symbolic conflict until Chaim Weizmann, Herzl's successor and a prominent chemist in England, persuaded the British government to endorse the Zionist idea. The Balfour Declaration of 1917 said merely that the British Government "view with favour the establishment in Palestine of a national home for the Jewish people." The nature of that home was not articulated with precision.

The English, who defeated the Ottoman armies during World War I, took over nominal control of Palestine under a trusteeship awarded by the League of Nations. American anti-Zionists, as they were labeled, were not indifferent to the fate of Jews in Palestine or its prospects for future development but they perceived it quite differently. Rather than a home for all Jews, they saw it as a refuge for Jews fleeing danger and discrimination elsewhere and as a spiritual destination for religious Jews drawn to the holy sites. They certainly did not consider Palestine a priority destination for Jews in the United States who had equal rights or for those in the more tolerant European democracies. Kaufmann Kohler (1918, 199), the president of Hebrew Union College, envisioned Palestine as a "centre of spiritual and intellectual life" for Jews but warned emphatically that "A homeland in Palestine in a political sense can only tend to unhome the Jew in other countries."

The American Jewish Committee (1918) accordingly issued a very measured response to the Balfour Declaration. Far more text was devoted to affirming the loyal citizenship of Jews in countries where they enjoyed human rights than to the promise of Palestine. In the end, AJC agreed to cooperate in bringing to Palestine those Jews "attracted by religious or historic associations" with the goal of developing there "a center for Judaism, for the stimulation of our faith, for the pursuit and development of literature, science, and art in a Jewish environment ...." In a letter to the AJC's British equivalent, Louis Marshall made Palestine sound more like a spiritual retreat than a reborn Jewish state: "... our Statement does not in any way commit us to Jewish Nationalism in the political as distinguished from the ethnical [sic] sense of the term ... we recognized no political allegiance whatsoever, save that flowing from our American citizenship." He further assured his British colleagues that AJC "did not look upon such a home as the home of the Jewish people, regarding them as a unit" (emphasis in original).

Even this concession to Zionist sentiment was too much for Simon Wolf, the long-time Jewish advocate in Washington, DC. He had hoped the Paris Peace Conference would put an end to Zionist ambitions. For Wolf, the priority was securing rights for Jews from the governments of the states that oppressed them. Were that problem addressed, "the problems of territory, creeds and races will solve itself [sic]" (Wolf 1918).

The debate between Zionists and anti-Zionists was not resolved by the Balfour Declaration although it was eclipsed on the communal agenda by concern about the growth of restrictive immigration during the 1920s and, in the 1930 and 1940s, by the mortal threats fascism posed to Jewish communities in central and eastern Europe. The AJC did not stand aloof from the British Mandatory government in Palestine during this period, cooperating with Zionists in raising funds for the existing Jewish community, pushing the British to open immigration to European Jews facing looming war and genocide, and actively supporting land purchases by Jews in Palestine. Yet, as Matthew Silver concludes in his biography of Louis Marshall (2013, 340), there was a "clear line of consistency" between the lukewarm response to the Balfour Declaration in 1918 and the AJC's position three decades later when the Jewish state had become fact.

During the period following the Balfour Declaration and World War I, the non-Zionist camp continued to reject statehood and focus instead on the "cultural and industrial upbuilding" of Palestine (*Non-Partisan Conference* 1924). Even as Palestine became ungovernable due to violence between Arabs and Jews and the British Government decided to end its trusteeship over the colony, the AJC still advocated a new international trusteeship "that will promote the greatest possible economic, social and cultural development" of Palestine" (*American Jewish Committee*

*Position on Palestine* 1948). But events undermined that goal and, following a United Nations vote, Palestine was partitioned and a Jewish state proclaimed in 1948.

Most non-Zionists accepted this outcome with reluctance as the only scenario that would provide a home for the thousands of Jews displaced by World War II. Even so, during the period between the United Nations vote for partition and the formal creation of Israel, the head of AJC hewed to the organization's traditional line by stressing that the new nation would follow the American practice of separating religion and state. Hence, he assured American Jews, it "will be a Jewish state only in the sense that the United States, with a preponderance of Christian population, might be termed a Christian state" (quoted in Solomon 2011, 24).

Even though the AJC greeted the creation of the state of Israel as "an event of historic significance" and welcomed it to the family of nations (quoted in Research Institute on Peace 1961, 63–64), the organization's official statement in 1949 did not include the word "Jewish." The ambivalence was apparent in the conclusion of the statement:

Citizens of the United States are Americans and citizens of Israel are Israelis; this we affirm with all its implications; and just as our own government speaks only for its citizens, so Israel speaks only for its citizens. Within the framework of American interests, we shall aid in the upbuilding of Israel as a vital spiritual and cultural center and in the development of its capacity to provide a free and dignified life for those who desire to make it their home.

In putting some distance between the two nations, the AJC apparently considered that the creation of the new state put at risk the integrity of American Jewry's liberal political culture. Rather than appear as citizens with the same deep attachment to the United States as everyone else, entitled to full rights and membership in the political community, vocal Jewish support for "a state of their own" might well intensify charges of dual loyalty and undermine their equal standing in the American polity. The organization was thus eager to put boundaries around the claims of the new Jewish state to play a political role among Jews in democratic nations.

The approach of non-Zionist Americans to Israel in the early years can best be expressed by the phrase "vigilant brotherhood," a term coined by Israel's United Nations ambassador with a very different connotation. The AJC was vigilant lest Israel promote the idea of Jews everywhere as members of a common "nation" and claim authority over Jewish communities outside the homeland. Elsewhere, this was described as the threat of "world Jewish nationalism" (Blaustein 1950, 9), hearkening back to the nationalities controversy after World War I. American Jewish leaders pushed back against what they perceived as Israeli efforts to delegitimate the narrative that Jews were fully at home in the United States.

In an otherwise exceedingly polite (and public) exchange with Israel's prime minister in 1950, the president of the AJC alluded to "burdens" that Israel had inadvertently placed on diaspora communities. Amidst statements of good will and fellowship, Jacob Blaustein nonetheless informed his host "I would be less than frank if I did not point out to you that American Jews vigorously repudiate any suggestion or implication that they are in exile" (quoted in Research Institute on Peace 1961, 68). The AJC leader made it clear that American Jews, who had put down deep roots in their own soil and already had a nation "of their own," would approach Israel as American citizens in a manner framed by their political culture:

The American Jewish community sees its fortunes tied to the fate of liberal democracy in the United States, sustained by its heritage, as Americans and as Jews. We seek to strengthen ... the American democratic and political system, American cultural diversity and American well-being. (67)

In the AJC archives, the press release about the encounter referred to " Blaustein–Ben Gurion Agreement" and treated the prime minister's comments as an "official declaration." A compendium of documents later published by AJC downgraded the exchange to a "Clarification Statement" (Research Institute on Peace 1961, 4), a more realistic title given subsequent confrontations when non-Zionists accused Israeli leaders of intellectual imperialism.

As recounted in AJC records (American Jewish Committee 1957), Ben Gurion himself went on record after the 1950 meeting by referring to Israel as the center of "the Jewish nation" and in the 1953–1954 yearbook of the Israeli government, he provoked even more ire by claiming "when a Jew in America or South Africa speaks of 'our Government' to his fellow-Jews, he usually means the Government of Israel" (5). This gave credence to the image of American Jews as a state within a state, an impression the American Jewish leadership had disparaged for decades.

Worried about the potential growth of "nationalism" among American Jewry, meaning precisely that these Jews would reject the United States in favor of Israel, the AJC announced that its research department would study the "extent and diversity" of such sentiments and, if necessary, "take such measures currently as seem appropriate to counteract these

attitudes" (Blaustein 1950, 11). One such measure was a series of pamph-
lets intended to shore up the liberal political culture. Published between
1950 and 1956 under the title *This Is Our Home*, the series reinforced the
notion that Jews were not a nation unto themselves. Volume IV contained
an attack on Jewish separatism entitled "The Absurdity of a Jewish
Parliament" (American Jewish Committee 1957, 10). It noted that Jews
were not a "national" group but completely integrated in American
society. Although the language was modern, the idea would not have
been out of place a century earlier.

In 1957, the AJC president was invited to speak in Israel (*Address by
Irving Engel*, June 23, 1957). The venue was the ZOA House in Tel Aviv,
a center established by the Zionist Organization of America. That the AJC
president spoke in a building funded by American Zionists was itself
remarkable given the enmity between the two groups since the late nineteenth century. But what was equally surprising was how much the AJC
tone toward Zionism had softened.

Irving Engel characterized his own organization, the AJC, as non-
Zionist rather than anti-Zionist. That phrase, he insisted, should not be
construed as negative because it meant only that the organization did not
accept "classical Zionist dogma." It rejected the idea that Jews living
outside Israel "are doomed to physical or spiritual extinction." He
reminded his audience that American Jews did not consider themselves
in exile but rather as "fully integrated citizens" who could "as Americans,
live a full Jewish life, maintaining our Jewish identity, our Jewish religion,
our Jewish culture." With that freedom, they intended to work hard to
strengthen the state of Israel.

By narrowing the basis of its criticism of Zionism and accepting the
Jewish state, the AJC certainly did move toward the center. This shift in
approach contrasted sharply with the implacable anti-Zionism of the
American Council for Judaism, an offshoot of the Central Conference of
American Rabbis that continued to stoke the traditional distaste for
Zionism among Reform Jews (Kolsky 1990). That said, the position of
American Jewry, in so far as it was reflected in the actions of the AJC, still
distanced it considerably from the kind of Zionism that Israeli leaders
promoted.

### ORIGINS OF AMBIVALENCE

Despite a change in the tenor of its approach to a Jewish state, the AJC did
not abandon its commitment to the American Jewish political culture.

Instead, as Engel's comments indicate, the leadership found a way to reconcile its new openness to Israel by embracing a form of Zionism that ultimately reinforced its long-held positions. They created a hybrid, combining "elements of acculturationism and integrationism with support for the national struggle of their compatriots left behind," which strongly resembled the ethnic consciousness of other minority groups in the United States (Mendelsohn 1993, 132). To the leaders of Israeli Zionism, whose perspectives were shaped in the eastern European milieu, the American formulation seemed, at best, a degenerate form of that ideology, at worst, an abandonment of Herzl's vision. The same year that Engel made his conciliatory remarks in Tel Aviv, an AJC memo by Lucy Dawidowicz (1957, 4–5) reported that "American Zionists have been the object of sharp criticism from the Israeli Zionists because of their loyalties to American traditions and laws."

To understand why Americans and Israeli Zionists interpreted Zionism so differently, it is necessary to contrast the political environments in the United States and eastern Europe when modern Zionism emerged in the late nineteenth century. The unique structural aspects of the two locales conditioned how each Jewish community responded to the rise of Zionism, how each would develop distinctive ends and means for its Zionist movements.

Eastern European Zionism developed in an area that was under the autocratic rule of a medieval monarchy that maintained an essentially feudal structure well into the early twentieth century. Jews were treated as a group or nationality with sharply limited opportunities for advancement and virtually no security for person or property. Emancipation did not come until the 1917 Russian Revolution and, even then, the situation of Jews remained dire. Hence the priority was to transfer Jews to places where they would not be oppressed and would be free to develop a full-fledged Hebraic culture, including restoring Hebrew as a *lingua franca*. The reorganization of Europe after World War I opened more space for Zionists to utilize political means to achieve their ends. That is, it created a different political opportunity structure. In the multicultural democracies that developed in parts of interwar eastern Europe, such as Poland, politics was an enterprise carried on by ethnic and religious nationalist groups. In such environments, Jews formed political parties and ran for public office, using their power to obtain tangible resources for their communities. These efforts were "Palestinocentric," meant to prepare young Jews for life in the soon-to-be Jewish homeland (Mendelsohn 1993, 58).

By contrast, American Jewry did not think it needed to be emancipated because Jews in the United States were included in the political community from birth, so to speak. That of course was a basic assumption of the American Jewish political culture. Rather than search for a new homeland where they would enjoy civil and political rights, their principal task was to ensure that the promises of equality during the American founding were implemented in full. As they were not legally considered a "nationality," there was no effort to create a comprehensive Hebraic culture or to get American Jews to speak Hebrew beyond the needs of worship.

Most communal leaders preached that Jewish children in the United States should be educated in public schools, not isolated from their fellow citizens in Jewish day schools, and that newcomers, whether adults or children, should be pushed to master English and become real Americans. There was no urgency among American Jewish elites to persuade American Jews to move to Palestine/Israel.[7] In pursuing their goals, American Jewish activists worked in an environment that disparaged "hyphenated Americanism" and where political parties based on hyphenated ethnic groups were considered illegitimate. Hence American Jewish advocacy functioned through voluntary interest groups that pressed their claims on the two "catch-all" political parties. If their lobbying was to be effective, Jewish advocates had to demonstrate that their goals served the national interest. That discourse was perfectly aligned with liberal political culture's charge that Jews should avoid particularism in their political activities.

It is natural to assume that Polish and Russian immigrants to the United States carried the eastern European perspective on Zionism in their cultural baggage, explaining the tension between the AJC and AJCongress movement. No doubt that was the case during the era from the 1890s to World War I. But by virtue of their immersion in the American setting, most of the so-called downtown Jews eventually came to appreciate life in the United States and consider it their permanent abode. As an astute American expert on Zionism observed playfully (Teller 1955, 344–345), "American Zionists were never committed to the East European Zionist *Shulchan Aruch,* and even the *mitzvot,* the ritual commandments that Zionists everywhere had in common, were performed differently in America than in Europe." This applied even to leaders on the Jewish left, who abhorred the uptown Jews from the AJC. Though sympathetic

---

[7] As part of their indifference to Hebraic culture, the AJC leaders pressed the Eastern European migrants to America to learn English and acculturate to American ways.

to socialism, prominent leftists "were not really Jewish nationalists of the East European type" (Mendelson 1993, 80–81). Their understanding of European Zionism, noted Ben Halpern (1956, 28), was vicarious.

The shift in thinking among American Zionists was already apparent at the first Congress of 1918. As I noted earlier, most speakers representing Zionist organizations sounded quite close to their former anti-Zionist antagonists in the American Jewish Committee (American Jewish Congress 1919). In welcoming the delegates on behalf of Philadelphia's Jewish community, an "ardent Zionist" referenced George Washington's famous praise of the "liberality of sentiment" that induced mutual respect among American religious groups. Their task at the Congress, he averred, was "to extend that liberality of sentiment to the most remote parts of the world" (7). As it tried to transplant American values abroad, he continued, they should not serve the interests of their own group alone but "should speak as well for all groups of oppressed people, for the Christians of Armenia, for the Moslems in the Balkan States" and others (8). In his inaugural address as Congress president, Judge Julian Mack assured the audience that Jews in America desired nothing for themselves because they already enjoyed equality of citizenship. Hence, he would not compromise or disavow his "exclusive and unqualified loyalty to the Government of the United States" (16). Most of the speakers representing Zionist organizations sounded quite close to their former antagonists in the AJC. As Auerbach (1990, 153) noted with some scorn, "American Zionists were led by men with little sympathy for Jewish national aspirations."

Subsequent American Jewish support for Israel thus focused primarily on providing material and, later, political assistance to the nascent state. Success was not defined in terms of mass *aliyah* – persuading young American Jews to become Israelis – but on building up the quality of Jewish life in Israel *from a distance* (Mendelsohn 1993, 79). This produced, as Ezra Mendelsohn described it, a Platonic relationship with Israel (132). The difference was captured nicely when a future president of the Zionist Organization of America distinguished between American Jews' "citizenship" in the United States and their "fellowship" with the Jews oppressed elsewhere in the world (*Jewish Exponent*, "On Behalf of World Jewry," January 28, 1938).

After lecturing Israelis that they should not intrude on American politics, American Jewish leaders had no choice but to pledge that they would not intervene in the Israeli political sphere. They eventually abandoned this stance and began increasingly to critique various aspects of Israeli society. As more than one Israeli has noticed, the American critics subsequently undertook efforts to transform Israel into something approximating a liberal state. As the United States attempted to export American values abroad, so did American Jewry vis-à-vis Israel, a story to be taken up in the next chapter.

## STATUS OF THE LIBERAL POLITICAL CULTURE AT MID-CENTURY

The overall strategy of downplaying the Jewish angle and promoting a position based more on the liberal concept of equal citizenship achieved its short-run goals in two of the three cases just examined. Both the minority rights clauses in the peace treaties and the framing of Zionism in nonnational terms were consistent with the thrust of the strategy worked out by the most influential Jewish organizations.[8] But as the meetings with President Taft over the Russian Treaty demonstrated, these strategies did not invariably bear fruit. Despite the attempt to frame the passport question in terms of constitutional values and the meaning of American citizenship, Taft could not see it as anything other than a Jewish issue. He opposed abrogation as a way to protect Russian Jews against increased anti-Semitic attacks and restrictive immigration legislation that would hamper emigration.

The protracted struggle over immigration in the 1920s is another case in which the attempt to frame the issue in terms of national interests and American values did not convince decision-makers. Before 1924, Jewish lobbyists had some successes fighting off or mitigating draconian policies that would have adversely affected their coreligionists seeking admission to the United States. As part of that campaign, spokesmen for Jewish organizations insisted that Jews should not be treated in racial or ethnic terms but simply as potential immigrants who shared a religious preference. They objected even to classifying Jewish immigrants from eastern Europe as Hebrews or Russian Jews in official statistics because those terms emphasized the differences between the newcomers and the host society. These Jews should simply be enumerated as Russians or Poles and treated more generously than the Asian or Africans whose might present significant challenges of assimilation justifying quotas or other restrictions.

---

[8] Of course, the minorities treaties proved toothless in practice without an enforcement mechanism and Zionism did achieve a nation-state after World War II.

For all their efforts to disclaim a Jewish angle in their rhetoric about immigration, Jewish advocates had to use a Jewish approach because their specific concerns reflected the conditions faced by would-be Jewish immigrants to the United States. Jews advocated recognizing Yiddish as one of the languages in which immigrants could demonstrate literacy, assuring that Jewish women denied schooling due to Russian anti-Semitism would not be thereby penalized in seeking admission to the United State. They also fought against proposals to deny entry on political grounds to Russian Jews who had been convicted of political crimes for resisting Czarist tyranny. These must have struck lawmakers as parochial claims.

When Congress considered slashing immigration quotas in 1924, targeting especially eastern and southern Europeans, it scheduled committee testimony by Jewish advocates on a single day and had the representatives of Jewish institutions sit together at one table (United States 1924). Jewish members of Congress on the House committee frequently broke into the discussion, challenging their fellow representatives on points of fact. Although those testifying tried to link their concerns to non-Jews affected by the reduced quotas – Italian, Slovakian, and Polish Christians – and called the proposals contrary to national values, most members of the House committee undoubtedly saw them as representatives of a distinct ethnoreligious group seeking special treatment. One imagines that the physical arrangement of the hearing room reinforced that impression for the Congressional representatives who ultimately slammed shut the doors against tens of thousands of aspiring Americans.

Effective or not, American Jewish leaders did not abandon their characteristic discourse in the post–World War II era. In fact, they were among the forces mobilizing for what became the Universal Declaration of Human Rights proclaimed by the United Nations in 1948 (Morsink 1999). Even before the war ended in 1945, the American Jewish Committee publicly presented a prototype that was suffused with the same language of liberal internationalism that had appeared in its discourse about Israel. Consciously trying to avoid the appearance of Jewish parochialism, it advocated the familiar blend of "civic patriotism and religious freedom at home with American-style democracy and human rights abroad" (Loeffler 2015b, 278). This component of the liberal political culture survived two world wars to remain a significant influence on the American Jewish worldview.

# JEWISH LIBERALISM AND THE DEMOCRATIC PARTY IN THE POST–NEW DEAL ERA

# 8

## Jewish Political Culture During the "Long Sixties" and After

The Jew likes this country very much as it is. He would like it a little better if it would be what the Constitution wants it to be and what the Constitution will yet decree it shall be.

– Moses Jacobson, *Is This a Christian Country?* (1913, p. 22)

As the chapters in Part III demonstrate, Jews in the post–New Deal era eventually determined that safeguarding the secular state required them to forge a stronger alliance with one of the American political parties. That linkage reached fruition in the late 1980s, following a period when a contentious domestic issue challenged the liberal political culture and temporarily weakened Jewish commitment to the Democratic Party. Throughout the period, the communal discourse continued to emphasize the priority of maintaining full and unalloyed Jewish membership in the polity and defending the idea of a liberal regime at home and abroad.

If we define the onset of the postwar era not by an arbitrary date like 1945 but by zeitgeist, the two issues described in this chapter really belong to a new age in American Jewish history. Both episodes grew out of the ferment of the 1960s and were unlikely to have emerged without the cultural changes of that era.

The "Long Sixties" (Strain 2017), a term that recognizes how the decade's impact stretched well beyond ten years, introduced major discontinuities in American society and, eventually, in Jewish politics. Although it is not clear which came first, a rise of ethnic consciousness coincided with an upsurge in identity politics. In the prewar period, politicized ethnic grievances had been treated as a symptom of sectarianism, a precursor to a dreaded outbreak of "hyphenated" politics.

The postwar era engendered an environment markedly more receptive to political claims based on overt expressions of ethnocultural identity and group interests. Those claims covered both domestic and foreign policy.

Liberated from prior constraints on public discourse by other identity-based social movements – the Black Power revolt, the gay rights movement, women's liberation, and others – Jews too became much less hesitant about invoking group interests explicitly in their advocacy of public policy (Medding 1992). Whether it was the movement to free Soviet Jewry or support Israel or any other specific issue, Jews no longer felt the same need to foreswear any particularistic motivations, to justify their preferences solely in terms of the national interest. The charge of dual loyalty was still heard but it now came from the political fringes and its advocates, such as Pat Buchanan, were routinely denounced by their conservative peers.

Apart from new issues and modified discourse, postwar American Jewry also adopted new techniques befitting its enhanced status and greater security in the United States. Jews no longer had to "go to head-quarters" to impress their priorities on government as headquarters increasingly came to them. Presidential administrations routinely appointed "outreach coordinators," essentially domestic ambassadors to the Jewish community (and other communities), and Jews routinely met with presidents by invitation in well-publicized and semipublic gatherings. Both major parties developed adjunct organizations specifically to promote their views among Jewish voters and donors: the Republican Jewish Coalition (founded in 1985) and the National Jewish Democratic Council (1990). Jews were increasingly represented in public office and many served openly as institutional activists on behalf of Jewish causes (Santoro and McGuire 1997). In sum, Jews *as* Jews were freer to act openly as self-interested agents seeking to influence public policy. The components of the liberal political culture that had preached against such developments did not survive the rise of identity politics. But as we shall see, other components, particularly the idea of the secular state, persisted and intensified even amid the changing political environment.

The second change, prefigured in the previous chapter, was the embrace of Israel by most of the American Jewish community. The Six-Day War in 1967, when Israel survived a joint attack by the Syrian and Egyptian armies, galvanized American Jewish public opinion and had the effect of putting support for Israel at the top of the community's domestic agenda. Along with fighting anti-Semitism, it became a major priority of organized Jewry (Woocher 1986). As long as Israel was perceived as a besieged nation surrounded by hostile powers that rejected all efforts at compromise, it enjoyed nearly universal Jewish support. That support was given more freely in an era when ethnic diasporas were accorded legitimacy in the policy-making process.

The two post–World War II episodes chosen for review in this chapter differ fundamentally from one another. In a narrow sense, one was domestic and the other international. The more important distinction is self-interest. In the first case, the rise of "affirmative action," it is not difficult to explain Jewish behavior from a rational choice perspective: Jews perceived a collective interest in resisting the spread of this policy because it appeared to threaten their opportunities for upward mobility.[1] It also marked the first time that the tension between the two variants of liberalism discussed in Chapter 4, economic egalitarianism and the classical version stressing individual rights, forced Jews to choose between them.

But the other case, the effort by American Jews to diminish religious influence in the *Israeli* public square, does not seem to flow from self-interest as that motivation is usually understood. In fact, one might have expected the post-1967 American Jewish community to refrain from criticism of Israel and focus its energies instead on defending the Jewish state and promoting its interests. It did so but, with time, the voices calling on Israel to become more like a liberal state gained more traction among American Jewry. As we saw in Chapter 7, many of the leaders of organized American Jewry, secular and religious alike, had rejected Zionism well into the twentieth century because it linked national and religious identity. As they had long fought against attempts to define US citizenship in religious terms, they did not countenance the linkage in Israel either. While most American Jewish leaders eventually made their peace with the existence of Israel, they worked (and continue to do so) to push Israel to dismantle institutions and practices that smacked of religious coercion by the state. Much of the tension between Israeli authorities and the American Jewish diaspora today is rooted in differing visions about Judaism in the public square.

The Jewish course of action in both case studies was very much rooted in the classic liberal assumption that the state should not differentiate

---

[1] Suggesting that many Jews saw affirmative action as a threat to their economic opportunities does not mean the issue was perceived solely in those terms. The aggrieved tone of many critiques suggests that it was also culturally problematic, violating community norms about how government should act. I take those concerns at face value.

among its citizens based on their religion, race, ethnicity, or gender. In the case of affirmative action in the United States, traditional liberalism argued that race-based policies were impermissible. But in dealing with Israel, the problem was perceived as the state favoring a specific type of Judaism over others, equally a violation of liberal norms regarding state neutrality toward religious groups. Paradoxically, in an era when social identity became the basis of group mobilization and political discourse, Jewish advocates insisted that it should not provide the foundation of public policy.

## THE DEBATE OVER AFFIRMATIVE ACTION

Many American Jews considered the passage of the Civil Rights Act of 1964 and the Voting Rights Act of 1965 as the climax of the long struggle for racial justice in the United States. Jewish leaders had enlisted in the movement from early days, co-founding the NAACP, providing legal support to the campaign against segregation, and supplying resources and counsel to the black leadership. Although Jewish support was never as wholehearted or complete as suggested by romantic images of a transracial coalition, Jews were distinctive among white American ethnic groups in their attachment to and identification with efforts to create more space for black people in the United States.

Although the new laws did increase the access of African Americans (and others) to the public sphere, many of the people in whose name these laws were passed remained dissatisfied with the results. Black poverty, educational disadvantage, and housing segregation – seen as the result of systematic racism in public policy – seemed impervious to the impact of laws promoting equality of opportunity. The movement for what became known as affirmative action grew out of this dissatisfaction. Advocates for racial progress argued that the state needed to take more positive steps to ensure not just equality of opportunity, as important as that was, but additional efforts to ensure more equitable outcomes for groups who faced persistent racism and resource gaps even after the passage of civil rights legislation.

This was, in the United States at least, a new form of liberalism although it hearkened back to the conception of "social citizenship" pioneered in Europe by T. H. Marshall. It can be understood as a shift in the role of the state. In the tradition of classical liberalism, the state was perceived as an agent that could threaten liberal values by imposing burdens on some citizens. Hence liberals generally favored "strong limitations on the activities of the state" ("Positive and Negative Liberty" 2016). Equality thus meant state neutrality toward its citizens – the state apportioning neither benefits nor costs based on individual traits.

The newer liberalism, spurred by the apparent intractability of economic inequality, called for the state to intervene on behalf of groups defined explicitly by qualities such as race, gender, and ethnic identity. Beyond removing burdens to promote a level playing field, it could undertake programs and provide opportunities uniquely for such groups. From this perspective, the state was an actor with the capacity to balance the scales of past injustice by compensating groups it had formerly burdened and oppressed. By promoting "positive" liberty, the state could facilitate efforts by members of previously subordinated groups to realize equality in fact as well as theory.

Affirmative action, the term given to efforts to promote better outcomes for groups that had not been treated equally in the past, became what philosophers call an essentially contested concept. The debate challenged even the labels applied to the program. Affirmative action, as it was known to its advocates, was framed instead by opponents as "affirmative discrimination" or "reverse discrimination." When some supporters used the language of reparations to justify these programs, critics seized on that term as further proof that the state was now playing favorites. The approach was in fact a significant departure from the classical liberalism that championed measures to promote equality of opportunity. Although government had previously distributed individual benefits based on age (Social Security), gender (workplace rules), and other criteria before affirmative action was proposed, these were justified as protective actions responding to unique social problems afflicting particular classes of the population. Critics considered the new approach to social benefits a radical departure from traditional norms.

Affirmative action programs were implemented at the behest of the federal government in a wide array of settings: admission to higher education, access to jobs and governmentally funded programs, even the drawing of boundary lines for election districts. These programs were not exclusively race-based, as various groups defined by language use, national origin, or gender were also potential beneficiaries. Yet the debate was driven politically more by race than any other affirmative action category. The new policies fueled an intense backlash among groups that had been part of the Democratic/New Deal coalition since the 1930s: labor unions, white Southerners, and white ethnic groups in particular.

Some of the early plans under the affirmative action rubric involved preferential hiring and quotas. Where past discrimination against groups could be documented, the public institutions responsible would be required to give additional weight to applicants from those groups in making personnel decisions. In some cases, hiring quotas would be set until the group constituted the same percentage of employees as it did of the population. These practices, known as "hard" affirmative action, earned virtually unanimous opposition from all the major organizations in the Jewish communal defense sector: American Jewish Congress (AJCongress), American Jewish Committee (AJC), National Jewish Community Relations Advisory Council (NJCRAC), and the Anti-Defamation League.[2]

That opposition drew in part on organized Jewry's longstanding resistance to any efforts by government agencies (including educational institutions) to collect racial, religious, or ethnic data as official policy. That opposition had emerged with impressive power during the debate over whether to include a question on individuals' religious affiliation in the 1960 population census. According to Kevin Schultz (2006, 362), Jews opposed the practice because it brought back memories of how the Nazi regime had used a special religious census to identify Jews living in Germany, targeting them for expulsion and then murder. They also worried that data demonstrating Jewish economic achievements would be used by anti-Semites to incite public opinion against them.

Jewish organizations routinely described the proposed religious question as an invasion of privacy and a potential assault on the religious liberty clauses of the Constitution. Using a stealth campaign that attempted to avoid any public awareness of their activities, lest that too arouse fears of excessive Jewish power, advocates for Jewish issues played a large role in killing the proposal. Furthermore, they organized an interfaith coalition that halted further analysis of a 1957 census survey that had tested the proposed question. Consistent with classical liberalism as they understood it, Jewish elites succeeded in preventing the state from imposing a potentially dangerous burden on their constituents.

Apart from constitutional beliefs, heritage and historical memory, the opposition of Jewish organizations to "hard" affirmative action implicated communal self-interest. Jews were highly sensitive to any developments that might threaten their success in the educational field. Like many

---

[2] This discussion draws heavily on the excellent work by Dennis Deslippe (2012).

other ethnic groups, Jews had a culture that valued education both for its own sake but also as a means of social mobility.

Throughout most of the twentieth century, that culture ran headlong into quotas on Jewish admission to prestigious universities. Jewish applicants for undergraduate study, graduate and professional education, and faculty and top administrative positions were limited by restrictive provisions in private colleges and universities (Lipset and Ladd 1971). Jews fared better in public education, rising to top positions in New York City and elsewhere. The bitter memory of these quotas – and the equally effective but informal devices by which Jews had been kept out of prestigious law firms, medical practices, top corporate positions, and other professional opportunities – fueled hostility to the very idea of government reserving positions based on group traits. Daniel Bell (quoted in Deslippe 2012, 74) concisely expressed this sentiment when said disparagingly of group quotas: "The person himself has disappeared. Only attributes remain."

This opposition was put into action in the first affirmative action lawsuit to reach the US Supreme Court. In *DeFunis v. Odegaard*, a Jewish applicant who was denied admission to law school claimed that he had better credentials than several applicants who were awarded places reserved for students from specified minority groups. This dual track admissions process, said one justice, was an undeclared quota. The three major Jewish defense organizations, AJC, AJCongress, and ADL, submitted friend of the court briefs on behalf of DeFunis. The Court did not rule on the principle of affirmative action in that 1974 case but confronted the issue in 1978 when another appellant, Alan Bakke, claimed he was denied admission to a California medical school under a system broadly like the Washington State process DeFunis had challenged. Once again, the three Jewish organizations joined to support the spurned applicant in rejecting quotas based on race and ethnicity.

Jewish elites were strong advocates of what was called "color-blind liberalism" but was in fact a traditional component of classical liberal doctrine. They came to the affirmative debate with a strong belief that "racial or gender differences should have no effect on the prospects" of applicants for jobs, programs, or admission to educational institutions (Deslippe 2012, 9). No wonder then that they battled with the advocates of affirmative action who believed that such differences should be considered in order to offset the deeply engrained racism and sexism that had blocked people of color and women from employment and advancement.

Peak organizations do not always represent accurately the views of their members or the constituency in whose name they speak. In this case, it does appear that antipathy to hard affirmative action measures was shared by rank-and-file Jews.

In justifying their opposition to race-based quotas and admission preferences, Jewish organizations reported a swell of grassroots resistance to these practices from ordinary Jews. In his ethnographic study of one community in Brooklyn, Jonathan Rieder (1985) found strong resistance to affirmative action among Jews and Italians. Much of that was rooted in financial insecurity, which bred a sense of indignation based on the perception that reverse discrimination enabled blacks and other minorities to get ahead of other, more qualified people due solely due to race. It manifested itself politically in sharp rejections of liberal politicians who supported quotas and preferences in admission, even among Jews who told the author they had supported the civil rights movement and earlier New Deal social programs. Such views were appreciably less common among the more affluent Jews of Manhattan.

Assessing the degree of Jewish antipathy to "hard" affirmative action is difficult to detect owing to data scarcity. There was no shortage of polling on affirmative action during the 1970s and 1980s but no single survey that was large enough to include a sizable subsample of Jews. In a 2000 Knowledge Networks survey, interviewers presented a series of questions about affirmative action to approximately 500 Jewish and 500 non-Jewish respondents, both samples selected at random. Researchers found no large differences between the two groups on affirmative action for blacks once background traits were included in the model (Wald and Sigelman 1995). Being Jewish didn't predict such attitudes very well. The very *absence* of differences is itself telling because being Jewish usually did predict preferences for liberal policies on race and social welfare.

### IMPACT AND NUANCE

Jews' oft-expressed hostility to "hard" affirmative action drove a wedge between them and black Americans. Once seen as allies in the struggle for equal rights, Jews were subsequently perceived as fair-weather friends for deserting the civil rights coalition on this crucial issue. Nowhere was this estrangement more apparent than in the 1968 conflict over control of public education in the Ocean Hill-Brownsville school district of Brooklyn.

Emboldened by a new state law promising "community control" of school boards, the newly elected community board involuntarily transferred several white teachers and administrators out of the district. The stated goal was to make the teaching and administrative staff more sensitive to the educational needs of the growing number of black students in the district. On the assumption that the state was using its power to discriminate against white educators who had done nothing to merit such treatment, the long-time liberal (and Jewish) president of the United Federation of Teachers intervened on behalf of the transferees. That prompted a strike by parents that was resolved only when the entire community control mechanism was shelved.

Because Jews were prominent in the teachers' union and most of the advocates of community control were African American, the conflict was understood in racial-ethnic terms. Both sides denounced their opponents, Jews accusing blacks of anti-Semitism, blacks in turn denouncing Jews as racists. Ironically, the bitterness of the conflict was attributable in part to their prior closeness in labor and civil rights activity. Noting that Jews had always justified their support for civil rights in terms of commitment to justice and equality, some black leaders charged that the motive was now revealed as a cover for mere self-interest. In a damning phrase from one influential black labor leader, "Jews in America had become white" (quoted in Greenberg 2006), finding their interests no longer aligned with the civil rights movement.

This stark view overlooks the subtleties of the Jewish views about affirmative action and ignores the underlying challenges affirmative action posed to a very well established ideological tradition. In his Canarsie study, Rieder noted that the Jews exhibited a different tone than their working-class Italian neighbors, expressing less overt racism and stronger belief that blacks had in fact suffered more serious discrimination than members of their own religious tradition. Even in 1969, when the mayor held responsible for affirmative action and the Ocean Hill-Brownsville controversy stood for reelection, Jews were two to three times more likely than Italians in the area to vote for the incumbent (Rieder 1985, 128–129).

At the organizational level too, Jewish elites differed from many of the declared opponents of affirmative action who rejected any government action on behalf of racial equality. Even as they opposed quotas and hiring preferences, Jewish leaders pushed for measures deemed "soft" affirmative action. These remedial programs would, it was hoped, lessen the need for such overly broad policies as quotas by equipping minorities with stronger skills and more resources. Jewish organizations continued to work in concert with the NAACP and American Civil Liberties Union, their partners in the civil rights movement, by mounting legal cases regarding school busing, public school funding, food stamps, and restrictive zoning (Deslippe 2012, 77–78).

By promoting integrated schools and housing, lobbying for additional funds for education and nutrition, the Jewish elites remained true to the tenets of color-blind and classical liberalism. Such programs would improve the conditions of black Americans, they believed, and thus enable them to take advantage of their newly won access to public and private resources. This approach remained very much in the mold of traditional liberalism with its emphasis on equality of opportunity for all rather than targeting specific groups for benefits based on group membership. In that sense, it did not come very close at all to the new form of liberalism that had emerged after the legislative gains of the civil rights movement. But the continuing drive to keep the state neutral was entirely consistent with the historic thrust of the American Jewish political culture.

## ISRAELI RELIGIOUS PLURALISM

Many American Jews who supported the new state of Israel in the early post–World War II period, most of whom probably would not have described themselves as Zionists, saw Israel as a place where liberal and progressive Jewish values could be realized. Steeped in the American model of liberal democracy, they held dear the values that were associated with the US Constitution, especially the basic rights and liberties guaranteed by that document. As we saw in the previous chapter, they attempted to reproduce this system in the eastern European states during the post–World War I peace conference in Versailles. They wanted the same values to operate in the political system of the Israeli state.

In an analysis prepared for the AJCongress, Will Maslow (1948) examined the draft Constitution for Israel that was expected to be passed by the Constituent Assembly scheduled to meet in 1949. Although the assembly postponed the adoption of a constitution until the indefinite future, the draft document itself heartened American Jews because it drew so heavily on the American founding and seemed consistent with their own political culture.

Although it began with a preamble making a strong statement about Israel's Jewish identity, much that followed in the constitutional draft was consistent with liberal principles. The document's bill of rights was strongly influenced by the first ten Amendments to the US Constitution and various provisions appeared to grant citizenship broadly and to emphasize fundamental equality among citizens (Maslow 1948, 15). Despite language making it clear that the state was created by Jews, the government it defined "is certainly not a theocratic one," Maslow argued. Like its American antecedent, Israel's blueprint did not provide for an established religion with state funding or establish a religious test for holding office. The absence of any provision to compel observance of Jewish religious rituals aligned closely with the free exercise clause of the First Amendment to the American Constitution.

Maslow highlighted another feature. As the Proclamation of Independence had promised a year earlier, Article IV sought to guarantee "equality of social and political rights to all inhabitants" by prohibiting discrimination based on religion, race, or sex. The implementation of that principle was less expansive in a constitutional provision that banned speech "that stirs up racial or religious hatred." Although differing from the American Constitution that treats freedom of speech as the default position, the Israeli document followed the practice of many countries in protecting collective religious rights at the expense of individual dissent. (This same principle, it should be noted, was enforced by blasphemy laws in much of the United States.)

Just a few years after the Maslow report was issued, an unpublished AJC report discovered that the assurances of religious freedom and conscience promised in the Proclamation of Independence had been severely compromised by the political realities of a parliamentary system (Committee on Israel 1955). The report attributed these deviations to political conditions in a parliamentary system. In the fragmented Israeli party system, Labor (the largest party) found it difficult to form governments with parties either to its left or right, forcing it to rely on several religious parties to achieve a majority coalition capable of controlling the Knesset. Labor found these parties amenable to its major priorities regarding defense and the economy while the religious parties, despite their unhappiness with Labor's secularism, appreciated the strategic advantages that came with the capacity to bring down the government. To maintain power, Labor granted to the Orthodox many policies and benefits "far beyond what the actual numerical strength of these parties would have appeared to justify – concessions which, on their merits, would never have won the support of more than a small fraction of the Knesset" (7).

The report then examined the consequences of these concessions in various sectors. As part of their bargain, the religious parties obtained expanded Orthodox control over the personal status of Jewish Israelis (marriage, divorce, adoption, etc.), legislation to further religious observance of the Jewish Sabbath, a ban on the conscription of Orthodox women for military or national service, and denial of recognition to non-Orthodox rabbis. Collectively, these victories composed what became known as the "Status Quo" regulating state–religious relations. The first two had been promised to the Orthodox in Ben Gurion's famous 1947 letter to the head of Agudat Israel, an organization representing ultra-Orthodox Jewry (reprinted in Shimshoni 1982).

From the American Jewish perspective, these features compromised religious and civil freedom in Israel and undermined any hope for the emergence of a secular state. By giving Orthodoxy power over the entire Jewish community in Israel and extending that authority "over fields which in the West have for centuries been considered the proper sphere of the civil authorities," Israeli law departed fundamentally from the no establishment and free exercise clauses in the US Constitution (Committee on Israel 1955, 31).

Consistent with the noninterference policy the AJC had declared regarding Israeli affairs, the report did not recommend any action. The sensitivity that might arise if this report did become broadly known – whether among Israelis, American Jews, or Israel's opponents – apparently accounted for the prohibition on its distribution, publication, or quotation and on language describing the report as representing only the views of the (unidentified) author rather than the AJC leadership or staff. In time, these concerns would be broadly known and become the basis for action by American Jews trying to mold Israel into something closer to a liberal democracy than an ethnic state.

Concerns about Israel's development into an ethnic democracy, a state that gives priority to the dominant group at the expense of minority prerogatives, grew gradually over time, intensifying amid the fervent religious nationalism on display when the Likud party displaced Labor as Israel's dominant political force in the "earthquake" election in 1977. The issue that most catalyzed subsequent American critics was, as anticipated by the 1955 AJC report, the preferred legal status of Orthodox Judaism. That issue has persisted over the decades, evolving as "a chronic source of conflict between Israel and the organized American Jewish community" (Brackman 1999, 795). Although other issues and controversies have contributed to criticism of Israel policies since the 1970s,

Steven Rosenthal (2001, 134) concluded, the privileged role of Orthodox Judaism in the Zionist state has generated "the most bitter and protracted of all the conflicts between American Jews and Israel."[3]

The "who is a Jew" controversy, as it was known, arose from an ambiguity in the Law of Return, the first piece of legislation passed by the Knesset. The law bestowed citizenship on Jewish immigrants on arrival in Israel. (Immigrants who were not Jewish had to go through a lengthy process of naturalization.) The regulations did *not* follow the religious code of law in determining who qualified as a Jew but adopted a much more lenient policy (a single Jewish grandparent) to encourage population growth. As some of the arrivals had been converted to Judaism in their prior country of residence, it was unclear who should decide whether they qualified for citizenship and registration as Jews. The Interior Ministry, the agency responsible for registering immigrants, was ordered by Israel's High Court in the early 1970s to accept as legitimate conversions performed abroad, even if the conversion was not done by Orthodox rabbis or did not meet Orthodox standards. As such, the converts were classified as Jewish on their identity cards. This did not affect conversions in Israel that were recognized as legitimate only if they followed the Orthodox procedure.

The High Court decision forced the hand of the Government. Insisting that classification of religion was the preserve of the rabbinate, the Orthodox political parties demanded amendment of the foundational Law of Return to specify its authority alone to rule on whether converts from abroad were in fact Jewish (and thus eligible for instant citizenship). In making the decision, the state rabbis were bound by *halacha*, the formal code of Jewish law as formulated and interpreted by Orthodox authorities. Under this rule, citizenship would be aligned with religious classification.

---

[3] The ongoing conflict over Israeli control of the West Bank, East Jerusalem, and the Golan Heights can be understood through this framework. Although Israeli spokespersons have provided secular justifications for these policies, arguing that they provide security for the Israeli heartland, public pressure to maintain these areas as part of "Greater Israel" has been stimulated in no small part by religious nationalism (Selengut 2017). Many Orthodox Jews who established what were once illegal settlements in the West Bank and who bought newly available housing in the old city of Jerusalem or state-funded settlements elsewhere did so to hasten the reconstitution of the ancient Jewish kingdoms. Referring to the West Bank by the historic names of Judea and Samaria makes clear the perceived biblical basis of the settlement project. The opponents of territorial maximalism are typically more secular and regard the religious ultra-nationalists as a danger to Israel's future as a Jewish and democratic state.

Without tracing every twist and turn of a long saga, the controversy over "who is a Jew" has recurred repeatedly over the decades, threatening to bring down governments dominated by various parties and destabilizing the state.[4] Setting up conversion courts that reflect the views of both Orthodox and non-Orthodox Jews, an arduous enough task in the United States, proved impossible under Israeli conditions. By 1997, the issue had become so contentious that the central organizations representing Conservative and Reform Judaism in the United States encouraged their communicants to withhold or reduce charitable contributions to Israel (Brackman 1999, 318).

Given the relatively small number of Israeli immigrants from the United States or elsewhere who converted under Reform or Conservative auspices, it might be hard to imagine why the issue resonates so strongly with American Jewry. In her invaluable history of the conflict, Nicole Brackman offers several hypotheses about why the conversion issue so consistently mobilizes American Jewish organizations. She does not ignore self-interest, noting that the non-Orthodox movements in the United States want Israel to legitimate conversions performed by their rabbis whether in Israel *or* abroad (Brackman 1999, 816). For American Jews, imbued with an individualistic view of religion, the nub of the conflict is "the refusal of the Israeli body politic, state, and religious authorities to allow American-style religious pluralism into Israeli law" (818). The conflict is inevitable because Israelis, even many who are not Orthodox, prefer to retain in law what they see as the traditional (that is, Orthodox) definition of Jewish identity.

From the perspective of the political culture of American Jewry, the root of the problem is that Israeli law assigns exclusive jurisdiction over *any* aspect of personal life to *any* religious group, including its own. American Jewish critics do not find Israel wanting merely because they prefer religious diversity or individuality in Judaism, although many do, but criticize Israel harshly for embracing policies that move it closer to an ethnic democracy. Precisely because Israel often speaks of itself as the

---

[4] In December 2016, the Israeli chief rabbinate promised to draw up a list of criteria for recognizing rabbis abroad whose conversions will be accepted as valid. This was occasioned by recent rejection of immigrants who had been converted by some of the most esteemed Orthodox rabbis in the United States. As the rabbinate continued to reject conversions performed by non-Orthodox rabbis, this policy would not address the core complaint of American Jews about Israeli policy. See July Maltz, "Israel to Publish Criteria for Recognizing Rabbis Who Perform Conversions Abroad," *Haaretz*, December 8, 2016, www.haaretz.com/israel-news/1.757795 (accessed March 7, 2017).

center of the Jewish nation, encompassing Jews both in Israel and the diaspora, the Israeli policy has implications for Jewry worldwide.

When the Knesset strengthened the Jewish ethnic component of the state by passing a new Basic Law in 2018, American Jewish leaders expressed deep concern about its antiliberal character. The philanthropist Ronald Lauder (2018), president of the World Jewish Congress, called attention to legislation that denied surrogacy rights to same-sex couples, demoted Arabic from its status as an "official" language, described Israel as *the* (rather than *a*) "nation-state of the Jewish people," and declared "Jewish settlement" as a national value. Collectively, he argued, this legislation and other administrative actions that enshrined Orthodox practices at the expense of secular rights tarnished the "sacred quality" of egalitarianism. In language that would not have been out of place when the American Jewish political culture was developed more than a century earlier, he lamented that these actions would "undermine the covenant between Judaism and enlightenment."

The "who is a Jew" conflict is merely one item in long list of concerns that have seemingly distanced some American Jews from the Jewish state. Identifying Israeli policies that contradict the core political culture of American Jewry, some American Jews have sought to intervene directly in Israeli public life. Although such "direct engagement" is not limited to the left wing of American Jewry, progressives have made noteworthy contributions to liberal organizations and movements in Israel (Sasson 2010).

As Shain (2000, 164) notes, American Jews

... have been instrumental in the struggle to challenge the Israeli Orthodox monopoly over Jewish marriage and conversion and its domination of religious councils. Such groups have also played a role in the fight for the rights of non-Orthodox Jews to be buried in non-denominational cemeteries and have taken the lead in redirecting Jewish diasporic fundraising away from general funds for Israel to targeted assistance of institutions and programs aimed at promoting tolerance, democracy, and religious pluralism.

The American Jewish contributions to this effort go beyond financial contributions. American Jews who moved to Israel have been deeply involved in Israeli social movements committed to liberal values. Although the movement has many home-grown activists (Woods 2004), American feminists such as Marcia Freedman helped found major Israeli women's organizations (Laskier 2000, 136). The civil rights lawyers who file lawsuits for many progressive Israeli social movements also have a strong connection to American Jewry. Noting the lack of a civil liberties Bar in Israel, a visiting American Jewish law professor recruited a corps of young lawyers who were subsequently trained in American law schools and "seasoned" by internships in leading American civil liberties organizations. The program funding came from the New Israel Fund, a Brooklyn-based philanthropy founded by American Jews (Laskier 2000, 129–130). Through these direct and indirect means, American Jewry has helped promote liberal values regarding the public role of religion in Israel.

American Jews have also been instrumental in importing American legal doctrines into Israeli law via the Jewish state's judiciary. Absent a bill of rights, Israeli jurists have drawn heavily on the US Constitution in developing that concept for their own country (Segal 1992, 22–28). One influential proponent of "transplantation," the American-born and educated Shimon Agranat, served as president of the Israeli Supreme Court from 1965 to 1976. He emphasized liberal American constitutional values in his decisions (Lahav 1981, 34–37). Social movements opposing what they called "religious coercion" achieved considerable legal success in Israel during the 1995–2006 Supreme Court presidency of Aharon Barak. A close friend and associate of the American legal scholar Alan Dershowitz, Barak effected a constitutional revolution built on "the enunciation of liberal-individualistic values and … utilization of American precedents" regarding religion and state.

The American precedents that Israeli jurists drew upon were often the work of Jewish legal scholars imbued with the classical liberal understanding of citizenship. Hence the leading American authority on the Israeli legal system described the result as the "Americanization" of Israeli law (Edelman 2000, 209). Even to an Israeli admirer (Lorberbaum 2012, 292), Barak's "liberal judicial activism" had the effect of effacing "the particular cultural and religious character of the Jewish public space of Israeli society."

That conclusion would not have disturbed many American Jews and their organizations who gave classic liberal values pride of place even when they constructed their image of a self-described Jewish state. This should not have been surprising. The Jewish state envisioned by Theodore Herzl in his novel, *Altneuland*, seemed saturated with Western liberalism rather than Judaism. Long before there was a Jewish state in Palestine, even the most engaged American Zionist activists believed the movement was not merely about restoring Jewish nationality for the first time since the expulsion from Jerusalem. Rather, to Stephen Wise (quoted in

Auerbach 1990, 173), Zionism was "the Jewish expression of American democratic values," a modern laboratory dedicated above all else to "the prophetic striving for social justice." Little wonder that postwar American Jews exerted so much effort to make Israel conform to their imagined community.

When American Jewish leaders in the late twentieth century perceived violations of the American Jewish political culture inherited from their predecessors, they did not hesitate to act in defense of liberal values. They acted whether the violations were observed in the United State or Israel. In the case of affirmative action, the policies of the US government seemed to threaten the classical version of liberalism based on the principle of meritocracy. This put American Jews at odds with some of their long-time allies in the Democratic Party who subscribed to the tenets of a newer form of liberalism. In the other case study, Israel's treatment of religion, American Jews reiterated ideas that had long been current among members of their community and they were willing to lock horns with the Israeli government when it diverged from American norms.

Contemporary American Jews remain strongly attached to classical liberal values and the Democratic Party. I have given more attention to those liberal values than to how the Democratic Party eventually became their carrier. Hence the next chapter examines how these classical liberal values became closely associated with the Democratic Party and cemented its status as the political home for most American Jews.

# 9

## Resurgence of Democratic Partisanship in the Post–New Deal Era

> When I hear the term "Christian America," I see barbed wire.
> —Rabbi quoted in Cohen (1993, 12)

Previous chapters have traced the development of classic liberalism as a political norm among American Jews and its persistent influence on their political actions during the nineteenth and twentieth centuries. This chapter reconnects that historical account to the central thread of the book, the puzzling attachment of contemporary American Jewry to the Democratic Party.

During the period when Jews were consolidating their political world-view, the American Jewish political culture of classical liberalism was not consistently linked to support for any political party. Jewish leaders stressed that Jews were not a cohesive electoral bloc but were divided internally on many political and economic questions.[1] Rabbis were noticeably silent on political controversies except those issues that clearly implicated Jewish interests, reflecting the wishes of politically divided congregations (Cohen 2008, 14). Before World War II, the parties were not defined by their attitudes to the secular state and challenges to the liberal regime could come from either Democrats or Republicans, as could allies who rallied to Jewish causes.

During the first era of stable Jewish attachment to the Democrats, from the 1930s through the 1960s, the appeal of the Democrats to Jews seems to have been largely economic in nature. It had little to do with concerns

---

[1] For an historical account of partisanship among American Jews before the polling era, see Forman (2001).

about a secular state or classical liberal principles. Still a predominantly working-class community composed mostly of immigrants and their native-born children, highly urbanized and attached to labor unions, Jews were hit hard by the economic decline that began in the late 1920s and expanded into the Great Depression during the 1930s. Like other working-class constituencies – Southern whites, African Americans, Roman Catholics, trade unionists and other manual laborers – Jews responded positively to the activist welfare state agenda that Democrats developed in response to the economic crisis. Franklin Roosevelt championed and extended the agenda through the New Deal, and his immediate successor, Harry Truman, tried to continue it into the post–World War II era.

There was little or no partisan polarization over religious issues during the Roosevelt–Truman–Eisenhower era. As late as 1953, when it was first proposed to add the phrase "under God" to the Pledge of Allegiance, party differences were hard to detect (Gallup Organization 1953). My analysis of polling data for that year revealed no significant variations in partisan support for the measure: 71% of Republicans, 69% of Democrats, and 67% of Independents favored the measure. These small differences failed to reach statistical significance. If Jews were looking for the party that better reflected their views on this issue, they had little basis to favor one over the other. The linkage between views on questions of religion and state and partisanship would begin to emerge a decade later when the parties began staking out competing positions on questions about the degree to which the law should permit government to embrace religious symbols and identity.[2] That change eventually reinvigorated Jewish attachment to the Democrats.

With the Depression and war receding from popular memory by the late 1960s, the Democratic coalition began to fray as new issues and concerns arose on the political agenda. Some, such as the conflict over affirmative action profiled in the previous chapter, tore into the fabric of the Democratic coalition, initiating a period of partisan change. Recall how we saw in Chapter 2 that Jewish electoral support for Democratic

---

[2] Even within the Jewish community, which had been leery of actions that stoked religious nationalism, the Pledge issue does not seem to have been particularly salient. The same Gallup survey shows that Jews were 17% less supportive than Protestants of changing the Pledge to include "under God" but only 12% behind Catholics in their objections to the proposal. Only the Protestant–Jewish comparison reached statistical significance and barely at that. As we will see below, those differences pale in comparison to Jewish/non-Jewish disparities on church–state issues that emerged in the 1970s and after.

presidential candidates dropped to a two-to-one advantage in the 1970s, still comparatively high but nonetheless lower than it had been in the 1950s and 1960s. Things became topsy-turvy in the 1980s and 1990s when Catholics, trade unionists, Southern whites, and other key components of the Roosevelt Coalition shifted sharply away from the Democrats, but Jews actually increased their attachment to the party.

The theoretical anomaly became much more significant when Jews, now a comfortably middle-class constituency, moved back toward the Democrats. None of the other groups that had formed the Roosevelt coalition returned to the Democrats as consistently or substantially as the Jews during this period. I provide evidence in this chapter that the Democratic resurgence among Jews owed much to new concerns about changes in church–state relationships. With the rise in conflict about the role of religion in the political system, the Democratic Party became the principal vehicle upholding classical liberalism's defense of the secular state.

To understand this process, I first review the connection among political issues, group identity, and political cleavage. This provides a framework for making sense of the Jewish pattern. The chapter then discusses the post–World War II revolution in jurisprudence that put questions about religion and state on the national political agenda,[3] contributing in time to a new line of partisan cleavage that further divided Democrats from Republicans. As the Reagan-era GOP came to depend on the votes of Evangelical Protestants, the party's new base, Jews began to wonder about the GOP's dedication to the secular state. When they could no longer trust Republicans to defend the classically liberal regime of religion and state they perceived in the Constitution, Jews redoubled their commitment to the Democrats.

THE RISE OF CHURCH–STATE JURISPRUDENCE

How do political questions become issues on the national agenda? How do such issues become aligned with party affiliation, a component of what divides Democrats from Republicans? And how do particular voter blocs within a party coalition absorb the party's issue positions as their own? Contemporary political science addresses these questions, respectively, through the framework of agenda setting, issue evolution, and social identification.

---

[3] This section draws from material in Wald and Calhoun-Brown (2018, chapter 4).

Agenda setting examines how and why public concerns and grievances about a matter become central to national political debate. Church–state relations became contentious in the 1960s largely because of growing differences among political elites in their understanding of the US Constitution. The theory of issue evolution helps us understand how questions about the proper relationship between religion and state came to divide the political parties at both the elite and mass levels. As I will argue, ambitious political entrepreneurs perceived partisan advantages in politicizing concerns about this issue and linking a specific position on the issue to their political party. Social identity theory, an approach rooted in social psychology, provides insights about how rank-and-file individuals come to consider themselves part of a group, how this affects the way they think about their group and its opponents, and how this becomes a component of their personal identity in a complex social world. In the case at hand, most people who identified as Jews perceived some specific groups as threatening their status by pushing a nonliberal interpretation of religion under the Constitution. This activated the strong underlying commitment to a secular state and attached it firmly to the Democratic Party.

## Church and State

The liberal political culture embraced by American Jewry has emphasized above all else the priority of maintaining a state that leaves religious life to the private sphere, largely unregulated, which neither recognizes a state religion nor limits the practice of religion unless necessary for public safety. Because Jews are a decided minority within the American religious economy, the religious equality provisions embodied in Article VI and the First Amendment have engendered a high degree of consensus among them.

Sensitivity to threats against religious equality operates like a physical antibody in the Jewish body politic. When Jews confront practices that grant preferred legal status to Christianity, it triggers almost immediate resistance and countermobilization. The pace of such defensive activity increased measurably in the post–World War II era when the federal courts assumed increased authority over questions of religion and state.

During the first century and a half under the Constitution, the federal courts seldom adjudicated the religious provisions of the Constitution. Very few cases touched on the prohibition of religious tests in Article VI or the First Amendment clauses regarding establishment and free exercise.

Although some important principles were established in cases decided during the nineteenth century, religious liberty was not a major topic on the Court's agenda.[4] When Jews challenged government actions to promote or restrict religion, they mostly targeted state or local authorities who were not bound by the religious provisions in the federal constitution. Although one Jewish judge believed that the Civil War amendments granting civic and legal equality to former slaves had effectively "annihilated" disfranchisement based on religion at the state level (Sulzberger 1904), this interpretation was not adopted by the Supreme Court during the nineteenth century.

The situation began to change in the mid-twentieth century when a majority of the Supreme Court judges gradually came to accept Justice Hugo Black's doctrine of "total incorporation." Justice Black argued that the Fourteenth Amendment, passed after the Civil War to protect freed slaves from oppressive state laws, was intended "to extend to all the people of the nation the complete protection of the Bill of Rights" (quoted in Wohl 1991, 44). Hence, the Court decided that the First Amendment, which began with "Congress shall make no law," now applied to *all* levels of government. This amounted to nationalizing the Bill of Rights.

Although religious freedom had been protected in a few cases on free speech grounds in the 1940s and 1950s, the Supreme Court gradually came to emphasize and expand the joint pillars of classical liberalism, the provision against establishment of religion *by* the government and the protection of individual religious liberty *from* the government. Thanks to incorporation, the government in question could be local, state, or national. Some of the Court's decisions generated enormous controversy, especially cases restricting religious exercises in the public schools (mandatory prayer and Bible reading in the early 1960s) and prohibiting government funding of religious schools. Critics of the Court's prayer and Bible reading opinions launched repeated attempts to overturn these decisions by constitutional amendment or, when those efforts failed, to evade them by slack enforcement.

Two camps emerged with very different understanding of the religious clauses of the First Amendment. Advocates debated whether the religion clauses were meant, as Jefferson said in 1801, to create a wall of separation between religion and state, or, in the view of critics, allowed

---

[4] Even the important *Pierce* decision of 1925 struck down an Oregon law prohibiting private school education on the grounds of parental rights, not religious freedom. The law targeted Catholic schools.

government to constitutionally recognize and provide nondiscriminatory aid to "religion in general" without running afoul of the establishment clause. The two contending approaches were known, respectively, as separationism and accommodationism.

Separationists regard many forms of government action on behalf of religion as impermissible on establishment grounds. This doctrine led the late-twentieth-century Supreme Court to strike down practices such as school prayers written by local authorities or tax-funded tuition scholarships for students in religious schools. Both were defined by the Court as forms of establishment that breached Jefferson's wall. They also broadened dramatically the defense of individuals' religious free exercise by, for example, excusing Amish children from mandatory high school attendance laws and insisting that a Seventh Day Adventist who refused to work on that denomination's (Saturday) Sabbath was entitled to unemployment compensation.[5] Government could restrict religious freedom only by meeting the very high threshold of "strict scrutiny," showing that the restriction was narrowly drawn, neutral toward religions, and served a compelling government interest. Religious minorities benefited disproportionately from these decisions simply because their beliefs and practices were more likely to encounter resistance from dominant religions (Weinrib 2003, 34–35).

Accommodationists were willing to tolerate policies that encouraged a significant degree of public religiousness. Given majority rule and the nature of religious affiliation, such decisions usually granted privileges to the dominant religious tradition in a community. But in free exercise cases, accommodationists usually felt that religion did not provide any exemption from what were called "neutral" laws of general applicability even if they impeded religious free exercise. They advocated a much lower threshold that required government to show only that it had some rational basis for restricting practices by religious groups, a doctrine that acquired the force of law in the 1989 decision *Employment Division v. Smith*. Under this policy, minority faiths were much less likely to enjoy constitutional protection for religious customs that went against the norms of majority faiths.

---

[5] Neither of these decisions impaired the religious freedom of other groups. The more recent claims by religious conservatives that the free exercise clause entitles individuals and corporations to deny services to employees (*Hobby Lobby*) or consumers (numerous cases related to same-sex marriage) does produce such a tradeoff, extending religious freedom to some at the expense of others (Nejaime and Siegel 2015).

## Issue Evolution

This conflict between contending elites – largely an intramural conflict among judges, lawyers, and legal scholars – underwent a process of "issue evolution" such that the contending sides eventually became strongly aligned with different political parties. The Democrats embraced separationism, the Republicans embodied accommodationism. As is common in what political scientists call partisan "sorting," the process took decades to complete.

Observing political ferment in the 1960s, Republican strategist Kevin Phillips (1969) perceived that the social upheaval of the time might provide a way to loosen party ties by politicizing these issues to the partisan advantage of the GOP, then the minority party. Based on electoral trends, he advised the party to try to detach two key components of the Democratic coalition, white Southerners and culturally conservative Catholics. Both groups were attracted to the economic policies of the Democrats but grew increasingly uncomfortable with the party's support for socially liberal policies. From the 1960s on, in pursuit of this objective, Republican activists remade their party into the voice of moral traditionalism. In so doing, they departed from classical liberalism by supporting state restrictions on many forms of what were considered unorthodox and/or immoral behavior. By the 1970s, these efforts began to bear fruit as Republicans increasingly became seen by voters as the party of faith. Evangelicals displaced mainline Protestants as the electoral base of the party, and their traditionalist priorities (packaged as "family values") usually dominated the party platforms. With this new alignment, the Republicans had reframed their party's image.

The Democrats, in turn, put their electoral fortunes in the hands of those who welcomed the social changes that Republicans condemned. Their "new liberalism" committed to enhancing individual freedom, fighting constraints based on race, gender, sexual orientation, and, of course, religion. Support for the separationist perspective, seen as a way to defend the interests of religious outsiders and minorities, fit in with their embrace of the ethos of the 1960s. They applauded Supreme Court decisions that classified government action on behalf of religion as violations of the Establishment Clause. At the same time, they endorsed the aggressive defense of individuals' religious freedom from the state, accepting limitations on free exercise only if they satisfied the strict scrutiny threshold. To reiterate, such positions were more sensitive to the aspirations of religious minorities than the values and prerogatives of religious majorities. They were also consistent with the emphasis on sovereign individualism in classical liberalism.

Thus, each party became publicly identified with the school of constitutional interpretation they considered likely to appeal to their target constituencies. As just noted, the Democrats reached out to young, progressive, and modernist voters who emphasized that individuals should have maximum freedom of religion and maximum protection from religious coercion by majority faiths. Aiming at conservative Catholics and (predominantly) white Southern evangelicals, Republicans took positions consistent with accommodationist doctrine. Judges appointed by Republican presidents championed a much narrower standard for defining government actions as a form of establishment and made it more difficult for individuals to challenge laws or practices that they claimed impeded religious free exercise.

These images stuck. More than one commentator likened the late-twentieth-century Republican Party to Iran's theocracy and other observers joked that GOP stood for God's Own Party. Yet it appears the Republicans had the last laugh. By referring repeatedly to the "San Francisco Democrats" after the party's 1984 national convention in that city, Republican activists succeeded in painting their opponents as morally threatening and antireligious. The shell-shocked campaign manager for Michael Dukakis in the 1988 presidential election observed that Republicans had used the Democratic embrace of the new liberalism to paint the party as out of touch with the electorate:

It is politically dangerous to take for granted that voters will automatically assume the Democratic candidate holds dear the country's basic values: God, patriotism, family, and freedom. In some historically perverse way, Democrats must – at least for now – work hard to somehow prove they are as politically wholesome and decent as Republicans. (quoted in White 1990, 156)

The durability of this impression was affirmed by a series of surveys conducted by the Pew Research Center. From 2003 to 2016, Pew asked respondents to rate the friendliness of each party to religion. These surveys revealed that Republicans were consistently seen to be friendlier to religion than Democrats. On average, Republicans outscored Democrats on this question by around 20%.

TABLE 9.1 *Perceptions of Party Principles by the American Public, 2006*
*Now, thinking about the two major political parties in this country,*
*which one would you say is most concerned with ...*

|  | Protecting religious values % | Protecting the freedom of citizens to make personal choices % |
|---|---|---|
| Republicans | 45 | 26 |
| Democrats | 29 | 53 |
| Both/Neither | 14 | 14 |
| Refused/DK | 9 | 7 |

*Source:* People for the American Way. Center for American Values (2006).

The divergence in party positions on this issue was laid bare in a 2006 survey that asked participants to assess the parties' commitment to a pair of conflicting priorities. Table 9.1 demonstrates that the public perceived the Republicans as committed to protecting religious values and the Democrats as a party devoted to protecting the rights of individuals to make their own moral choices. Although this perception covered a range of specific political issues, it clearly extended to questions about church and state.

With the issue of accommodation versus separation now defined, put on the political agenda, and thoroughly politicized, we examine how Jews found themselves clearly on the Democratic side. Their long project to define the US Constitution in classical liberal terms made it easy for Jews to redouble their commitment to the Democratic Party once the separationist/accommodationist divide came to align with partisan loyalties. We will first examine these efforts in the post–World War II period and then interpret them through the lens of social identity theory.

## JEWISH LEGAL EFFORTS

Considering their strong commitment to the classical liberal understanding that the state has no religious identity and should allocate neither benefits nor costs based on religious affiliation or values, Jews were drawn almost to a person to the "high wall" interpretation. As previous chapters have noted, Jews were traditionally sensitive to any government action that appeared to embrace religion, seeing such efforts as stealth attempts to impose Christianity by law. They perceived as exclusionary even symbolic actions such as official Thanksgiving proclamations steeped in Christian imagery.

By the same token, they regarded many seemingly neutral public policies as effectively abridging their religious freedom. Laws that mandated Sunday closing of businesses were particularly problematic for observant Jews who were forced to abstain from work on two days a week, both their Sabbath on Saturday and on Sunday. Even Jews who did not follow religious law perceived such limitations as covert attempts to confer official status on the Christian sabbath. Because restrictions on the availability of birth control, the criminalization of same-sex activity, severe limits on abortion, and other forms of moral regulation were rooted in traditionalist Christianity, Jews also approached them as religiously based penalties that undermined political secularism. Their interests in preserving and strengthening the liberal church–state regime aligned Jews very closely with separationism.

As Gregg Ivers (1993) detailed in his painstaking analysis of church and state cases, Jews were central to the coalition that promoted separationism in the legal sphere. The American Jewish Congress (AJCongress) and the American Jewish Committee (AJC), two organizations whose conflicts over Israel were detailed in Chapter 7, were among the key interest groups litigating cases under the religion clauses of the First Amendment. This work was supported by Jewish denominational organizations associated with the Conservative and Reform wings of Judaism as well as trans-denominational organizations like the Anti-Defamation League. Some secular groups which joined in this effort, such as the American Civil Liberties Union (ACLU) and People for the American Way, enjoyed disproportionate financial support from Jews and included a significant number of Jewish lawyers and researchers on their staffs.

At the same time, this was not solely a Jewish effort. The roster of organizations that did the legal work on behalf of separationism – identifying potential cases, recruiting litigants, funding research, composing amicus briefs, arguing cases in court – included many secular and religious groups not formally associated with the Jewish community. Aside from those already mentioned, groups such as Americans United for Separation of Church and State and the Baptist Joint Committee on Public Affairs devoted considerable efforts to maintain the high wall of separation and promote individual religious free exercise.

It is equally important to remember that many of these organizations did not restrict their efforts to cases implicating only Jewish interests or to religious cases involving other denominations or even to lawsuits about the religion clauses. Rather, the groups comprising the Jewish communal defense sphere advocated more broadly on behalf of minorities facing various threats to their First Amendment rights. Much of the leadership of the NAACP Legal and Defense Fund was provided by Jewish lawyers who worked closely with attorneys from the black community. These groups also lobbied for the passage of both the Civil Rights Act of 1964 and the Voting Rights Act of 1965. Hence, the campaign for constitutional protection against establishment, religious tests, and limits on free exercise was part of a broader commitment to promoting pluralist values that would incidentally but not exclusively provide benefits to the Jewish community.

The degree of American Jewish involvement in promoting the separationist doctrine is apparent from looking at how Jewish judges diverged from their non-Jewish counterparts in cases involving religion and state.[6] The first systematic study on that topic, Frank Sorauf's *Wall of Separation* (1976), discovered that Jewish judges on appellate courts reached separationist decisions in 82% of the religious cases between 1953 and 1971. During the same period, Roman Catholic judges promoted accommodationist interpretations 84% of the time. The differences between Jewish judges and those from other religious traditions has been replicated in a wide variety of subsequent studies using statistical controls for other background factors (Blake 2012; Sisk, Heise, and Morriss 2004; Wasserman and Hardy 2013). The finding was also reaffirmed by the behavior of the three Jewish justices on the US Supreme Court in recent church–state cases. They voted against an Arizona scholarship program that used tax funds to send students to private religious schools, Christian public prayers before the meetings of the city council in a small New York town, and granting a private business the right to deny contraceptive coverage to employees based on the owners' religious objections.

The same pattern was apparent from studies of amicus briefs, the written legal arguments filed by groups and individuals with an interest in a legal case under review. In First Amendment religion cases argued between 1969 and 1988, Ivers (1990) reported that

---

[6] The next few paragraphs follow the argument presented in Wald (2016). I compare Jewish and Catholic views because both are minorities in a predominantly Protestant country and because most of these studies combined mainline and Evangelical Protestants who are likely to hold very different opinions on the religious clauses.

more than four-fifths of these briefs filed by Jewish organizations favored a separationist decision. Of the briefs submitted by Roman Catholic organizations, an even higher percentage advanced an accommodationist perspective. Kathryn Oates (2010) found that Jewish organizations were particularly active filing briefs in cases in which the government was alleged to grant a tangible benefit – funding, official status, or another perceived privilege – rather than merely symbolic recognition. Jewish organizations opposed virtually all benefits that government provided to religions. They did so even when those benefits flowed to Jewish organizations.

Elite debates between separationism and accommodationism are not restricted to the courtroom. Elected officials may also have a say. Such a case came before the US Senate in March 1984 when it considered a proposed amendment to the Constitution. Aimed at a long line of separationist Supreme Court decisions that limited official state-composed prayers in public schools and at ceremonial occasions, Senate Joint Resolution #73 would have permitted "organized, recited prayer in public schools and other public places." The amendment was openly seen as intended to promote Christian devotion in the public square. Although the Senate voted 56–44 in favor of the amendment, it failed to reach the sixty votes needed for submission to the states.

The yawning religious gap on this vote was noteworthy. Of the ten senators who were either Jewishly identified or had some Jewish heritage, just two voted for the amendment. That was 40% below the level of support for the resolution from the other ninety senators. Even though the amendment was supported by then-president Ronald Reagan and the GOP congressional leadership, five of the seven Jewishly connected Republican senators and their Democratic coreligionists rejected accommodationism by voting against the amendment.

## JEWISH PUBLIC OPINION

### Abstract Principles

Do rank-and-file Jews share the perspectives of Jewish elites on religion and state? The best way to assess this claim is to examine the responses of Jews and other religious groups to a question that obliges respondents to choose between the two major constitutional interpretations of the religion clauses. Three national surveys have posed the following question:

Which comes closer to your view?

1.  The government should take special steps to protect America's religious heritage.

OR

2.  There should be a high degree of separation between church and state.

The wording of the first option taps the underlying logic of accommodation in church–state relations. In 1952, Justice Douglas asserted that Americans are "a religious people whose institutions presuppose a Supreme Being."[7] Hence, he reasoned, the Court embodies our national heritage when it "respects the religious nature of our people and accommodates the public service to their spiritual needs." The second option is a restatement of Jefferson's classic letter to the Baptists of Danbury, Connecticut that called for a "wall of separation" between church and state. The question is designed to encourage respondents to choose between the alternatives by omitting other options such as "both" or "neither." Respondents who did not answer initially or volunteered "both" or "neither" were asked the question a second time, and those who still did not answer or insisted on both options were dropped from analysis. Fewer than 5% of respondents were eliminated for those reasons.

The question was asked in a 2000 national opinion survey conducted by Knowledge Networks and in 1998 and 2012 surveys of the American public sponsored jointly by the Kaiser Family Foundation and the *Washington Post*. The samples included enough Jewish respondents to support a meaningful comparison of Jews and non-Jews and even more focused contrasts between Jews and members of other specific religious traditions.

According to the 2000 survey data in Table 9.2, American Jews share the separationist faith of their elite coreligionists. They were almost unanimous in their preference for the Jeffersonian option over the accommodationist alternative. Given the minority/majority dynamic underlying church–state philosophy, it was not surprising that Jews were 50% more supportive of separationism than Christian respondents. Yet even when compared with members of other minority faiths and those who reported no religious affiliation, Jews still stood

---

7 Reports, 343 U.S. 310 [1952].

TABLE 9.2 *Attitudes to Church–State Relationships by Religion, 2000*

|  | Jewish (%) | Christian (%) | Minority (%) | None (%) |
|---|---|---|---|---|
| Protect America's religious heritage | 12 | 61 | 54 | 33 |
| High degree of separation | 88 | 39 | 46 | 67 |
| Total percentage | 100 | 100 | 100 | 100 |
| Number of cases | 450 | 433 | 37 | 51 |

*Source:* Calculated from Greenberg and Wald (2000).
*Note.* The composition of the sample, almost evenly divided between Jews and non-Jews, makes it inappropriate to apply the overall divisions in this sample to the public. Respondents who chose both/neither or held no opinion were dropped from the analysis.

out in their near-unanimity about this question. Jews were about 40% more supportive of separation than members of other minority faiths and 20+% ahead of the nonaffiliated in supporting this option. All these differences reached conventional levels of statistical significance.

The Kaiser–*Washington Post* surveys showed a closely divided public in both 1998 and 2012. Overall, there was a 51% to 49% split between protecting religious heritage versus separation in 1998; by 2012, the ratio had swung 52% to 48% in the other direction. Regardless of the overall differences between the two surveys, as Figure 9.1 demonstrates, roughly nine out of ten Jewish respondents preferred the second option in both 1998 and 2012. The gap between Jews and all groups other than the religious "nones" was statistically significant in both surveys. Unlike its 1998 counterpart, which lumped them in the "other" religious category, the 2012 Kaiser survey recorded the religious affiliation of three non-Jewish religious minorities – Hindus, Muslims, and Buddhists – who collectively favored a high degree of separation by a two to one ratio (data not shown). Even compared to this distinctive group, however, Jews were more committed to the liberal regime by a margin that reached statistical significance.

These data make clear that Jews are distinctive in their preference for a state that keeps religion in the private sphere.[8]

---

[8] The results were further confirmed by a 2010 survey conducted by the Public Religion Research Institute (2010). This survey asked respondents to agree/disagree with the statement, "We must maintain a strict separation of church and state." Jews exceeded all groups in their support for strict separation, with 95% in favor and more than three-fourths in complete agreement with the statement. The gap between Jews and the religious nones was statistically significant.

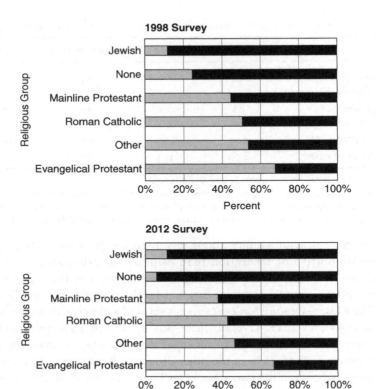

FIGURE 9.1 Attitudes to church–state relationships by religion, 1998 and 2012.
Source: Calculated from Kaiser Family Foundation (1998, 2012). Respondents
who selected any other option were dropped from this analysis.

## Tangible Issues

No matter how the question is worded, it seems, American Jews emerge as
strongly separationist when compared to other religious groups. The
pattern holds when we move from abstract principles to tangible policy
issues. I reach this conclusion based on findings from what appears to be
the only comprehensive study of American Jewish attitudes on specific
forms of church–state interaction, the "Jews and the American Public
Square" surveys funded by the Pew Charitable Trusts (Cohen 2000a,
2000b, 2000c).

On a series of eight questions about religion in the schools, there was almost a 30% average difference between Jews and non-Jews, with the former embracing the separationist position on each issue. On many of these issues, Jews were two to three times as likely to oppose religion in the schools as their non-Jewish counterparts. A diverse set of questions about religion in public life yielded almost equally massive gaps along religious lines. Whether asked about legislative prayers, "God talk" by public officials, displays of religious objects in public space (including Jewish items), or the contribution of religion to American culture, Jews were much less enthusiastic about such practices than the general public. Similarly, the Jewish public showed itself to be much more liberal on social issues often debated in moral terms: abortion, homosexuality, pre-marital sex, and birth control. Such attitudes are likely to translate into sympathy for minority plaintiffs seeking free exercise protection from a majority committed to traditionalist social values. While Jews agreed much more than non-Jews that "Organized religion should stay out of politics," they were more forgiving and much closer to non-Jews in their willingness to allow clergy and congregations free speech on political issues.

During the 2000 presidential campaign, the Democratic Party named a Jewish candidate for vice president, Sen. Joseph Lieberman of Connecticut. Thinking that the nomination of an observant Jew might make Jews more likely to accept religious appeals by candidates, the sponsors of the Pew Trusts survey commissioned a follow-up wave of interviews late in the campaign. Table 9.3 reprints one of the tables from that follow-up survey.

On principle, as the first and last questions in Table 9.3 make clear, Jews were much less enthusiastic than non-Jews about the use of religious language in campaigns. They were notably more negative than the general population about actions taken by George W. Bush, Richard Cheney, and Al Gore that expressed Christian religious convictions and/or a willingness to support religion in the public square. But the most telling finding is that Jews were less than half as positive as non-Jews when Joseph Lieberman, a Jewish nominee, referenced God and the Bible in his remarks after his selection for the Democratic ticket. A majority of Jews disapproved of religious language by one of their own while a plurality of non-Jews found nothing objectionable in Lieberman's religious language! As the study director commented dryly (in Cohen 2000c), "Far from having moved them toward more tolerance for religion in public life, Sen. Lieberman's campaign seems to have convinced many Jews to continue

TABLE 9.3 *Attitudes toward Candidates' Expressions of Faith*

| | Jews who approve(%) | Non-Jews who approve(%) |
|---|---|---|
| Politicians speaking about their faith in God and quoting the Bible in public. | 16 | 52 |
| George Bush's proclamation of "Jesus Day" in Texas. | 3 | 24 |
| Al Gore's comment that he never makes a major decision without asking himself what Jesus would do. | 10 | 42 |
| Joseph Lieberman's references to God and quoting from the Bible in his speech in Tennessee after being selected by Gore. | 21 | 45 |
| Richard Cheney's sponsorship of a constitutional amendment to permit prayer in schools. | 16 | 59 |
| Religion in the campaign disturbs me. (% agree) | 53 | 30 |

*Source:* Cohen (2007c).
Reprinted with permission of Center for Jewish Community Studies.

to oppose it." That finding demonstrates the depth of resistance by Jews to religion in public political discourse even if the messenger and the message come from their own tradition.

Do the data collected at the turn of the century still describe accurately Jewish views on specific church–state controversies two decades later? As no single study has fully replicated the 2000 Pew-funded survey, we turn instead to data from the annual survey of American Jewish opinion conducted on behalf of the AJC. Because the survey is topical, policy questions are rotated on and off the questionnaire, leaving us scattered measures of church and state through 2005 and none whatsoever after that date. Moreover, as a survey administered solely to Jewish respondents there is no way to compare the responses of Jews to the general public. But those data nonetheless emphasize the continuity of Jewish resistance to accommodationist policies regarding the schools.

On the most frequently asked church–state question in the AJC survey, the level of Jewish opposition to government aid to parochial schools ranged between 68% and 78%. The survey also asked four times about

TABLE 9.4 *Jewish Attitudes to Religion in the Schools*

| Percent oppose | 1998 | 2000 | 2001 | 2002 | 2003 | 2004 | 2005 |
|---|---|---|---|---|---|---|---|
| Government aid to parochial or other religious schools? | | 68 | 78 | 76 | 73 | 72 | |
| A school voucher program that would allow parents to use tax funds to send their children to the school of their choice, even if it were a private school? | 53 | 61 | | | | | |
| Taxpayer funds for social service programs run by religious institutions, such as churches or synagogues? | | | 76 | 73 | 73 | | 66 |

*Source:* American Jewish Committee, Annual Survey of American Jewish Opinion, selected years. Retrieved from: http://www.jewishdatabank.org/Studies/details.cfm?StudyID=765 (accessed June 30, 2017).

the Bush II-era Faith-Based Initiative. The goal of this program was to increase the capacity of religiously affiliated social service organizations – particularly those associated with Evangelical Protestantism – to compete for government-funded contracts and grants (Wineburg 2007). Two-thirds to three-fourths of Jewish respondents opposed this program in the AJC surveys even though the question explicitly indicated that synagogues could participate. There is no convincing reason to assume that the views recorded in Table 9.4 have changed much over the last decade.

## SOCIAL IDENTITY AND GROUP AFFECT

The data presented in this chapter have established that Jews, masses and elites alike, adhere to the separationist position consistent with the classical liberalism embraced by their forerunners. I show now that concern about defending the liberal regime on this issue contributed to stabilizing and reinforcing American Jewish commitment to the Democratic Party from the 1980s onward.

Social identity theory helps us make sense of why Jews alone among the core groups in the Roosevelt coalition have remained loyal to the Democratic Party.[9] Facing a complex and diverse social order, how do

---

[9] Some of this material is reported in Wald and Calhoun-Brown (2018).

individuals answer the fundamental question of "Who am I"? The process turns out to be group-centered through a process known as social categorization. Using experimental designs, social psychologists have demonstrated that individuals easily develop cognitive ties to social groups, a sense that certain groups contain people like themselves. Even though some such ties are weak and membership may be arbitrary, they nonetheless exert significant impact on behavior. Specifically, individuals come to attach meaning and positive value to membership (real or imagined) in the group. In addition to strong, positive feelings about members of the in-group (known as positive group affect), social identity may also promote antagonism to out-groups.

Negative orientations (affect in social science jargon) are especially likely to develop toward any out-group perceived to pose a threat to the values and interests of the group that defines the individual's social identity. The threat may be objective, when the membership group and another group compete for tangible benefits, but is equally if not more potent when it is defined by differing cultural and social values (Huddy 2013, 752).[10] In practice, the dynamics of social identity operate very much like loyalty to a tribe, a brand, or a sports team.

Some social identities acquire political content. In Huddy's definition (2013, n. 8, 741), a political identity is "a social identity that is either defined on the basis of a common political outlook, or has become political through the emergence of explicitly political group norms governing members' outlook and action." As I have argued throughout this book, the American Jewish political culture transmits explicit political norms that structure behavior in the public realm, especially when it comes to the regime of religion and state. We thus expect that Jewish social identity will promote a commitment to classical liberalism and, through that, to the Democratic Party.

If this hypothesis is correct, we should thus expect to see that Jews exhibit (1) negative affect toward social groups and social movement organizations perceived as carriers of threats to classical liberalism regarding church and state; (2) positive affect to organizations that are believed to counter those threats; and (3) partisanship based in part or whole on perceptions of Democrats as advocates of classical liberalism and Republicans as less committed to that value.

American Jews have come to perceive organizations associated with Evangelical Protestantism (variously labeled) as major threats to Jewish

---

[10] For an analysis of the political power of symbolic cultural threats, see Leege et al. (2002).

interests and values. Though the two groups were once components of the Roosevelt coalition, they increasingly began to part company over issues such as racial segregation and, in time, the Vietnam War, civil liberties, and questions of church and state. Most Jews, particularly those outside the Orthodox camp, perceive evangelicals' organizations that champion their causes and values as inimical to Jewish political interests. They are seen to support conjoining state and religion and as more willing to impose penalties on individuals based on traditionalist moral codes, both departures from classical liberalism.

Those perceptions became staples of Democratic campaigns. Consider, for example, a letter sent in 1994 to Jewish voters in Florida by nineteen current and former elected Jewish officials on behalf of the reelection effort of Governor Lawton Chiles, a Democrat. Chiles' opponents, it warned, had been embraced by the "radical right" whose agenda was to "dismantle the separation of church and state; abolish religious tolerance; and end pluralism and diversity." Because the GOP candidate for Lieutenant Governor had been honored by Pat Robertson-sponsored organization, the Republican nominees were further accused of wanting to introduce prayer into public schools. The letter urged recipients to call their friends and let them know about these threats to "our individual rights and freedoms."[11]

Although Protestant evangelicals are a diverse group with conflicting opinions on many questions, including the relationship of church and state, the Jewish perception of them is not entirely without foundation. Social scientists disagree about whether evangelicals and fundamentalist embrace more negative stereotypes about Jews than the general population. But when compared to other Americans, there is strong evidence that evangelicals are less tolerant of atheists (Cox, Jones, and Navarro-Rivera 2015) and Muslims (Shortle and Gaddie 2015) and believe that Christianity is an integral element of American national identity (Jacobs and Theiss-Morse 2013). Such ideas are inconsistent with the American Jewish political culture rooted in classical liberal values.

Data from a 1996 national survey by the AJC demonstrate further that evangelicals are less respectful than others of Judaism as a theological system and appreciably more likely to believe that Christian values should

---

[11] The undated letter is in the possession of the author. Given Florida's relatively large Jewish community, letters of this sort from both parties are commonly distributed during election season. No doubt other religious groups receive similar communications stressing issues likely to resonate in their communities.

drive public policy. The survey was designed to identify participants who demonstrated affinity with politicized organizations that promoted the Christian America perspective. This was done is two ways: asking Protestant respondents directly if they identified with the social movement known as the Religious Right and, for those participants who did not recognize the term, isolating a subgroup of Protestants that held evangelical theological beliefs and identified themselves as conservatives in politics and/or social values. Just under 40% of Protestant respondents fell into this combined category and its members, when compared to the Protestant respondents outside the group, were strongly committed to the religious and political views commonly detected among evangelical Christians.[12] For that reason, I will refer to them as evangelicals.

How do the views of such Protestants affect the image of evangelicals in Jewish eyes? Table 9.5 shows that the religious and political views of this subgroup would surely raise concern among Jews in the United States. On a question about the need to convert Jews to Christianity, Protestants with Religious Right sympathies were much less likely to demonstrate what Jews would consider as respect for their religious tradition. While two-thirds of other Protestants believed that Jews did *not* need to be converted to Christianity, only a third of evangelicals close to the Christian Right accepted this view. Moreover, although the percentages were small, Protestants aligned with the Religious Right were still twice as likely as others to believe that Jews must take responsibility for killing Jesus.

As Jews define anti-Semitism, it does appear to be more prevalent among the kinds of Protestants attracted to the Christian Right. The gap between evangelicals and other Protestants was even wider on the political question that undergirds Jewish attachment to the liberal regime of religion and state. Approximately 150 years after the proposal was first introduced in Congress, a majority of Protestants with Religious Right

---

[12] The Protestant respondents with an affinity for the Religious Right were much more persuaded than other Protestants (1) that there was only one "correct" Christian position on most political issues, (2) the world would end with a battle between God and Satan, and (3) to express admiration for the political leaders of Christian conservatism and closeness to groups like Christian Coalition. In Smith's (1999) report on this survey, the aligners and supporters (as he called the two groups) included respondents of all religious backgrounds including a significant number of Roman Catholics and religious "others." My analysis was confined to Protestants alone because that tradition is home to most evangelicals.

TABLE 9.5 *Religious and Political Views of Non-Jews by Affinity to the Religious Right*

| How much do you agree or disagree with the following statement? | Affinity to Religious Right | No affinity to Religious Right | Difference |
|---|---|---|---|
| Jews do not need to be converted to Christianity. (percent agree/agree strongly) | 34 | 64 | 30 |
| Now, as in the past, Jews must answer for killing Christ. (percent agree/ agree strongly) | 20 | 9 | 11 |
| We should pass a constitutional amendment declaring the United States is a Christian nation. (percent agree/agree strongly) | 51 | 18 | 33 |

*Source:* American Jewish Committee (1996).

affinity believed the Constitution should declare the United States a "Christian nation."[13] That idea was endorsed by fewer than a fifth of Protestant respondents who were not close to the Religious Right. The reputation of evangelicals among Jews, though overbroad and ignoring intragroup differences, does reflect the reality that many conservative Christians consider Judaism incomplete and Jews as a tolerated minority in a Christian nation.

Even if Jews were not aware of these tendencies, their images of theologically conservative evangelicals were likely influenced by the attitudes and actions of violent Protestant religious extremists in the United States. Although extreme and unrepresentative, such actions

[13] Early in the race for the 2016 Republican presidential nomination, a polling firm surveyed Republican primary voters ("Walker Takes the Lead" 2015). Based on their answer to a series of questions about evolution and their favorable assessments of Mike Huckabee and Ben Carson, it appears that a plurality of the respondents were likely to be Evangelical Protestants or conservative Catholics. Among this population, 57% indicated support for establishing Christianity as the official religion of the United States, with 30% against and the remainder unsure. The support is roughly twice as high as in surveys of the general population.

leave an impression on the public mind. Advocates of the Christian Identity movement subscribe to the notion that white Europeans are the lost tribes of Israel chosen by God. They regard Jews as the spawn of Satan who are engaged in an effort to enslave white Christian Americans through what they call the Zionist Occupation Government (ZOG). Such views have led naturally enough to acts of political terrorism against Jews ranging from hate crimes to murder (Barkun 1994). Jews have also been exposed to accounts of Christian Reconstructionism, a theological movement that calls on its supporters to refashion the United States as a theocratic state (Ingersoll 2015). Although the organizational wing of this movement has not formally endorsed violence or anti-Semitism, many of its key themes have been echoed by anti-Semites who do launch physical attacks against Jews and Jewish institutions. As unrepresentative as these extreme forms of Christianity undoubtedly are, their prominence in news accounts probably reinforce negative Jewish views of Evangelical Protestantism.

When they survey the universe of religious groups, individuals are likely to find traditions both congenial and uncongenial. To determine how each group assessed its religious competition, so to speak, the Pew Research Center (2014) undertook a unique survey in 2014. During the interview, a large sample of Americans was administered a "feeling thermometer," a measuring device widely used by political scientists. Individuals were presented verbally and/or visually with the image of an analog thermometer with a minimum value of zero and a maximum of 100, separated by cut lines every ten degrees. Researcher asked participants to rank each specified group on the gauge. In the Pew Survey, respondents were told "A rating of zero degrees means you feel as cold and negative as possible. A rating of 100 degrees means you feel as warm and positive as possible. You would rate the group at 50 degrees if you don't feel particularly positive or negative toward the group." Figure 9.2 shows how Jews rated other religious groups.

Like most social groups, self-identified Jews have very warm feelings toward their coreligionists, assigning them 89 degrees on the feeling thermometer, almost thirty points higher than the average score given to the other seven groups they rated. Most of the other groups were ranked by Jews in the 50- to 60-degree range, which Pew described as neutral to positive. Jews, however, had a negative affect toward the remaining two groups, American Muslims and Evangelical Protestants, assigning scores to both groups in the bottom third of the thermometer scale. The Jewish stance toward Muslims

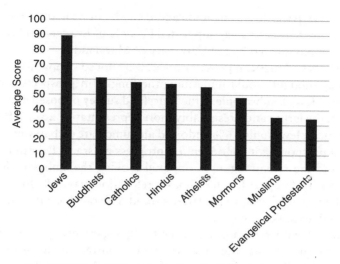

FIGURE 9.2 Mean thermometer score assigned by Jews to religious groups, 2014.
Source: Derived from Pew Research Center (2014), p. 13.

probably reflects the tensions over conflict in the Middle East but the antipathy to Evangelical Protestants cannot be explained in those terms.

The low scores assigned by Jews to evangelicals surprises many observers who point to the central role of those Protestants in the movement known as Christian Zionism (Spector 2009).[14] Although Christian support for the return of Jews to their homeland predates the establishment of the state of Israel in 1948, it did not become a mass movement until Israel's remarkable military victories in 1967. Since then, evangelicals have become fervent advocates of a particular vision of Israel. Leaders of the movement today have opposed peace proposals that would require Israel to cede territory to Palestinians and generally support the right-wing agenda associated with the Likud party. This includes retaining Jerusalem as the undivided capital of Israel. Accordingly, Donald Trump's promise

[14] Although evangelicals commonly assert that they are Israel's "best friends" in the United States (Mayer 2004), there is considerable doubt about whether rhetorical support for the state of Israel actually translates into philo-Semitic attitudes and genuine (as opposed to symbolic) political support (Wald et al. 1996, 161ff). Jews continue to express substantial doubts about the depth of evangelicals' commitment to Israel and note that scenarios about Jesus' return to the Holy Land in Revelations usually end up with the death of most Jews who refuse to accept Jesus as messiah. American Jews are also far more supportive than evangelicals of a negotiated settlement between Israel and the Palestinians that would produce a Palestinian state.

to recognize Jerusalem as Israel's capital city by moving the United States Embassy there was strongly supported by 57% of Evangelical Protestants in a survey conducted by the University of Maryland.[15]

The bulk of American Jews, however, were not so sympathetic to a plan that they thought would undermine the long-term prospects for peace. The small Jewish subsample in the Maryland survey opposed it by 39% to 61%. In the larger and presumably more representative 2017 AJC survey of American Jews, only 16% endorsed an immediate embassy move, 36% favored postponing it contingent on progress in Israeli–Palestinian peace talks, and the remaining 44% opposed moving the embassy altogether (SSRS 2017). Support for the embassy relocation was 44% lower among Jews than evangelicals, so the latter's stand on Israel has not helped them much in Jewish perceptions.

Israel notwithstanding, many Jews still regard evangelicals as committed to policies that are perceived to be contrary to Jewish interests. As I noted earlier, the poor image of evangelicals among Jews reflects a long-standing association in the Jewish mind between Evangelical Protestants and religious intolerance. This position is rooted in supersessionist doctrine, also known as replacement theology, which contends that God abandoned the Jews because they rejected the Messiah and Christians have thus displaced Jews as God's chosen people. Although the doctrine was once associated primarily with Catholicism, the church has largely repudiated it and explicitly advised Catholics to foreswear converting Jews to Christianity. However, conversionist Protestant evangelicals have not taken that same step and, fortified by the values displayed in Table 9.5, its missionaries continue to encourage Jews to reject their own traditions and accept Jesus as the son of God. Because this position denies the authenticity of Judaism and the Mosaic covenant, many Jews regard it as fundamentally anti-Semitic and express revulsion when Christians emphasize their loving duty to persuade Jews to accept Jesus as the messiah foretold in the Hebrew Bible.

We can test this idea more directly by looking again at the 2000 survey of Jews conducted as part of the "Religion in the Public Square" project. This project included an unusually comprehensive set of questions asking respondents to gauge the degree of anti-Semitism among religious and ethnic groups. As shown in Figure 9.3, Jews assigned the highest levels of

---

[15] The figures on evangelical and Jewish attitudes to the location of the US Embassy were provided to me by the study director, Dr. Shibley Telhami of the University of Maryland and the Brookings Institution. I am grateful for his collegiality in sharing the data.

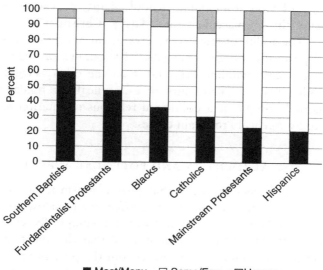

FIGURE 9.3 Jewish perceptions of anti-Semitism by groups, 2000.
Source: Derived from Cohen (2000b), pp. 13–14.

anti-Semitism to Southern Baptists, with three-fifths of respondents believing that many or most members of the group harbored anti-Jewish views. When asked about "Fundamentalist Protestants," almost half the survey participants reached a similar judgment.

Jews clearly differentiated among Christians in estimating levels of anti-Semitism. Fewer than a third of Jewish respondents saw Catholics or the predominantly Catholic Hispanic community as having a high proportion of anti-Semites. Similarly, fewer than one-fourth of Jews believed that anti-Semitism was common among mainline Protestants, a term that likely captured denominations such as Methodists, Episcopalians, Lutherans, and Congregationalists. It bears repeating that even during a time of tension between Jews and blacks, Jews were twice as likely to ascribe a high degree of anti-Semitism to Southern Baptists (a predominantly white denomination) than to African Americans.

Some critics have charged that low thermometer scores assigned to Evangelical Protestantism reflect religious bigotry (Bolce and DeMaio 1999). That perspective is popular among people who assert that American culture is saturated with anti-Christian sentiment, citing the "expulsion" of God from public schools, bans on teacher-led group prayer, and the displacement of "Merry Christmas" by "Happy Holidays." The ability of Jews to perceive significant differences in anti-Semitic dispositions between Evangelical Protestants, on the one hand, and Catholics and mainline Protestants on the other, suggests not a blanket indictment of Christianity or evangelicals or fundamentalists but a nuanced critique of a politicized religious orientation most pronounced in Evangelical Protestant circles.

## SOCIAL IDENTITY AND POLITICAL AFFECT

The available evidence indicates that Jews conform to social identity theory by developing a strong positive affect for their own group and a correspondingly negative affect toward theologically conservative religious communities. I have hypothesized that the negative disposition to evangelicals among Jews arises from the perception that evangelicals (broadly conceived) hold political values and interests inimical to Jews and contrary to the Jewish political culture. I conclude that Jews have indeed developed a politicized ethnic identity in the American political arena organized around their concern to preserve the secular state.

Partisan and ideological conflicts are often rooted in group attachment stemming from social identity. This awareness followed decades of research that raised doubt American citizens had sufficient cognitive sophistication and political attentiveness to analyze the political world through meaningful ideological lenses. Despite the prevalence of terms such as "liberal" and "conservative" (or left and right) in political parlance, classic research suggested that most citizens could not meaningfully organize their opinions on issues within a framework based on those labels. They simply lacked enough information to make sense of ideological positions, nor were their issue opinions sufficiently stable to cohere around an ideological pole.

If not based on issues, how then did people choose to take sides in political conflicts or to identify themselves with ideological labels? Subsequent work suggested the group basis of ideological and partisan loyalties. Conover and Feldman (1981) hypothesized that seemingly content-free symbols and labels "derive their affect from their association with other symbols of social conflict such as various groups and issues" (622). In deciding whether to adopt the liberal or conservative label, to identify with one or the other of them, individuals were directly influenced by their affect toward conservatives and liberals. Those dispositions were, in turn, largely driven by the kind of groups mentally associated with each label.

Conservatism was cognitively connected in the public mind to groups promoting social order, capitalism, and racial traditionalism. Liberals were linked to left-wing movements and various symbols of rapid social change. A similar dynamic undergirds the process by which individuals decide which position they favor in political debates (Sears et al. 1980). Unable to master all the information necessary to take a position, individuals rely instead on cognitive short-cuts, "heuristics" that are saturated with affect toward groups. In many cases, individuals simply look at the groups aligned on either side of a political conflict and pick the position associated with the symbols and groups they most esteem.

If Jews follow the pattern indicated by these studies, we should then find evidence that they evaluate political organizations according to their association with groups that favor or oppose classic liberalism. I look at four kinds of evidence: Jewish versus non-Jewish ratings of various organizations, partisan issue advantage, preferences for and against religious groups as candidates for office, and the impact of group affect on voting decisions. All these affirm that contemporary Jewish social identity has acquired a (pro-Democratic) political component.

To examine the group factor in how Jews assess political organizations, I draw again on the AJC's periodic surveys of community opinion. The question about anti-Semitism in that series is similar to the question we looked at in Figure 9.3, although the groups are not the same and the term used to describe the social movement supported by religious conservatives has changed over time. Table 9.6 traces Jewish attitudes to three groups – the Religious Right, Fundamentalists, and Evangelical Protestants – as more or less anti-Semitic. The two entries for each question report the absolute and relative perceptions of the target groups by Jews: the "absolute" percentage of Jewish respondents who considered the group to have a high degree of anti-Semitism and, for the relative measure, the difference between the absolute figure for the specified group and the average figure respondents assigned to the other five ethnoreligious groups asked about in the surveys. I consider the relative figure a superior estimate of Jewish perceptions of the group being assessed.

Christian organizations committed to bringing Evangelical Protestant values into political life have flourished since the 1970s. Although specific organizations have come and gone, the Religious Right label probably had a constant underlying meaning when the surveys were administered.

TABLE 9.6 *Jewish Perceptions of Absolute and Relative Anti-Semitism by Groups, 1998–2015*
*In your opinion, what proportion of each of the following groups in the United States is anti-Semitic: most, many, some, very few, or none?*
*(Percentage responding most or many)*

| | 1998 | | 2001 | | 2002 | | 2006 | | 2007 | | 2015 | |
|---|---|---|---|---|---|---|---|---|---|---|---|---|
| | Abs | Rel | Abs | Rel | Abs | Rel | Abs | Rel | Abs | Rel | Abs | Rel |
| Religious Right | 44 | +24 | 46 | +28 | 39 | +19 | | | | | | |
| Fundamentalists | 28 | +8 | 26 | +8 | | | | | | | | |
| Evangelical Protestants | | | | | | | 24 | +2 | 22 | +2 | 35 | +3.0 |

"Abs" indicates the percentage responding "most" or "many" for the group indicated in the table. "Rel" indicates the difference between the absolute percentage and the average percentage of five other ethnoreligious groups in the question sequence: blacks, Hispanics, Asians, Muslims, and Catholics. A plus sign in the relative column indicates that the group was considered to have a higher level of anti-Semitism than the other five ethnoreligious groups that respondents rated. In 1998, 44% of Jewish respondents considered most or many members of the Religious Right to be anti-Semitic, 24% higher than the average level of anti-Semitism they perceived among the five comparison groups.
*Source:* Calculated from American Jewish Committee, Annual Survey of American Jewish Opinion, selected years. Retrieved from: http://www.jewishdatabank.org/Studies/details.cfm?StudyID=765 (accessed June 30, 2017).

Between 40% and 50% of Jews in these AJC surveys believed that most/many members of Religious Right organizations held anti-Semitic views. Moreover, as the relative score tells us, the Religious Right was presumed by Jews as home to a much higher proportion of anti-Semites (roughly 20% to 30%) than the comparison groups. Both absolutely and relatively, Jews considered the Christian Right to be saturated with anti-Semites. By contrast, the categories of "Fundamentalists" and "Evangelical Protestants" were not presumed by Jews to be much more anti-Semitic than the comparison categories. Indeed, the percentage who thought the level of anti-Semitism among Fundamentalists and Evangelical Protestants exceeded that of the comparison groups never reached double digits. Rather than religious bigotry, it seems quite clear that Jewish survey participants distinguished between a religious tradition and a political movement that aims to restore what it calls Christian America (Singer 2000). That was certainly the message conveyed by Jewish defense organizations that mobilized wholeheartedly against the Christian Right.[16]

[16] See Cantor (1994), Cohen (1993), Forman (1994), and Moyers and Rifkind (1996) for examples.

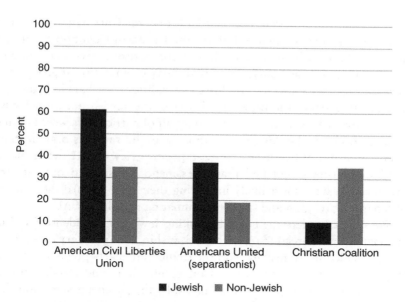

FIGURE 9.4 Favorability ratings of three organizations involved in church–state matters, 2000. (Percent rated very favorable/favorable by respondents)
Source: Calculated from Cohen (2000c).

The "Religion the Public Square" survey, previously referenced, also had a series of questions that asked respondents to rate various political organizations active in American politics. The scale ranged in gradations from very favorable to very unfavorable. In Figure 9.4, I have reported the percentage of Jewish respondents who rated three of these organizations as very/mostly favorable. Because Cohen conducted a parallel survey of non-Jews, the figure compares the ratings of the three organizations by Jews and a general population sample.

The ACLU and Americans United (AU) are two of the most influential groups promoting separationism through public education, intervention in lawsuits, and other forms of advocacy.[17] The Christian Coalition, a group formed by Pat Robertson after his defeat in 1988, reflected his view that the Constitution does not require separation between religion and state. Hence social identity theory would predict that Jews would be more favorably inclined toward ACLU and AU than the Christian Coalition.

---

[17] AU subsequently changed its name to Americans United for Separation of Religion and State.

As expected, Jews preferred the ACLU over the Christian Coalition by 50+% and similarly rated AU above the Christian Coalition by almost 20%. In the Jewish versus Non-Jewish comparison, Jews were roughly twice as favorable as non-Jews toward the two separationist groups and decidedly less favorable to the Christian Coalition. The bars in Figure 9.4 actually understate the difference between the Jewish and non-Jewish samples toward AU because only about half of participants were familiar enough to rate it. Looking just as those who did rate this organization, almost four out of five Jews expressed positive views of AU while only a third of non-Jews matched that assessment. Those who did rate the organization were most likely indicating their view toward the concept of separating religion and state, the animating principle of AU.

We now complete the circle by linking Jewish social identity and its associated traits directly to Jewish partisanship. It is necessary to establish that Jews identify so heavily with the Democratic Party precisely because they perceive it as an advocate of the secular state and classical liberal values. That effect is probably enhanced by the parallel assumption that the Republican Party largely relies on support from voters who reject the secular state.

The concept of "issue ownership" refers to the idea that "voters identify the most credible party proponent of a particular issue and cast their ballots for that issue owner" (Bélanger and Meguid 2008). The mechanism operates only on voters who consider the issue salient. For many years, the Democratic Party was said to "own" Social Security while Republicans had equal dominance over national security and gun rights.

Figure 9.5 demonstrates how the Democratic Party owns the church and state issue in the eyes of American Jews. The 2012 AJC survey of Jewish opinion, fielded before the presidential election that year, asked participants to determine which party was "likely to make the right decisions" on various political issues. The size of the bars in Figure 9.5 represents the difference between the percentage of Jewish respondents who put their trust in the Democrats rather than Republicans to better handle each issue. We would expect a disproportionately Democratic group like American Jews to have more confidence in the Democrats regardless of issue and, to nobody's surprise, Jews did in fact repose more trust in the Democrats on all eleven issues presented to them.

But the *magnitude* of the partisan gap between Democrats and Republicans was not the same from one issue to the next. Only a third or fewer Jewish respondents were more confident about Democratic superiority

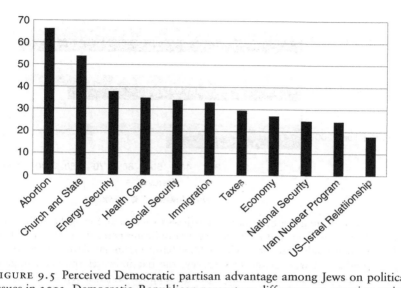

FIGURE 9.5 Perceived Democratic partisan advantage among Jews on political issues in 2012. Democratic–Republican percentage difference on question series: "Regardless of how you usually vote, do you think the Republican Party or the Democratic Party is more likely to make the right decisions in dealing with the following issues: ..."
Source: Calculated from American Jewish Committee, *2012 Annual Survey of American Jewish Opinion*. Retrieved from: www.jewishdatabank.org/Studies/de tails.cfm?StudyID=594 (accessed June 30, 2017).

over Republicans on issues as important as taxes, immigration, economic policy, and the Iranian nuclear program. Two issues stood out by the degree to which Jews believed that Democrats were much more reliable: abortion (in which almost two-thirds of Jews trusted Democrats more than Republicans) and church and state. The clear majority who thought the Democrats would make better decisions on church and state indicates that Democrats own the issue in Jewish eyes and that Jews perceive greater distance between the parties on this than any other issue excepting abortion.

We also see the linkage between social identity and Democratic partisanship among Jews by considering the kinds of people they prefer as presidential nominees. Americans are prone to claim they vote for the person and not the party but evidence gathered since the 1930s suggests that only certain kinds of people are acceptable to different constituencies. The earliest surveys showed that blacks, Jews, Catholics, and women were not particularly appealing to the general public but that the animus against these groups has diminished considerably over time. Contemporary surveys show that Mormons, Muslims, and atheists are

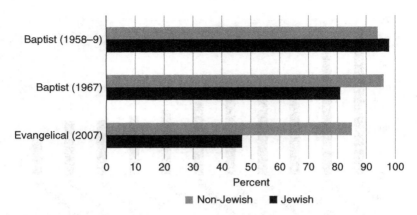

FIGURE 9.6 Willingness of Jews and non-Jews to accept an Evangelical/Baptist as a presidential nominee. For AIPO survey, bar indicates percentage of respondents who said they would vote for a well-qualified Baptist nominated for the presidency by respondent's party. In the Pew survey, the bar indicates the percentage of respondents who said either they would support an Evangelical Protestant presidential candidate or it wouldn't make any difference in their decision.
Source: Calculated from AIPO1958-604, AIPO1959-622, and Pew Religion and Public Life Survey 2007.

now the least welcome groups when it comes to presidential candidates. Questions of this nature will enable us to see if Jews factor group affect into deciding what kind of candidates to support for the presidency.

Figure 9.6 shows that American Jews have come to perceive Evangelical Protestants as undesirable presidential candidates over the past forty years. Gallup surveys provide data from the late 1950s and mid-1960s while the Pew Center asked a similar set of questions about this subject in 2007.[18] Given the difference in wording between the Gallup and Pew questions (see the note in the figure), we must be cautious in making direct comparisons. But the data in Figure 9.6 do suggest that, relative to the rest of the population, Jews have lost their appetite for evangelicals seeking the presidency.

In the late 1950s, Jews were a few points *more* willing than non-Jews to vote for a Baptist – then as now the largest grouping among evangelicals. They swung by nearly 20% against that idea in 1967, even as the rest of

---

[18] Gallup has continued to collect information on this topic along with other survey organizations but the drop in overall sample size has reduced the number of Jewish respondents below the level needed for reliable analysis. The 2007 Pew survey, primarily administered online, has a sufficient Jewish subsample to conduct further analysis.

the population became a bit more open to the prospect of a Baptist presidential candidate. Even so, most Jews in 1967 were still willing to vote for a Baptist candidate. But by 2007, when 85% of the rest of the population was open to the presidential candidacy of an Evangelical Protestant, fewer than half the Jewish respondents (47%) felt the same. The finding is remarkable considering that Jews were equally or more supportive of virtually all other kinds of presidential candidates in the three surveys. Even in 2007, Jews indicated a greater willingness than the public to support a Muslim presidential nominee, which underlines just how powerfully they have turned against the prospect of an evangelical presidential nominee.

It is important to emphasize that Jews have in fact voted overwhelmingly for Evangelical Protestant presidential candidates in the contemporary period. Jews supported Jimmy Carter in 1976 and again in 1980, voted for Bill Clinton in 1992 and 1996, and for Al Gore in 2000. In fact, the evangelical who received the Democratic nomination in those elections won a greater percentage of votes from Jews than from Evangelical Protestants (compare Mellman et al. 2012, 5 with Kellstedt et al. 2007, 272–273)! Carter, Clinton, and Gore were all Southern Baptists, a group that we recall from Table 9.6 was very negatively assessed by Jews in 2000. Why then did Jews prefer Carter, Clinton, and Gore over their Republican rivals when Jews have reacted so negatively to the generic evangelical/Baptist presidential candidate in survey questions?

Apparently, Jews did not see these three candidates as "typical" evangelicals. To be sure, each was deeply embedded in Southern Baptist culture: Carter emphasized his born-again experience and taught Sunday School, Clinton was known to attend religious revivals throughout his home state, and Gore studied at a seminary before opting for a legal/political career. Although Carter said little about his religious views during his presidency, Clinton emphasized covenantal themes that appear in both the Hebrew and Christian bibles and Gore asserted the spiritual foundations of his commitment to preserving the environment. Yet while each could attest personally to their religious ideas, they did not much engage in God talk. None of them spoke of Christian America, engaged in sectarian language, acted as if they wanted Jews to convert to Christianity, or asserted that all their political views came from God. In sum, they did not conform to the stereotype of evangelicals as rabid conversionists who seek a Christian America.

I conclude this section by examining a pair of studies that assess directly how Jewish political behavior responds to the perceived threat posed by social groups committed to undermining classical liberalism. As far as I can discern, these studies identified and utilized the *only* extant data sets that permit such direct analysis because they contained two essential ingredients: large Jewish and non-Jewish samples of presidential voters (in one of them) and a sufficient set of questions enabling a full-scale test of voting behavior. Uslaner and Lichbach (2009) tested voter choice models of Jews and non-Jews in 2004 using two different data sources, a specialized Jewish-only survey conducted by the National Jewish Democratic Council and the 2004 general population survey known as the National Election Study. Both surveys included feeling thermometers that captured attitudes to groups associated with evangelical Protestantism and the Christian Right. The two datasets did not have identical questions but the language was sufficiently comparable to make careful group contrasts.

The authors tested separate comprehensive models of vote choice by Jews and non-Jews. By comprehensive, I mean that the predictors of the presidential vote in 2004 included a wide range of factors shown to influence voting decisions over the decades. The most striking finding is that even after taking account of pro-Democratic skew and sociodemographic traits, Jews' perceptions of Christian conservatives still exerted a significant, independent impact on Jewish voting. The evangelical feeling thermometer (a relative number which subtracted the average thermometer score assigned to all other groups from the score assigned to evangelicals) was the second largest influence on voting for the Democratic nominee: A Jewish voter who had the *least* favorable assessment of evangelicals was fully 25% *more likely* to vote for the 2004 Democratic nominee, John Kerrey, than a coreligionist who thought favorably of evangelicals. In the equivalent vote choice model for the non-Jewish sample (which excluded self-described fundamentalists), the thermometer score for fundamentalists did *not* affect the voters' choice between candidates.

The study was replicated in 2012 using another Election Day survey of Jews and the general public (Uslaner 2015). The Jewish survey had no measure of attitudes to evangelicals but it did contain a question about the Tea Party. Because prior research had shown that Jewish views of the Tea Party and Christian conservatives were closely related, Uslaner used the Tea Party measure as a proxy for affect to politicized evangelical

Protestants.[19] In 2012 as in 2004, attitudes toward an out-group perceived as threatening – in this case, the Tea Party – was the second most powerful influence (after partisanship) on the disposition of Jews to vote for the Democratic presidential nominee. Comparing Jewish respondents with the highest and lowest levels of approval of the Tea Party, they found the latter 32% less likely to favor Mitt Romney, the Republican nominee. Although there was no parallel analysis of a general population sample, the finding provides additional evidence that Jews have incorporated negative affect toward cultural conservatives as part and parcel of their political calculus.

## WHAT ABOUT JEWISH REPUBLICANS?

The data just arrayed suggest strongly that most American Jews have incorporated a commitment to the Democratic Party as part of their social identity. The partisan skew, I contend, is due in considerable degree to a strong negative affect toward political organizations associated with Evangelical Protestants who are believed to reject the idea of a secular state. One might wonder if Republican and politically conservative Jews – perhaps a fifth or a quarter of the community according to most surveys – are also sensitive to the Christian America theme when it is deployed by evangelical Protestants in their party. If so, Jewish Republicans are likely to be cross-pressured, their Republican identification pulling them toward Republican candidates, their concern about religious sectarianism driving them away from the GOP.

Studying Jewish political behavior is challenging, as I have complained about often enough in these pages, simply because Jews typically turn up in small numbers in general population surveys. Finding a decently sized Jewish Republican subsample is even more of a snipe hunt. The few surveys that contained more than a handful of Jewish Republicans and asked questions relevant to this inquiry do suggest that Jewish Republicans are distinctive from their fellow non-Jewish partisans in their views of religion and state. Concerns about the party's position on this issue appear to threaten their commitment to the GOP.

In a large survey of delegates to the 1984 national party conventions, Jewish Republicans parted company with other Republican delegates on several issues connected to the idea of a secular state (calculated from

---

[19] For evidence of the powerful role of Christian Nationalism in Tea Party attitudes, see Wald and Peña-Vasquez (2018).

Abramowitz et al. 2001). When asked a question about prayer in schools, a majority of non-Jewish Republican delegates approved starting the public-school day with prayer. Jewish Republicans preferred instead a softer option that allowed only for silent prayer. When asked to provide a feeling thermometer score for Moral Majority, then the principal political group promoting a Christian America platform, Jewish Republicans averaged 20 degrees versus the 46 degrees assigned to the organization by the other Republican delegates in the survey. On this question, Jewish Republicans at the 1984 convention were closer to Jewish Democratic delegates than to their fellow Republicans.[20]

Four years later, the 1988 presidential campaign provided a natural experiment to show how Jewish Republicans felt about the growing prominence of Evangelical Protestants within their party. The campaign for the Republican nomination featured the prominent Christian minister, Pat Robertson. One of the leaders of the Christian Right, the man who would found Christian Coalition the next year, Robertson had gone out of his way to appeal to Jewish voters. He embraced the cause of Israel with real fervor and pointedly denounced religious bigotry of any kind. Yet Robertson was also a Southern Baptist minister, a prominent televangelist, and somebody who had been an ardent advocate of Christian America.[21] He had also explicitly claimed that the Constitution does not separate religion and state. So how did Jewish Republicans react to the prospect of a Christian Right stalwart as their party's nominee? Did his pro-Israel language offset his association with his history of Christian America rhetoric?

Apparently not. In the annual American Jewish Committee survey of 1988, conducted before the national party conventions, Jewish Republicans were asked how they would vote in November should Robertson be added to the ticket. *Without* Robertson on the ticket, 70% of Jewish Republicans expected to support the GOP presidential slate. But should that ticket include Robertson as the vice presidential

[20] The 1984 convention delegate study shows the Jewish delegates also differed from their fellow partisans. Jewish Democrats were more likely than non-Jewish Democratic delegates to reject school prayer altogether and reported a higher level of membership in civil liberties organizations.

[21] Years later, he dabbled in bizarre conspiracy theories that recycled old anti-Semitic innuendo about "European bankers," long a code word for Jews in anti-Semitic discourse. For a sample of how Jewish communal leaders reacted to Robertson, see Rudin (1986).

nominee, only a third of Jewish Republicans were sure that they would vote for the Republican nominee. Roughly a third were unsure how they would vote under the circumstances and another third committed to supporting the Democratic presidential candidate. That represents almost a 40% drop in probable Republican support because of Robertson's inclusion on the ticket (Wald and Sigelman 1997, 153). Despite campaigning as a philo-Semitic candidate, Robertson's association with the Christian Right and the evangelical tradition seriously damaged the Republican brand among the Jews in his own party.

## CONCLUSION

Jews became part of the coalition of minorities that sustained the Roosevelt Democratic coalition from the late 1920s through the 1970s. They joined Roman Catholics, African Americans (to a lesser degree), white Southerners, and union members in common cause to support Democratic candidates. But as the New Deal party system began to fray in the 1960s when new issues rose to prominence, Jewish attachment to the Democratic Party also started to waver. Still high by the standards of most ethnoreligious voting blocs, Jews' pro-Democratic commitment dropped in elections from 1972 through 1988 before rebounding and reaching or exceeding earlier levels beginning with the election of 1992. Catholics, another religious minority that had once defined the Roosevelt coalition, moved permanently away from the Democratic Party to become swing voters (Wald 2006). White Evangelical Protestants moved even more rapidly away from the Democrats to displace mainline Protestants as the Republican Party's most dependable constituency. Jews swung back to the Democrats.

Jews returned to their Democratic partisan home once the Republican Party became closely identified with the political movement known as the Christian Right. Although that alliance dramatically improved the GOP's overall electoral performance, particularly in the South and border states, it seems to have cost Republicans the inroads they were making among Jews in the 1960s and 1970s.[22] The concern with the role of politicized evangelicals in the GOP was not a matter of religious bigotry but rather

---

[22] For evidence that this reliance on conservative Christians also hurt the party with women and mainline Protestants, see Leege et al. (2002).

apprehension about the movement's perceived designs on the secular state. By putting the maintenance of classical liberalism at the head of their political priorities, Jews in the late twentieth and early twenty-first centuries echoed the concerns that had long dominated American Jewish political culture.

# 10

# The Persistence of the Jewish Liberal Tradition

This book is organized around a central puzzle: American Jews have traits normally associated with conservative opinions and Republican loyalty yet they generally hold liberal views and vote Democratic to a greater degree than any other white ethnoreligious group. In unpacking that puzzle, I identified two subsidiary enigmas: (1) American Jews today are the only Jewish diaspora community identified with the left side of their nation's political spectrum and (2) American Jews have exhibited a degree of political volatility, drifting away from the Democratic Party in the 1970s and 1980s, but returning in force by the early 1990s. They have continued to vote roughly 3-to-1 Democratic in presidential elections through 2016.

The solution to the major puzzle is context: American Jews are politically liberal because they are *American* Jews. Thanks to a favorable political opportunity structure, Jews found in the United States a country that, if not entirely welcoming to them at first, nonetheless embraced principles of equality that enabled them to participate without hindrances in public life. That was a new development in the long history of the Jews, far exceeding the relatively brief experiences of toleration in fifteenth-century Spain and the late eighteenth century Dutch Batavian Republic. Yossi Klein Halevi (2016), an American-born Israeli commentator, captured the uniqueness of the setting when he observed that American Jews "live in the most benign and welcoming environment Jews have ever known." It has imbued them with a deep commitment to the classical liberal value that the state has no religious identity and no authority to allocate benefits or costs based on religious affiliation. I have traced how a political culture built on those values guided Jewish political deliberations over time and eventually acquired a partisan component that persists to this day.

The Jewish experience in the colonial period was uneven. The passage of the Constitution in 1787 was critical because it separated citizenship from religion and, as Jews saw it, created a secular national state. Jews came to attribute their successes in the American Republic to this innovative approach to religious differences and they embraced the idea of political secularism in what I have called the American regime of religion and state. Maintaining that system has been the highest priority on the American Jewish political agenda but it was not clearly tied to any political party until the post-New Deal era. When the major parties began to differ on this topic in the 1970s and 1980s, Jews strengthened their identification with the party more committed to maintenance of separationism in law and policy (the Democrats).

This approach also addresses the subsidiary puzzles regarding space and time. Precisely because they claim equal citizenship under the Constitution of a secular state, a position generally associated with the left, American Jews differ politically from their compatriots abroad who live under different political norms. American Jews oscillated politically in the late twentieth century because they worried about their party's apparent abandonment of classic liberal values but they returned to the Democratic fold when they sensed even greater danger in the Republican Party's alliance with the Christian Right, a social movement seeking to undo or soften the separation of religion and state.

This final chapter first presents evidence that Jews do not only identify with and vote for the Democratic Party but have become a significant share of its activist base. The next section addresses a key limitation of the theory, the existence of two Jewish subgroups that decidedly reject the liberalism and pro-Democratic attachment of most American Jews. After discussing that topic, I turn to the 2016 presidential election to demonstrate the contemporary relevance of American Jews' attachment to the classic liberal regime of religion and state. I conclude the book by considering the relevance of the Jewish experience to other ethnoreligious groups seeking to defend their interests in American public life.

## BREADTH OF JEWISH ATTACHMENT TO THE DEMOCRATS

In a classic textbook, V. O. Key, Jr. argued that the term "political party" actually encompasses three different if overlapping formations: the party in the electorate, the party organization, and the party in office. Most of this book has focused on Jews as an electoral constituency, one manifestation of their strong Democratic attachment. To demonstrate how fully Jews have invested in the party most closely associated with defense of the secular state, I need to discuss their activism and office-holding as well

Jewish activism on behalf of the Democratic Party organization extends to fundraising and volunteer activity. Jews, more affluent (on average) than non-Jews, contribute disproportionately to candidates and parties than other voters.[1] But do they favor Democratic recipients with those contributions, both absolutely and relatively?

In a study of donors to political action committees (PACs) during the 1982–1983 election cycle, Guth and Green (1990) documented both the religious affiliation of donors and the recipients of their contributions.[2] There was a dramatic difference in the partisan division of contributions between Jews and other respondents in the survey. While the entire sample was divided almost evenly between those who contributed to Republican and Democratic-oriented PACs, almost 90% of Jewish donors sent their money to the Democrats. The skew was similar if a bit less pronounced when the same authors surveyed major donors to the political parties and PACs during the 1988 presidential election cycle (Green, Guth, and Fraser 1991). Almost 80% of Jewish contributors favored Democratic candidates, 33% more than the non-Jewish donors in the survey.

More recent data point in the same direction. The public records of the Federal Election Commission list donors by name but not religious affiliation. Hersh and Schaffner (2016) classified political donors in the 2012 election cycle as Jewish if their last names appeared on a list of Distinctive Jewish Names (DJN). This technique provides a rough and ready means of identifying Jews and has been widely used by scholars of Jewish life (Lazerwitz 1986). In the 2012 presidential campaign, they found that 70% of the money given by Jews to presidential or other candidates for national office flowed to President Obama and the Democratic Party, with the remaining 30% to Mitt Romney or GOP organizations. Keep in mind that this is the split in the *amount* of contributions, not the partisan split among donors per se.

---

[1] They also contribute disproportionately to charitable causes sponsored both by Jewish and non-Jewish organizations. In the world of "development," a euphemism for fundraising, Jews are also perceived as super donors. Politics is no different.

[2] "Major" donors are defined as contributors of $200 or more, the minimum threshold at which donor information has to be reported to the Federal Election Commission. My thanks to John Green and Jim Guth for making these data available to me.

Do Jews also contribute more time and energy to Democrats than other groups? Clark and Prysby (2004) surveyed Southern grass-roots political activists in 2001. They examined the attitudes and behavior of almost 7,000 people who had been involved in county-level activity through political parties. Even with this distinctive sample, the authors found sharp differences between Jewish and non-Jewish activists. While the non-Jews in the study were evenly divided between Republicans and Democrats, the Jewish activists were four times as likely to be Democrats as Republicans. The partisan gap in the percentage of Democrats between the Jewish and non-Jewish activists was 30%.

Looking at the national level, a team of four scholars surveyed delegates to the Democratic and Republican presidential nominating conventions in 2000 (Layman et al. 2010). Many of the more than 2,000 participants in this survey had attended more than one such convention. Of the almost 200 Jews in the sample, fully 90% were Democrats. Sixty-four percent of the delegates who were not Jewish also favored the Democrats, yielding a 26% partisan gap very much in line with what the state-level surveys have revealed. In a compilation of delegate surveys from 1972 through 2008, Bowman and Rugg (2008) found that the ratio between the Democratic and Republican percentages of Jewish convention delegates was typically three or four to one in favor of the Democrats.

Beyond their importance to the party organization, Jews are also prominent among the party in government. The ultimate political activists are people who seek and achieve public office. Jews have been appointed to a wide range of government positions and elected as governors, US representatives, and senators. I will use data on members of Congress to summarize the partisan orientation of Jews in public office.

Figure 10.1 begins with the US House of Representatives in the 55th Congress elected in 1896, the first to have five Jewish members, and runs through the 114th Congress which governed through the end of 2016. Jews are statistically overrepresented in Congress because they share the social background traits of people who make up the political elite. Hence, their high level of representation among political elites is no surprise.

Looking at the trend lines for Democratic and Republican US representatives in the top panel of Figure 10.1, we see the partisanship of Jewish representatives didn't crystallize until the 1930s. Before then, neither party typically dominated among Jews in the US House and a surge in one election was often cancelled or reversed two years later. But in the 1930s, the trend lines began to scissor apart in a pattern that further intensified in the 1980s and persists to the current day.

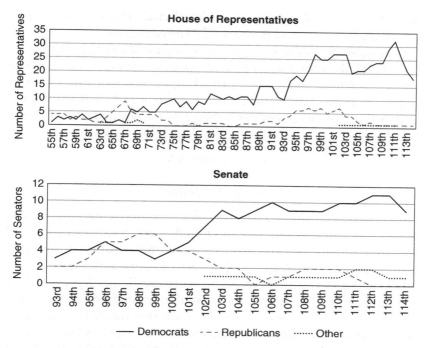

FIGURE 10.1 Partisanship of Jews elected to the US House and Senate.
Calculated from Stone (2010).

The Senate data in Figure 10.1 reveal a similar pattern. Owing to lower turnover rates in the Senate, the partisan split that became apparent in the House in the early 1970s did not occur until about a decade later in the Senate. The Senate information depreciates the degree to which Jews in the Senate are disproportionately Democratic by excluding two Jews elected as Independents, Joseph Lieberman of Connecticut and Bernie Sanders of Vermont, who both caucused with the Democratic Party. Even with these biases in the classification of religion and party, Jewish senators have been disproportionately Democratic for most of the past forty years.

The pro-Democratic skew among Jewish legislators extends to the state level. In a 1995 national survey of state legislators, Jews in the sample were split 84% to 16% in favor of the Democrats (calculated from Carey, Niemi, and Powell 1995). The almost 50/50 partisan divide among the non-Jewish legislators produced a total partisan gap of 31% between Democrats and Republicans favoring the former. Whether we examine the state or national legislatures, Jewish elected officials share the pro-Democratic orientation of rank-and-file American Jews.

Looking at the data in this section, one might well conclude that Jews as a group do indeed constitute a cohesive political community that is almost entirely loyal to the Democratic Party. Despite their very strong orientation to the Democrats, we will now see partisan and ideological differences within the Jewish community based on religion and ethnic origins.

## THE DISSENTERS

### Orthodox Jewry

The truism that Judaism is a religion of deed not creed is particularly apt in discussing the differences between Orthodox and non-Orthodox Jews.[3] The two groups do *not* part company principally on theology. The roughly 10% of American Jews who identify with the Orthodox movement are distinctive from their coreligionists in the degree to which they legitimate and observe the 613 Biblical commandments that compose the core of *halacha* or Jewish law. The Orthodox regard the commandments as binding and draw on centuries of commentary by learned scholars to interpret the meaning of the language. Apart from the centrality of religious practices, the Orthodox tend to differ from their fellow Jews in family size, gender norms, and modes of dress. The Orthodox "stream," as it is sometimes labeled, comprises two major communities usually called Modern Orthodox (*datím* with the i pronounced as ē in Hebrew) and ultra-Orthodox (*haredim* with the same "i" pronunciation as in *datim*). In the United States, unlike in Israel, the former predominates numerically.

Just as non-Orthodox Jews differ from one another based on their affiliation with Reform, Conservative, Reconstructionist, or secular humanistic forms of Judaism, so too do the two Orthodox groups. The Modern Orthodox are generally comfortable with modernity (hence the terminology) and have acculturated to American norms in many respects. Engagement with society is not seen by them, as in the ultra-Orthodox world, as a major threat to communal integrity. Even though they often send their children to religious schools, the Modern Orthodox

---

[3] A prominent rabbi who grew up in an ultra-Orthodox environment in Baltimore recalled that conversations at home never concentrated on theology but were rather about the behavior prescribed by Jewish law (Hertzberg 1996).

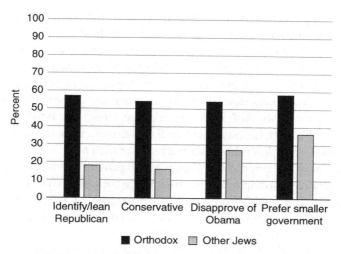

FIGURE 10.2 Differences in political views between Orthodox and non-Orthodox Jews.
Source: Derived from Pew Research Center, *Portrait of Jewish Americans* (2013), chapter 6.

typically insist that the curriculum must address a full range of "secular" subjects including science, literature, and other fields, so the children are equipped for membership in modern society. By contrast, the ultra-Orthodox community looks warily on secular education, seeing it as a potential pathway to assimilation, and upholds the ideal of full-time Torah study for men. Whatever their differences, the two wings of Orthodoxy in the United States have largely come to cohere on Israel. Although the ultra-Orthodox world once rejected Zionism as a dangerous heresy, putting redemption in the hands of (often secular) human beings instead of God, those differences are much less salient among Orthodox American Jews today. Both groups are much more sympathetic to the right-wing perspective on Israel, supporting Jewish settlements in occupied territory, opposing an independent Palestinian state, and attributing a divine imperative to a Jewish state.

As Figure 10.2 shows with data from the 2013 Pew study of American Jewry, there are sizable political gaps between the two Orthodox streams and the rest of the American Jewish community. Compared to the non-Orthodox, the Orthodox are much more likely to identify with the Republican Party, to describe themselves as politically conservative, to disapprove of Democratic presidents (Obama in 2013), and to reject the idea of big government. The Orthodox are in fact closer to the general public than their fellow Jews in partisan identification, their attitude to President Obama at the time of the survey, and their preference for a reduced role for government. The two Jewish groups are roughly equidistant from the American population on ideological positioning, with the non-Orthodox being less likely to identify as conservative and the Orthodox more so. Although conservative views on social issues play a role, it's likely that attachment to Israel drives many in the Orthodox world away from liberalism and the Democratic Party.

Laurence Kotler-Berkowitz (1997, 2015) provides compelling evidence that differences among religious streams are the major source of political disunity in the Jewish community. The impact of identification with different Jewish denominations is particularly marked in partisanship, ideology, social issues, and Israel. Yet, when he compared the political orientations of all US voters and Jews, he found that the former were *more* divided by religion, race, and ethnicity than were Jews. Although social characteristics structure political orientations among American Jews, they are less potent than commonly imagined.[4]

Historically, the idea of separation of religion and state, the operational dimension of classical liberalism, also differentiates Jews by stream. When Congress was considering a constitutional amendment to permit organized prayer in public schools shortly after the Supreme Court banned it on establishment grounds in 1962, the leader of the ultra-Orthodox Lubavitch religious movement famously supported the effort with both theological and sociological arguments (Schneerson 2014). The Orthodox Union, the association representing the Modern Orthodox, has also long supported more expressions of religion in the public schools and pushed for increased state funding of private religious education (Jewish Link Staff 2017). Do these elites speak for Orthodoxy?

Unfortunately, the 2013 Pew Survey of American Jewry did not ask questions about this issue and the American Jewish Committee (AJC) surveys summarized in Table 9.4 asked only about two issues: government funding for religious schools and government-funded social service programs run by religious institutions. While the Orthodox much more strongly favor these programs than the non-Orthodox, we cannot dismiss the role of self-interest in these views. The Orthodox have much larger families on average and put a much higher priority on sending their

---

[4] I found the same pattern – greater religious cleavages among non-Jews than Jews –when I examined attitudes to same-sex marriage (Wald 2008a).

children to Jewish day schools. Because they are also much more likely to be attached to synagogues, the Orthodox would benefit directly if their religious centers were subsidized by public funds supporting religious education and social services on-site. To get at views that have less of a basis in self-interest, I turn again to the 2000 survey of Jews by the Religion in the Public Square Project. As the survey mainly focused on Jewish attitudes to religion and state, the questionnaire covered a wide range of policies and actions as well as questions about broad principles associated with classical liberalism.

Only thirty-three participants defined themselves as Orthodox. Despite their small number, the Orthodox respondents in that 2000 survey were distinctive precisely in the same way that Pew found the Orthodox different from non-Orthodox Jewry in the 2013 survey displayed in Figure 10.1: They were much more likely than the non-Orthodox to

- describe religion as very important in their lives
- attend religious services regularly
- report that most/all their friends were Jewish
- have visited Israel
- light Sabbath candles on Friday night
- belong to a synagogue

All these differences were statistically significant, suggesting this small sample is sufficient to detect meaningful differences if they exist.

To reduce the large number of items to more manageable dimensions, I created composite measures of attitudes to religious displays in public space (including public schools and public property) and religion in politics. The scores of Jews in Figure 10.3 indicate the level of support for positions that were consistent with the accommodationist interpretation of the Constitution by lowering the wall of separation. The higher the bar, the more the Jewish group in question was open to and supportive of religion in public space and as a factor in American political and governmental life. The first scale ranged from 1 to 19 and the religion and politics composite scale varied between 1 and 40.[5]

Even though the difference between the two groups of Jews does not look very large, Orthodox and non-Orthodox Jews differed significantly on religion in the schools and on public property. The Orthodox were far more accepting (meaning the difference was positive and statistically significant) of religious songs during school holiday celebrations and

[5] The standardized reliabilities of the two scales were 0.75 and 0.78.

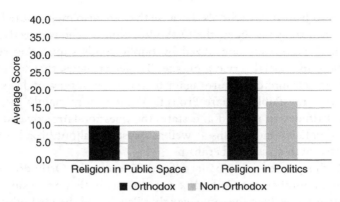

FIGURE 10.3 Average score of Orthodox and non-Orthodox Jews on Religion in Public Life Scales, 2000.
Source: I calculated these figures from the first wave of the "Religion and Public Square" survey conducted by Steven M. Cohen in 2000. I am grateful to him for making these data available to me. Calculated from Cohen (2000c).

publicly funded vouchers for private religious schools. Somewhat surprisingly, both groups were close together in their opposition to classroom prayer and their support for a moment of silence in lieu of group prayer.

There were much larger differences between the two groups on the items comprising the scale of religion in government. As a rule, the Orthodox welcomed displays of religiosity in government, society, and culture while the non-Orthodox were skeptical or firmly opposed to such policies. Specifically, compared to the non-Orthodox, Jews who identified as Orthodox were more positive about

- religion shaping American society
- laws regulating moral behavior
- political leaders expressing faith in God
- opening Congress with prayers
- increased religious influence in American life

These views grow out of the belief, articulated by David Novak (quoted in Birnbaum 2008, 2432), that "Jews ought to encourage non-Jews to pray in public in order to show how much they believe the world, including the political order, is dependent upon God."

The Orthodox participants in the survey also believed that an increase in religious influence would make the country less receptive to anti-Semitism, a better place for Jews, and improve the quality of democracy. Not all the questions in the scale yielded the same pattern of polarization between Orthodox and other Jews. The two groups were indistinguishable and very much divided among themselves over whether religious institutions should express political views and clergy should discuss candidates from the pulpit. Both groups also agreed to roughly the same degree that organized religion should stay out of politics.

On balance, the Orthodox are less committed than other Jews to maintaining the classical liberal regime of religion and state. How are we to understand the differences between these two groups?[6] The political gaps between the Orthodox and other American Jews appear to stem largely from different social identities. In their study of the Orthodox community in the United States, Heilman and Cohen (1989, 5) identified an inward-turning face of Jewish Orthodoxy that prioritizes faith, tradition, and observance and largely rejects "many of the essentials of contemporary secular American society and culture." Those most imbued with this "parochial" perspective, who try to live outside the purview of the dominant American (and Jewish) society, have tended to practice a form of ethnic particularism and separatism. The perspective is strongest among the ultra-Orthodox but apparent as well in the Modern Orthodox community.

Seeking to minimize interaction with the secular world, these parochials are willing to vote but normally seek to trade their electoral assets for tangible policy benefits (Kazis 2016). Like voters in the days of urban political machines, they care less about ideology and more for the tangible resources they can accrue in exchange for their votes. In so doing, they do not much worry that state actions might accord benefits based on religion or give legal recognition to certain religiously based social values, a preoccupation of Jews who defend the liberal regime.

Rather, the Orthodox parochials often seek a share of the public benefits provided by state programs championed by Christian conservatives and opposed by the bulk of non-Orthodox Jewry. They perceive state funding for religious education as a tool to facilitate communal integrity.[7] This style of exchange typifies clientelist politics wherein groups exchange political support for selective benefits. Precisely because they do not wish to assimilate, the practitioners are less

---

[6] These paragraphs are from Wald (2014).

[7] The prospect of state funding for religious education also attracted support from the Neoconservatives (Dalin 2002).

concerned about the state's religious identity. Accordingly, their social identity as Jews does not include the same strong Democratic component as Jews who wish to be integrated into (but not necessarily assimilated by) the American political system. The Orthodox who are not parochial apparently favor conservative candidates and issue positions for their intrinsic value.

## Russian Jewry

In speaking of "recent" Russian immigrants in this chapter, I am *not* referring to the great wave of eastern Europeans who arrived in the United States between the Civil War and World War I but rather to those who arrived after the end of Soviet communism in 1989. With a thaw in relations between the United States and the new Russian Federation, Soviet-era restrictions on emigration were relaxed and many Jews left the country for the United States.[8] They tended to cluster in specific American cities, particularly New York.

Those who left the Soviet Union and its successor states are often portrayed as a right-wing political constituency in both Israel and the United States, their major destinations. Drawing on political socialization theory, scholars have attributed this conservative political outlook to their experience in Russia. Their exposure to Soviet communism may have imbued them with an overriding hostility to the political left and a preference for market solutions to social and economic problems. Probably more important, they were attracted to the Republican Party by admiration for the Republican Party's assertive military stance against the Soviet Union during the Reagan era and its perceived position on Israel (Kliger 2011). In a memoir of his childhood in Russia, Gary Shteyngart credited those factors with generating "the intense Republicanism that is the birthright of every Soviet Jew in the time of Reagan" (2014, 136).

The Jews from the former Soviet Union arrived in the US presocialized to political orientations that were quite different from other American Jews. As Kotler-Berkowitz (2017) has recently argued using data from the 2013 Pew survey of American Jews, this is likely to be a short-term phenomenon. American-born Jews who had at least one Russian-born

---

[8] A 2004 survey of Russian-Jewish Americans in New York City, supported by the American Jewish Committee, indicated that more than three-fourths of the immigrants arrived in 1990 and later (American Jewish Committee 2004).

parent were not significantly different from other American Jews in their political views. As the children of this post-1989 cohort develop a strong identity as Americans, they apparently shed the political dispositions imbibed by their parents. This is consistent with what scholars have found for second-generation Cuban Americans (Hill and Moreno 1996).

## OTHER EXCEPTIONS

Orthodox Jews and post-1989 Russian émigrés do not exhaust the list of groups or occasions when the Jewish commitment to liberalism has been, at best, uneven. In their accounts of American Jewish politics, scholars have identified times and places when Jews did not cohere in response to threats to core constitutional values (Dollinger 2000). How does the argument presented in these pages help us understand these lapses?

When Franklin Roosevelt signed his infamous executive order interning Japanese Americans in 1942, the organized Jewish community did not rally in defense of the rights of their fellow Americans who were imprisoned solely based on ethnicity. While this reticence in the face of an assault on the Constitution might be explained by Jews' obsession with the threat faced by Jewish communities in war-torn Europe, their commitment to the Democratic president, or a sense that security demanded extreme measures, it does not obscure the inaction displayed by American Jewry.

The internment of Japanese Americans was not the only occasion when Jews seemed to soft pedal their liberal commitments. Although scholars have paid a great deal of attention to the Jewish role in the civil rights movement in the 1950s and 1960s, they have also documented the general hesitance of Jews in the South to engage wholeheartedly in the black struggle for civil rights. Although many Northern Jews embraced the movement fervently, their Southern compatriots were much less likely to support the Freedom Riders, demonstrators, marchers, and other actors who put their bodies on the line (Webb 2001). Unlike the debate over affirmative action in the 1970s and 1980s, the civil rights movement was explicitly anchored in the classic liberal values that Jews held dear. Why did Southern Jews hold back? We might explain such behavior in terms of Jewish concerns that identifying with the black cause would threatened their status as "white" in the bifurcated racial order, undermining their own liberty and security.

These cases *would* challenge a theory of American Jewish liberalism that was invariant regarding time or place. My explanation specifically takes account of these factors. Although liberalism has become central to the American Jewish political creed, it can be "backgrounded," as scholars like to say, if other concerns come to the fore. In the case of the Japanese internment, Jews may well have calculated a trade-off between taking public action to defend the Constitution as their political culture would suggest they should do or, as they did, remaining silent lest their own loyalty be called into question. Similarly, although Southern Jews may have been far more sympathetic to black aspirations for political equality than other white Southerners, taking such a position would increase the danger to their own community as Jews were already suspected of collusion owing to the aggressive civil rights support by national Jewish organizations. Time and place can reshape the political opportunity structure, a key variable in the approach I've taken. Asking if liberalism is "good for the Jews" may sometimes elicit a negative response.

The distinguished historian of Judaism, Jonathan Sarna (1989), has suggested another exception although it is a primarily a matter of the breadth of American Jewish liberalism rather than its variability across time or space. Sarna contends that American Jews did not embrace the separation of religion and state wholeheartedly until the late nineteenth and early twentieth centuries. Jews grew alarmed by efforts to Christianize the state, as they saw it, manifest in the Christian Amendment to the Constitution, increasing attempts to promote Bible reading in the public schools, and other actions taken in response to perceptions of growing immorality and licentiousness among the population. That pushed them into strategic alliance with various non-Jewish organizations that sought a thorough-going secularism that would forbid government from favoring religion over irreligion altogether.

Before then, he argues, American Jews often sought not to end the religious privileges accorded by governments but to share in them. When states provided funding for private or religious schools, Jews often sought a piece of the pie on a par with Christians. Even if military chaplains were perceived as constitutionally suspect, Jews only wanted to ensure that their coreligionists had the same access to spiritual guidance and counseling as members of other religious traditions. Rather than abolish Sunday closing laws that burdened observant Jews, many Jewish defense organizations called only for exemption for Jews who ceased from work on the Sabbath. Jews opposed test oaths that discriminated against them but did not call for their abolition across the board. Even in the twentieth century when Jewish organizations joined the separationist movement, they acted pragmatically by accepting certain practices that appeared to support religion in general even if these actions violated the strictures of Madison, Jefferson, and other founders.

When I compare Jewish discourse from the late eighteenth to the mid-nineteenth century with the language that emerged after the Civil War, I do not find much of a disjuncture. I suspect there was slippage between word and deed based on how Jewish elites understood political realities but, again, am not sure much changed from one period to the next. The explanations I offer for American Jewish liberalism are probabilistic, not absolute, and I accept that Jewish political behavior is situational. The central tendency of the American Jewish political culture has been liberal while allowing for a degree of variability. The ideology American Jews have built around classic liberalism is not a straitjacket.[9]

## REAFFIRMING CLASSIC LIBERALISM IN 2016

Even though the presidential campaign of 2016 was unusually disruptive, a sharp departure from the norms that traditionally govern the nomination/election process, it also revealed the continuity of Jewish concerns about the liberal regime of religion and state. Exit polls indicated the usual 3-to-1 split in the Jewish presidential vote favoring the Democrats. Considering that some Jews may have been more sympathetic to a Republican nominee who had promised to withdraw from the Iranian nuclear agreement and whose daughter was an observant Jew, the drubbing Trump experienced at the hands of Jewish voters was even more notable.[10] The partisan gap might have increased further had Jews foreseen what happened in 2017 when the proportion of American Jews who considered anti-Semitism a very serious problem doubled to 41% from the 2016 figure.

In December 2015, the AJC, which emphasizes its nonpartisan character, broke a long tradition by offering public comments about the Republican presidential candidate. Specifically, the organization issued a statement condemning as "offensive and inflammatory" Donald Trump's proposal to ban Muslims from entering the United States.

---

[9] It is important to remember that even John Locke, often considered the foremost influence on American founders' view about religion and state, did not advocate the complete separation of religion and state. Locke excluded atheists and those outside religion altogether from equal participation in liberal society (Alzate 2014).

[10] Ironically, of the three leading candidates for the 2016 presidential nominations, two had Jewish grandchildren. The exception was Bernie Sanders!

Almost a year later, after Trump had been elected but before he was sworn into office, the AJC publicly denounced the "noxious proposition" suggested by his transition team that the United States establish a registry of Muslims within its borders. The statement criticized the proposal as unconstitutional, among other shortcomings, probably because the organization believed (correctly, I am sure) it would violate the religious test clause in Article VI and both religion clauses of the First Amendment. The AJC and the Anti-Defamation League, which similarly criticized the candidate for his departure from classic liberal values, represent centrist perspectives in the Jewish community so their comments were not altogether unexpected.

The organizational wing of American Jewry mirrored the views of the community in general. The gap between the two candidates was even larger among Jews who were more politically engaged. In a preliminary analysis of the 2016 election cycle, Hersh and Schaffner (2016) found that Hillary Clinton received an astounding 95% of the funds from donors with distinctively Jewish names. That represents a 25% increase in Democratic skew over 2012.

Even the most affluent members of the Jewish donor class seem to have been affected negatively by Trump's language and behavior. To assess Jewish contribution patterns in 2016 with more precision, I analyzed a list of the top 100 donors in the Federal Election Commission file consulted by Hersh and Schaffner. The sums contributed by mega-donors ranged from a low of almost $2 million to a high of $57 million. Rather than use the DJN method to identify Jews by their surnames, I compiled data on the donors' religious backgrounds by searching newspapers, biographies, directories of prominent Americans, and consulting a knowledgeable reporter. This hunt produced forty-one donors who were identified as Jewish and fifty-one who were affiliated with another religion or had no discernible connection to Judaism.[11]

Of the Jewish donors, twenty-two of forty-one gave all their money to Democrats (54%) compared to just seven of the forty-five non-Jews (16%). Despite the relatively small pro-Democratic skew among Jewish mega-donors compared to other Jews, the real story is the nearly 40% gap

---

[11] I found several donors with names that could have been Jewish but who turned out to belong to other religious groups and it also revealed that most Jewish donors had last names that were not on the standard DJN list. I should emphasize that this is not meant to indict the DJN approach. I was looking at a very small group of people and the list performs better with a larger and more representative target sample. I mention the false negatives and positives only to show that the alternate approach in this analysis seemed to bear fruit.

in Democratic contributions between elite Jewish and non-Jewish donors in the top donor category. Even at the very top end of the income range, where we would expect the Republican Party's emphasis on low corporate taxes and reduced regulation to appeal to the self-interest of the wealthiest donors, Jewish contributors still stood out from non-Jews by their relatively greater attraction to Democrats.

The reaction to Donald Trump on the Jewish right, the politically conservative wing of the community, presented even more compelling evidence that American Jews still value the classic liberal regime of religion and state. Conservative commentators and observers voiced strong objections to Trump's perceived assault on norms about religion and ethnic identity in American politics. They were overrepresented in the "Never Trump" movement. I make no claim that such views are representative of the Jewish rank-and-file if only because the critics are public intellectuals. But the great virtue of focusing on intellectuals is precisely that they articulate assumptions that might well be latent among coreligionists who do not write essays.

Trump's Jewish critics in the media, academia, politics, and other sectors did not ignore the candidate's explicit and implicit attacks on Jews. The catalog of complaints covered Trump's use of anti-Semitic stereotypes about Jews when addressing AIPAC supporters, his preposterous claim that Americans would be forced to say "Merry Christmas" rather than "Happy Holidays" in December, and his final campaign advertisement that spoke of global financial conspiracies with photographs of leading Jewish figures such as Janet Yellin of the Federal Reserve; financier and philanthropist George Soros; and the head of Goldman Sachs, Lloyd Blankfein. Both his "America First" slogan and his dark claims about "international bankers" connoted symbols and themes long popular in anti-Semitic discourse.

Throughout the campaign, the respected Politifact website noted Trump's habit of "using social media to broadcast material that comes from sources with a history of spreading racism, anti-Semitism or white supremacy" (quoted in Bruni 2017). His top political adviser, Steve Bannon, styled himself the chief enabler of the Alt-Right, a movement of loosely connected white nationalists with particular animus against Jews. After his inauguration, Trump was also denounced for omitting the attempted genocide of the Jewish people from the White House statement on Holocaust Remembrance Day, failing to speak out against a wave of vandalism and bomb threats against Jewish institutions in the United States, skipping a visit to a major Holocaust memorial during his visit to Poland, and breezing through Israel's *Yad Vashem* Holocaust memorial.

Yet it was not only or chiefly Trump's indifference to Jewish communal interests that motivated his critics on the right. Their concerns centered on the candidate's perceived rejection of pluralism and diversity, ideas more commonly celebrated on the political left. They were alarmed by Trump's negative statements about other ethnic and religious minorities, his trafficking in "reprehensible sectarian tribalism" as Jonah Goldberg (2016) of *National Review* put it. The candidate's insults against Muslims, Mexicans, women, gays, the handicapped, and others, James Kirchik (2016) wrote, raised danger signs for Jews in the United States:

A country that is politically pluralistic, open to new ideas and new people, ethnically diverse, and respectful of religious difference, is a country that will naturally be safer for Jews than a country that is none of these things.

Liel Leibovitz (2016) similarly urged Jewish voters "to reject a man who lacks any respect for the very principles of pluralism that have made this country such a welcoming home for Jews and have allowed us to thrive here for more than two centuries." Noting the animosity that Trump had stirred up against other minority groups, a prominent Republican Jewish adviser (quoted in Pomorski 2016) confessed "I find it difficult to see how some Jewish voters don't recognize the danger in someone like this."

Bret Stephens (2016), then a columnist for the *Wall Street Journal*, found the Trump campaign's "America First" slogan chilling. The motto, used originally by nativists urging the United States to keep out of war against Germany in the 1940s, rested on the assumption that "there are some Americans who put their country second, or last, presumably behind their ethnic loyalties . . ." As used before World War II, the phrase identified "Wall Street bankers" and the "Jewish lobby" (sometimes interchangeably) as the enemies. By 2016, it singled out "globalists," including, prominently, the investment banking firm of Goldman Sachs and financier George Soros. Stephens argued that Trump's ideas undermined the American creed "which disavows traditional concepts of blood and soil nationalism in favor of a broader ideal of citizenship – identity defined primarily by participation and aspiration, not ancestry." Under Trump, he feared, there was a real danger that "ethnic bigotries" would become "the animating spirit" of the Republican Party.

Another writer, Bethany Mandel (2016) of the *New York Post*, called attention to the silence of Trump's Jewish daughter and son-in-law about the hateful anti-Semitism directed at Jewish journalists who wrote critically about the candidate. (Mandel herself was a major target.) Because the Jewish members of the Trump family did not denounce the "pervasive anti-Semitism" exhibited by Trump supporters, the author warned, "we shouldn't hold out any hope that their response would play out differently in real life."

In the conclusion to his *Tablet* essay, James Kirchik admitted that his conservative self-image had been shaken by his confrontation with the Trump phenomenon: "I've come to appreciate the Jewish identification with liberalism (both in its classical and modern American political form) more than at any other point in my life, and in a way no history book or sermon by a rabbi could relate." The Trump candidacy had reminded him that Jewish well-being in the West "is inextricably bound to democracy, pluralism, religious tolerance and ethnic harmony." Underscoring this point, the entire essay was entitled "Donald Trump is turning me liberal."

While I am not privy to the intricacies of politics on the Jewish right, it was striking that criticisms of Trump from that quarter do not seem to have generated significant blowback from Jewish conservatives or their funding sources. In fact, the concerns expressed by the intellectual critics were apparently shared by an unlikely group – Republican Jewish super-donors (*Haaretz* 2016). A mere 19% of the members of the Board of Directors of the Republican Jewish Coalition had contributed to the Trump campaign just days before the election – representing a 60% decline from the two previous elections. By contrast, when two leading Protestant evangelicals declared that Trump did not represent the beliefs of their community, they were threatened with reprisals and pressured to recant their heresy. Something similar may have occurred among the Jewish right but it was not publicized.

Some observers of the Jewish right have tended to dismiss the comments of these critics as a reaction by neoconservatives to Trump's foreign policy. The Neoconservatives, Jews who had left the Democratic Party and found a home in the GOP, were particularly active in challenging the Soviet Union and pushing for the use of force in Iraq, Afghanistan, and elsewhere. They objected to Trump, in part, because he broke with Republican orthodoxy by stating his willingness to accept Russian power in the Ukraine and Crimea and form an alliance with Vladimir Putin. His foreign policy statements during the campaign cast doubt on US commitments to NATO and the many post–World War II defense agreements worked out with American allies around the globe.

Although I do not gainsay that Trump's conservative critics objected to different aspects of his candidacy, there was nonetheless an undertone, sometimes an explicit assertion, that the most disturbing aspect of his campaign was his rejection of pluralism and diversity, principles intimately tied to classical liberalism and central to the American Jewish understanding of the regime of religion and state. In line with the evidence from Chapter 9 about how Jewish Republicans were appalled by Pat Robertson's presidential candidacy in 1988, commitment to the secular state has imprinted on the minds of American Jews across the political spectrum. Its latency, its "taken-for-grantedness," if you will, demonstrates its potency more than a century after it became the core political priority of American Jewry.

This concern became even more salient in the wake of the massive Alt-Right demonstration in Charlottesville, Virginia in August 2017. Among other provocations, the demonstrators screamed "blood and soil" and "you will not replace us" in front of a synagogue while Sabbath services were underway. They also threatened violence against journalists who "looked Jewish," shouted Nazi slogans, and proudly displayed swastikas on placards and brown-shirt uniforms. Far from being a side issue, according to veteran antiracist campaigner Erik Ward (2017), "Anti-Semitism forms the theoretical core of white nationalism." When President Trump attributed the violence to "both sides" and clumsily suggested that there were "very fine people" among the protestors defending a Confederate memorial, one of his Jewish advisers publicly denounced the comments and threatened to resign. Even the Republican Jewish Coalition appeared to rebuke the president.

The American Jewish commitment to liberalism goes back much further in time than most commentators have acknowledged. Belief in the United States as a secular state grew out of the colonial experience and became central to Jewish opinion with the adoption of the Constitution in the late eighteenth century. It persisted over the centuries, adapting and adjusting to new political issues both domestic and international. A venerable tradition with a long history, the American Jewish political culture casts a long shadow, visible even in the stormy, overcast skies of the 2016 presidential contest.

## THEORETICAL IMPLICATIONS

As readers will discern, I believe the study of religion as a political factor should be nested in the same theories and perspectives that drive research on American political behavior. Alan S. Zuckerman (1999, 936) once bemoaned the yawning "intellectual distance between contemporary social science and the study of Jewish communities" and called for more integration between them. He insisted that studies of Jewish political behavior "address fundamental questions of political science and the scientific understanding of contemporary political and social life" (937).

By focusing on the North American context and applying various social scientific approaches to the Jewish "case," I have tried to honor Zuckerman's clarion call. Instead of explaining Jews' distinctive political loyalties and choices by reference to "internal" factors such as religious beliefs, this perspective counsels us to examine more carefully structural aspects of the political system. Peter Medding's political interests theory of Jewish political behavior can be generalized to other groups that face threats to their status. The emphasis on the political opportunity structure in the political process model can also be exploited to apply the findings about Judaism to other religious groups.

From this perspective, the state is an actor that structures opportunities and may impose limits on religious expression in the public square. The interplay or balance between freedom and constraint affects the nature of political activity by religious communities. States are also dynamic. With changing political conditions, groups must adapt tactics to fit whatever "strategic repertoire" is appropriate under new circumstances (Koopmans 1999, 96). As we saw in the case of Jews, they moved away from the Democratic Party when it appeared to lose its commitment to classic liberal values in the 1960s but shifted back toward the Democrats when the Republican Party became closely identified with groups that Jews perceived as more hostile to their political interests.

The same dynamic seems to operate among other minority groups in the United States. In the presidential election of 2000, most American Muslims of Middle Eastern heritage appear to have voted Republican, a trend partly explained by conservative social values, the many small business owners and operators among them, and the promise of the Republican presidential candidate to eliminate "nation-building" as a goal of US foreign policy. After the attacks on the World Trade Center and the Pentagon in 2001, Muslims in the United States reported heightened levels of discrimination, harassment, and ethnic profiling, part of a syndrome they called Islamophobia. Perceiving the Republican Party as the major carrier of these sentiments, Muslims shifted strongly to the Democratic Party where they remain today (Mogahed and Pervez 2016). The religious values of Islam do not help us much to understand such rapid transitions. Their perceived treatment by the GOP, which changed the political opportunity structure, mattered more than religious values. The party's attempt to enforce a "Muslim ban" for immigration in the Trump Era suggests the partisan transformation of American Muslims will not be reversed anytime soon.

Like Jews, Latino Catholics, Asian Americans, African Americans, Muslims, and Mormons are best conceived as "ethnoreligious" groups whose political behavior may be anchored simultaneously in race, religion, nationality, or other markers of identity (Campbell, Green, and Monson 2014). When the political system sends cues that disfavor them, group solidarity may drive them toward one political party or away from another, depending on the party's attitude toward the group's interests. The political opportunity structure in 2016 – in the form of a Democratic Party seen as more tolerant and open to multiculturalism than the Republicans – apparently mattered more than religious beliefs or creed, moving all these groups away from the GOP presidential nominee.

Sometimes, religion is simply an indicator of group attachment and an idiom for political discourse. For that reason, as is evident in this book, I discount the theological element in studies of mobilization by religious groups. In this case study of American Jewish political liberalism, I have attributed Jewish distinctiveness not to theology but to the status of Jews as a minority group who have long identified state-supported religion as a threat to their well-being. The American context, particularly the favorable political opportunity structure they encountered, gave them a basis to claim full membership in the American polity. The depth and salience of that perception have been reinforced over the centuries and it shows little sign of abating. Parallel research on other minority groups will help determine whether and how these dynamics operate beyond the Jewish case.

As suggested earlier, there is an intriguing parallel between the political behavior of American Jews and American Muslims. The latter community is, of course, strikingly diverse in its ethnic, racial, and national-origins composition, making collective action a challenge. Nonetheless, some Muslims have openly identified Jews as the "model minority" the Muslim community should emulate in its political practices (Mazrui 2004). The similarities between the Arab American Anti-Discrimination Committee and the venerable Jewish organization, the Anti-Defamation League, suggest that some borrowing has already taken place.

In the current era, American Muslims seem focused mostly on the kinds of projects pursued by American Jews during the 1940s and 1950s, promoting interreligious understanding and tolerance. In time, the

Muslim community may develop a political ethic that promotes the idea of a secular state as a core value. Islam is the state-sponsored or preferred religion in Muslim-majority nations so developing a communal commitment to political secularism in the United States may be especially challenging for those with foreign ancestry. On the other hand, American Muslims have already seen some value from the principle of state neutrality toward religions. The oddly named federal legislation, the Religious Land Use and Institutionalized Persons Act (RLUIPA), has consistently negated discriminatory zoning laws adopted to prevent the construction of mosques and Muslim community centers in many localities. American Muslims may yet come to resemble Jews in regarding a secular state as the best guarantor of their political and social equality.

# References

Abelson, Paul. Undated. "Meaning of America." Paul Abelson Papers Ms. 004. Box 3, item 6c. American Jewish Archives, Cincinnati, OH.

Undated. "Religious Liberty." Paul Abelson Papers Ms. 004. Box 3, item 3c. American Jewish Archives, Cincinnati, OH.

Abraham, Lewis. 1875 (July 16). "The Centennial." *The Jewish Messenger*, 5.

1895. "Correspondence between Washington and Jewish Citizens." *Publications of the American Jewish Historical Society* 3: 147–168.

Abramowitz, Alan I., John McGlennon, Ronald B. Rapoport, and Walter J. Stone. 2001. "Activists in the United States Presidential Nomination Process, 1980–1996." ICPSR 06143. 1996. Distributed by Inter-university Consortium for Political and Social Research.

Adams, Hannah. 1817. *A Dictionary of All Religions and Religious Denominations*. New York: James Eastburn and Co.

"Address by Mr. Irving Engel at ZOA House, Tel Aviv, Israel, June 23, 1957." Israel-Visits-Speeches File. Foreign Affairs Department Collection. FAD-1. Speech by Irving Engel, ZOA House in Tel Aviv 1957. AJC Archives. Retrieved from ajcarchives.org (accessed August 16, 2018).

Adler, Cyrus. 1916. "Letter to *American Hebrew*, March 21, 1916." Cyrus Adler Papers. Box 3, FF 2. Katz Library, University of Pennsylvania.

1932. "Twenty-Fifth Anniversary Address." New York: American Jewish Committee.

Allinsmith, Wesley, and Beverly Allinsmith. 1948. "Religious Affiliation and Politico-Economic Attitudes: A Study of Eight Major U.S. Religious Groups." *Public Opinion Quarterly* 12: 377–389.

Alzate, Elissa B. 2014. "From Individual to Citizen: Enhancing the Bonds of Citizenship through Religion in Locke's Political Theory." *Polity* 46: 211–232.

American Jewish Committee. 1942. *Jewish Post-War Problems: A Study Course*, Vol. 3. Research Institute on Peace and Post-War Problems. New York: American Jewish Committee.

1950. *This Is Our Home.* New York: American Jewish Committee.

1957a. "Relations between Israel and Other Jewish Communities." AJC Archives. Israel-American Jews and Israel File. Foreign Affairs Department Collection. FAD-1. Memoranda, including a report by Lucy Dawidowicz on relationship of American Jews to Israel, 1956–1961. AJC Archives. Retrieved from ajcarchives.org (accessed August 16, 2018).

1957b. *This Is Our Home.* New York: American Jewish Committee.

1996. "American Jewish Committee Religious Right Survey, 1996." Study AJCRR96. Study Distributed by Association for Religious Data Archives. Retrieved from www.thearda.com/Archive/Files/Downloads/AJCRR96_DL .asp (accessed August 16, 2018).

2004. "AJC Survey: Russian Jews Lean More Conservative." Retrieved from ajc .org/site/apps/nlnet/content2.aspx?c=70JILSPwFfJSG&b=8479733&c t=12482395 (accessed September 15, 2017).

American Jewish Congress. 1919. *Report of Proceedings of the American Jewish Congress 1918.* New York: American Jewish Congress.

1920. *Proceedings of Adjourned Session of American Jewish Congress Including Report of Commission to Peace Conference and of Provisional Organization for Formation of American Jewish Congress; Philadelphia, May 30–31, 1920.* New York: Provisional Organization for Formation of American Jewish Congress.

Anderson, Dewey, and Percy E. Davidson. 1943. *Ballots and the Democratic Class Struggle: A Study in the Background of Political Education.* Palo Alto, CA: Stanford University Press.

Angel, Marc. 1973. "The Sephardim of the United States: An Exploratory Study." *American Jewish Year Book* 74: 77–137.

"As to a Jewish Congress." *The Menorah* 40 (January): 83–92.

Antin, Mary. 1912a. "The American Miracle." *Atlantic Monthly* 109 (January): 52–67.

1912b. "Making of a Citizen." *Atlantic Monthly* 109 (February): 211–224.

1912c. "The Immigrant's Portion." *Atlantic Monthly* 109 (April): 518–525.

1916. *At School in the Promised Land; or, the Story of a Little Immigrant.* Boston: MA: Houghton Mifflin.

Auerbach, Jerold S. 1990. *Rabbis and Lawyers: The Journey from Torah to Constitution.* Bloomington: Indiana University Press.

Ball, Terence, Richard Dagger, and Daniel O'Neill. 2014. *Political Ideologies and the Democratic Ideal.* Boston: Pearson.

Barkun, Michael. 1994. *Religion and the Racist Right.* Chapel Hill: University of North Carolina Press.

Barnea, Marina F., and Shalom H. Schwartz. 1998. "Values and Voting." *Political Psychology* 19: 17–40.

Barnett, Michael N. 2016. *The Star and the Stripes: A History of the Foreign Policies of American Jews.* Princeton, NJ: Princeton University Press.

Bartels, Larry M. 2008. *Unequal Democracy: The Political Economy of the New Gilded Age.* Princeton, NJ: Princeton University Press.

Barton, Allen H. 1968. "Survey Research and Macro-Methodology." *American Behavioral Scientist* 12: 1–9.

Beaulieu, Anatole Leroy. 1917. "Jewish Immigrants and Judaism in the United States." In *Judaean Addresses*, 33–51. New York: Bloch.

Be'chol Lashon. 2018. "Counting Jews of Color in the United States." GlobalJews .org. Retrieved from www.bechollashon.org/population/north_america/na_ color.php (accessed April 11, 2018).

Beck, Paul Allen. 1979. "The Electoral Cycle and Patterns of American Politics." *British Journal of Political Science* 9: 129–156.

Bélanger, Éric, and Bonnie M Meguid. 2008. "Issue Salience, Issue Ownership, and Issue-Based Vote Choice." *Electoral Studies* 27: 477–491.

Bennett, W. Lance. 1975. "Political Sanctification: The Civil Religion and American Politics." *Social Science Information* 14: 79–102.

Ben-Ur, Aviva. 2009. *Sephardic Jews in America: A Diasporic History.* New York: New York University Press.

Berkowitz, Henry. 1889. "Public Schools Praised." Henry Berkowitz Papers. Box 6, Folder 2. American Jewish Archives, Cincinnati.

　　1905. *Course in American Jewish History. A Syllabus of Topics, Historical and Biographical, with Suggested Subjects for Debates or Informal Discussions.* Philadelphia: Jewish Chautauqua Society.

Berlin, Adele and Marc Zvi Brettler, eds. 2004. *The Jewish Study Bible.* New York: Oxford University Press.

Bhargava, Rajeev. 2009. "Political Secularism: Why It Is Needed and What Can Be Learnt from Its Indian Version." In *Secularism, Religion and Multicultural Citizenship.* Ed. Geoffrey Brahm Levey and Tariq Modood, 82–109. New York: Cambridge University Press.

Biale, David. 1987. *Power and Powerlessness in Jewish History.* New York: Schocken.

Bien, Julius. 1898. "Past and Future of the Order." *The Menorah* 24: 230–236.

Birnbaum, Pierre. 2008. "On the Secularization of the Public Square: Jews in France and in the United States." *Cardozo Law Review* 30: 2431–2443.

Blake, William. 2012. "God Save This Honorable Court: Religion as a Source of Judicial Policy Preferences." *Political Research Quarterly* 65: 814–826.

Blau, Joseph L., and Salo W. Baron, eds. 1963. *The Jews of the United States, 1790–1840: A Documentary History.* 3 vols. New York: Columbia University Press.

Blaustein, Jacob. 1950. *"Voice of Reason."* New York: American Jewish Committee.

Board of Delegates of American Israelites. 1862. *Third Annual Report.* New York: Joseph Davis.

Board of Education. City of New York. 1922. "Short Unit Syllabus for Special Naturalization Classes in Evening Elementary Schools (Tentative)." Board of Education Records. Series 666. Courses of Study and curriculum Resources Materials. Non-Serial Publications. 1900–1942. Box 6, Folder 104. New York City Municipal Archives.

Bolce, Louis, and Gerald De Maio. 1999. "The Anti-Christian Fundamentalist Factor in Contemporary Politics." *Public Opinion Quarterly* 63: 508–542.

Borden, Morton. 1984. *Jews, Turks and Infidels*. Chapel Hill: University of North Carolina Press.

Bowman, Karlyn, and Andrew Rugg. 2008. "AEI Special Report: Delegates at National Conventions, 1968–2008." Retrieved from images.politico.com/global/2012/08/convention_delegates_survey.html (accessed August 16, 2018).

Brackman, Nicole. 1999. "Who Is a Jew? The American Jewish Community in Conflict with Israel." *Journal of Church and State* 41: 795–822.

Bradley, Gerard V. 1986. "The No Religious Test Clause and the Constitution of Religious Liberty: A Machine That Has Gone of Itself." *Case Western Reserve Law Review* 37: 674–747.

Brady, Henry E., David Collier, and Jason Seawright. 2017. "Toward a Pluralistic Vision of Methodology." *Political Analysis* 14: 353–368.

Brubaker, Rogers. 1996. "Nationalizing States in the Old 'New Europe' – and the New." *Ethnic and Racial Studies* 19: 411–437.

Brumberg, Stephan F. 1986. *Going to America, Going to School: The Jewish Immigrant Public School Encounter in Turn-of-the-Century New York City*. New York: Praeger.

Bruni, Frank. 2017 (July 8) "Why Does Donald Trump Keep Dissing Jews?" *New York Times*.

Campbell, David E., John C. Green, and Geoffrey C. Layman. 2011. "The Party Faithful: Partisan Images, Candidate Religion, and the Electoral Impact of Party Identification." *American Journal of Political Science* 55: 42–58.

Campbell, David E., John C. Green and J. Quin Monson. 2014. *Seeking the Promised Land: Mormons and American Politics*. New York: Cambridge University Press.

Cantor, David. 1994. *The Religious Right: The Assault on Tolerance and Pluralism in America*. New York: Anti-Defamation League.

Carey, John M, Richard G. Niemi, and Lynda W. Powell. 1995. "State Legislative Survey and Contextual Data, 1995." ICPSR 2031. December 8, 2000. Distributed by Inter-University Consortium for Political and Social Research, Ann Arbor, MI.

Carnes, Nicholas and Noam Lupu. 2017 (June 5). "It's Time to Bust the Myth: Most Trump Voters Were Not Working Class." *Washington Post*. Retrieved from washingtonpost.com/news/monkey-cage/wp/2017/06/05/its-time-to-bust-the-myth-most-trump-voters-were-not-working-class/?noredirect=on&utm_term=.464c8fa43fec (accessed April 23, 2018).

Central Conference of American Rabbis. 1906. *Why the Bible Should Not Be Read in the Public Schools*. Central Conference of American Rabbis, Committee on Church and State.

1909. *Yearbook of the Central Conference of American Rabbis*. New York: Central Conference of American Rabbis.

Chyet, Stanley F. 1958. "The Political Rights of Jews in the United States: 1776–1840." *American Jewish Archives* 10: 14–75.

*Cincinnati Daily Enquirer.* 1868 (June 6). "City Matters: The New Jewish Temple at the Corner of Eighth and Mound Streets," 1.

Claassen, Ryan L., Paul A. Djupe, Andrew R. Lewis, and Jacob R. Neiheisel 2016. *Malum Religiosorum Factionum*: Beliefs about the Religious Divide in Politics. Paper presented to the annual meeting of the American Political Science Association, Philadelphia.

Clark, John A., and Charles L. Prysby, eds. 2004. *Southern Political Party Activists: Patterns of Conflict and Change, 1991–2001.* Lexington: University Press of Kentucky.

Clements, Ben. 2017 (August 11). "Religious Affiliation and Party Choice at the 2017 General Election." British Religion in Numbers. Retrieved from www .brin.ac.uk/2017/religious-affiliation-and-party-choice-at-the-2017-general-election/ (accessed April 12, 2018).

Cohen, Henry. 1893. *National Loyalty: A Jewish Characteristic.* New York: Philip Cowen.

Cohen, Josiah. 1864 (February 19). "Correspondence." *Jewish Messenger,* 53.

Cohen, M. I. 1857 (November 6). "This Memorial." *Israelite,* 142.

Cohen, Naomi W. 1989. "In Defense of Equality: American Jews and the Constitution." In *In Celebration: An American Jewish Perspective on the Bicentennial of the United States Constitution.* Ed. Kerry M. Olitzky, 6–26. Lanham, MD: University Press of America.

    1993. *Natural Adversaries or Possible Allies? American Jews and the New Christian Right.* New York: American Jewish Committee, Institute of Human Relations.

    2008. *What the Rabbis Said: The Public Discourse of Nineteenth-Century American Rabbis.* New York: New York University Press.

Cohen, Steven M. 2000a. "Religion and the Public Square: Attitudes of American Jews in Comparative Perspective – a Follow-up Study." Center for Jewish Community Studies. Retrieved from cjcs.net/survey4.htm (accessed June 23, 2017).

    2000b. "Religion and the Public Square: Attitudes of American Jews in Comparative Perspective – Part 1." Jerusalem Center for Public Affairs. Retrieved from jcpa.org/article/religion-and-the-public-square-attitudes-of-american-jews-in-comparative-perspective-part-one/ (accessed June 23, 2017).

    2000c. "Religion and the Public Square: Attitudes of American Jews in Comparative Perspective – Part 2." Jerusalem Center for Public Affairs. Retrieved from jcpa.org/jl/jl435.htm (accessed June 23, 2017).

Cohen, Yinon, Yitzchak Haberfeld, and Irena Kogan. 2011. "Who Went Where? Jewish Immigration from the Former Soviet Union to Israel, the USA and Germany, 1990–2000." *Israel Affairs* 17: 7–20.

Committee on Israel. American Jewish Committee. 1955. "Religion and State in Israel." AJC Archives. Retrieved from ajarchives.org (accessed August 16, 2018).

Committee on Post Office and Post Roads. 1830. *Report No. 271.* Washington, DC: U.S. House of Representatives.

"Conference of the American Jewish Committee at the Hotel Astor." 1916 (July 16). American Jewish Committee Archives. Retrieved from ajcarchives .org (accessed August 16, 2018).

Conover, Pamela Johnson, and Stanley Feldman. 1981. "The Origins and Meaning of Liberal/Conservative Self-Identifications." *Journal of Politics* 25: 617–645.

Costain, Anne N. 1992. *Inviting Women's Rebellion: A Political Process Interpretation of the Women's Movement*. Baltimore, MD: Johns Hopkins University Press.

Cousins, Norman, ed. 1958. *In God We Trust: The Religious Beliefs and Ideas of the American Founders*. New York: Harper and Brothers.

Cox, Daniel, Robert P. Jones, and Juhem Navarro-Rivera. 2015. "Nonreligious Tolerance: American Attitudes toward Atheists, America's Most Unpopular Religious Group." In *Religion and Political Tolerance in America*. Ed. Paul A. Djupe, 133–150. Philadelphia: Temple University Press.

Dalin, David G. 2002. "Jewish Critics of Strict Separationism." In *Jews and the American Public Square: Debating Religion and Republic*. Ed. Alan L. Mittleman, Jonathan D. Sarna, and Robert Licht, 291–310. Lanham, MD: Rowman & Littlefield.

Dawidowicz, Lucy S. 1957 (September 10). "Memorandum to Milton Himmelfarb on Session of Executive Board Meeting on Israel-Zionist Interrelations." Israel-American Jews and Israel File. Foreign Affairs Department Collection. FAD-1. Memoranda, including a report by Lucy Dawidowicz on relationship of American Jews to Israel, 1956–1961. AJA Archives. Retrieved from ajcarchives.org (accessed August 16, 2018).

De la Motta, Jacob. 1820. *Discourse Delivered at the Consecration of the Synagogue of the Hebrew Congregation*. Savannah, GA: Russell & Edes.

De Lancey, Edward Floyd, ed. 1886. *The Burghers of New Amsterdam and the Freemen of New York*. New York: New York Historical Society.

DellaPergola, Sergio. 2001. "Some Fundamentals of Jewish Demographic History." In *Papers in Jewish Demography*. Ed. Sergio DellaPergola and Judith Even, 11–33. Jerusalem: Institute of Contemporary Jewry, Hebrew University of Jerusalem.

Department of Civics. Educational Alliance. 1905 (September 21). "General Statement." Paul Abelson Papers MS0004. Box 2, Folder 7. American Jewish Archives, Hebrew Union College, Cincinnati.

Deslippe, Dennis. 2012. *Protesting Affirmative Action: The Struggle over Equality after the Civil Rights Revolution*. Baltimore, MD: Johns Hopkins University Press.

Diner, Hasia R. 1994. "Jewish Self-Governance, American Style." *American Jewish History* 81: 277–295.

2017. "Looking Back on American Jewish History." In *American Jewry: Transcending the European Experience?* Ed. Christian Wiese and Cornelia Wilhelm, 352–365. London: Bloomsbury Academic.

Dollinger, Marc. 2000. *Quest for Inclusion: Jews and Liberalism in Modern America*. Princeton, NJ: Princeton University Press.

Durkheim, Emile. 2005 [1897]. *Suicide*. Ed. George Simpson. Trans. John Spaulding and George Simpson. London: Routledge Classics.

Dushkin, Alexander M. 1918. *Jewish Education in New York City*. New York: Bureau of Jewish Education.

Eagles, Munroe, ed. 1995. *Spatial and Contextual Models in Political Research*. Bristol, PA: Taylor & Francis.

Edelman, Martin. 2000. "The New Israeli Constitution." *Middle Eastern Studies* 36: 1–27.

Endelman, Todd M., ed. 1997. *Comparing Jewish Societies*. Ann Arbor: University of Michigan Press.

Evans, Geoffrey. 2000. "The Continued Significance of Class Voting." *Annual Review of Political Science* 3: 401–417.

Fein, Leonard. 1988. *Where Are We? The Inner Life of America's Jews*. New York: Harper and Row.

Feingold, Henry L. 2014. *American Jewish Political Culture and the Liberal Persuasion*. Syracuse, NY: Syracuse University Press.

Fetter, Henry D. 2016. "Review of Michael N. Barnett's *The Star and the Stripes: A History of the Foreign Policies of American Jews*." Retrieved from http://historynewsnetwork.org/article/163004 (accessed August 5, 2017).

Fink, Carole. 2004. *Defending the Rights of Others: The Great Powers, the Jews, and International Minority Protection, 1878–1938*. New York: Cambridge University Press.

Fishman, Sylvia. 2000. *Jewish Life and American Culture*. Albany: State University of New York Press.

Foner, Philip Sheldon. 1946. *The Jews in American History, 1654–1865*. New York: International Publishers.

Forbath, William E. 2014. *Jews, Law and Identity Politics*. Working Paper, University of Texas School of Law, Austin, TX.

Forman, Ira N. 2001. "The Politics of Minority Consciousness." In *Jews in American Politics*. Ed. Louis Sandy Maisel and Ira N. Forman, 141–160. Lanham, MD: Rowman & Littlefield.

Forman, Lori. 1994. *"The Political Activity of the Religious Right in the 1990's: A Critical Analysis."* New York: American Jewish Committee.

Fox, Jonathan. 2007. "Do Democracies Have Separation of Religion and State?" *Canadian Journal of Political Science/Revue canadienne de science politique* 40: 1–25.

2015. *Political Secularism, Religion, and the State: A Time Series Analysis of Worldwide Data*. New York: Cambridge University Press.

Frankel, Jonathan. 1976. "Jewish Socialists and American Jewish Congress Movement." *YIVO Annual of Jewish Social Science* 16: 202–341.

Friedman, Murray. 2005. *The Neoconservative Revolution: Jewish Intellectuals and the Shaping of Public Policy*. New York: Cambridge University Press.

Friedman, William. 1908 (January 16). "Jews within Their Rights." *Israelite*, 1.

Fuchs, Lawrence H. 1956. *The Political Behavior of American Jews*. Glencoe, IL: Free Press.

Gallup Organization. 1953. "Gallup Poll: Finances/Automobiles and Driving/Russia/Korea/Sports [Dataset]." USAIPO1953-0513. Distributed by Roper Center for Public Opinion Research.

Gamm, Gerald H. 1989. *The Making of New Deal Democrats: Voting Behavior and Realignment in Boston, 1920–1940.* Chicago: University of Chicago Press.

Gelb, Leslie H. 1992 (March 20). "Foreign Affairs: The Anti-Israeli Leaks," *New York Times*, 33.

Gelman, Andrew, Lane Kenworthy, and Yu-Sung Su. 2010. "Income Inequality and Partisan Voting in the United States." *Social Science Quarterly* 91: 1203–1219.

Gitlin, Todd. 2015 (February 17). "Why 'The Enlightenment Project' Is Necessary and Unending." *Tablet*. Retrieved from www.tabletmag.com/jewish-news-and-politics/189001/the-enlightenment-project (accessed February 17, 2017).

Glaser, James M. 1997. "Toward an Explanation of the Racial Liberalism of American Jews." *Political Research Quarterly* 50: 437–458.

Glendon, Mary Ann. 1991. *Rights Talk: The Impoverishment of Political Discourse.* New York: Free Press.

Goldberg, Jonah. 2016 (March 22). "For Trump Supporters, a Reckoning Is at Hand." National Review Online. Retrieved from nationalreview.com/article/432160/donald-trump-supporters-must-face-reckoning (accessed July 14, 2017).

Goldberger, Henry H. 1922. *America for Coming Citizens.* New York: C. Scribner's Sons.

Goldscheider, Calvin and Alan S. Zuckerman. 1984. *The Transformation of the Jews.* Chicago: University of Chicago Press.

Goldstein, Israel. 1926 (September 16). "The Jew in America's Jubilee." *Jewish Advocate*, A3.

Goodin, Robert E., and Charles Tilly, eds. 2006. *The Oxford Handbook of Contextual Political Analysis.* New York: Oxford University Press.

Green, Donald P., Bradley Palmquist, and Eric Schickler. 2002. *Partisan Hearts and Minds: Political Parties and the Social Identities of Voters.* New Haven, CT: Yale University Press.

Green, John C., James L. Guth, and Cleveland R. Fraser. 1991. "Apostles and Apostates? Religion and Politics among Party Activists." In *The Bible and the Ballot Box: Religion and Politics in the 1988 Election.* Ed. James Guth and John C. Green, 113–133. Boulder, CO: Westview.

Greenberg, Anna, and Kenneth D. Wald. 2001. "Still Liberal after All These Years? The Contemporary Political Behavior of American Jewry." In *Jews in American Politics.* Ed. Sandy Maisel and Ira N. Forman, 167–199. Lanham, MD: Rowman & Littlefield.

Greenberg, Cheryl Lynn. 2006. *Troubling the Waters: Black-Jewish Relations in the American Century.* Princeton, NJ: Princeton University Press.

Greilsammer, Ilan. 1978. "Jews of France: From Neutrality to Involvement." *Forum* (Winter): 130–146.

Guth, James L., and John C. Green. 1990. "Politics in a New Key: Religiosity and Participation among Political Activists." *Western Political Quarterly* 43: 153–179.

*Haaretz*. 2016 (November 3). "Few Donations for Trump from Republican Jewish Coalition Leaders." Retrieved from www.haaretz.com/world-news/f ew-donations-for-trump-from-republican-jewish-coalition-leaders-1 .5456618 (accessed April 17, 2018).

Halevi, Yossi Klein. 2016 (June 6). "A Jewish Centrist Manifesto." Times of Israel. Retrieved from blogs.timesofisrael.com/the-state-of-the-jewish-world -2016/ (accessed July 14, 2017).

Halpern, Ben. 1956. *The American Jew: A Zionist Analysis*. New York: Theodor Herzl Foundation.

Hanson, Russell L. 2013. *Secularizing the American State, 1876–1905*. Bloomington: Department of Political Science, University of Indiana.

Hartz, Louis. 1955. *The Liberal Tradition in America: An Interpretation of American Political Thought since the Revolution*. New York: Harcourt, Brace.

Hassler, Isaac. 1907 (May 31). "The United States as a 'Christian Nation'." *Jewish Exponent*, 7.

  1907 (June 7). "A Reply to Justice Brewer's Lectures: "The United States as a 'Christian Nation'." *The Jewish Exponent*, 7.

Hebrew Education Society of Philadelphia. 1899. *Fifty Years' Work of the Hebrew Education Society of Philadelphia 1848–1898*. Philadelphia: Hebrew Education Society.

Heilman, Samuel C., and Steven M. Cohen. 1989. *Cosmopolitans and Parochials: Modern Orthodox Jews in America*. Chicago: University of Chicago Press.

Herda, Daniel. 2013. "Innocuous Ignorance? Perceptions of the American Jewish Population Size." *Contemporary Jewry* 33: 241–255.

Hersh, Eitan, and Brian Schaffner. 2016. "The GOP's Jewish Donors Are Abandoning Trump." FiveThirtyEight. Retrieved from fivethirtyeight.com/fea tures/the-gops-jewish-donors-are-abandoning-trump/ (accessed August 14, 2017).

Hertzberg, Arthur. 1996 "My God, Myself." *Hadassah Magazine* 77 (November): 74.

Higham, John. 2002. *Strangers in the Land: Patterns of American Nativism, 1860–1925*. New Brunswick, NJ: Rutgers University Press.

Hill, Kevin A., and Dario Moreno. 1996. "Second-Generation Cubans." *Hispanic Journal of Behavioral Sciences* 18: 175–193.

Hout, Michael, Clem Brooks, and Jeff Manza. 1995. "The Democratic Class Struggle in the United States, 1948–1992." *American Sociological Review* 60: 805–828.

Howe, Irving. 1976. *World of Our Fathers*. New York: Simon and Schuster.

Huddy, Leonie. 2013. "From Group Identity to Political Cohesion and Commitment." In *Oxford Handbook of Political Psychology*. Ed. Leonie Huddy, David O. Sears, and Jack S. Levy, 737–773. New York: Oxford University Press.

Huhner, Leon. 1905. "Francis Salvador." *New Era Illustrated Magazine* 7 (July): 36–40.

Hunt, Gaillard, ed. 1910. *The Writings of James Madison, Comprising His Public Papers and His Private Correspondence*. New York: Putnam's Sons.

Hyman, Paula E. 1992. "Was There a 'Jewish Politics' in Western and Central Europe?" In *The Quest for Utopia: Jewish Political Ideas and Institutions through the Ages*. Ed. Zvi Gitelman, 105–118. Armonk, NY: M. E. Sharpe.

Illowy, Bernard. 1861 (January 3). "Civil and Religious Liberty." *Occident*, 248–249.

Ingersoll, Julie. 2015. *Building God's Kingdom: Inside the World of Christian Reconstruction*. New York: Oxford University Press.

*International Encyclopedia of the Social Sciences*. 2008. "Political Culture." Retrieved from www.encyclopedia.com/social-sciences/applied-and-social-sciences-magazines/political-culture-0 (accessed November 28, 2017).

Isaacs, Isaac. 1865 (December 15). "Thanksgiving Address." *Jewish Messenger*, 188.

*Israelite*. [Anonymous articles. The newspaper was also published as the *American Israelite*.]

    1854 (December 15). "Thanks Giving." 188.

    1855 (May 11). "Sunday Trading Bill: His Holiness King Stowe, vs. the Jews of California." 345.

    1855 (December 14). "Thanksgiving at the Greene Street Congregation." 187.

    1857 (October 2). "This Memorial: Supplement to the Swiss Question." 100.

    1861 (November 29). "That Chaplain Law." 172.

    1862 (March 28). "Breakers Ahead!" 308.

    1867 (April 26). "Bigots at Work." 6.

    1872 (July 26). "The Declaration of Independence of the United States; or, the Redemption of the World." 13.

    1889 (June 27). "A Jewish Demonstration Proposed." 4.

    1916 (October 12). "Right, Not Toleration." 4.

Isser, Natalie. 1993. "Diplomatic Intervention and Human Rights: The Swiss Question, 1852–1864." *Journal of Church and State* 35: 577–592.

Isserman, Ferdinand. 1937. "Keeping America the Land of the Brave and the Free." Ferdinand M. Isserman Papers. Box 14, FF7. Katz Library, University of Pennsylvania.

Ivers, Gregg. 1990. "Organized Religion and the Supreme Court." *Journal of Church and State* 32: 775–793.

    1993. *Redefining the First Freedom: The Supreme Court and the Consolidation of State Power*. New Brunswick, NJ: Transaction.

Jacobs, Carly M., and Elizabeth Theiss-Morse. 2013. "Belonging in a 'Christian Nation': The Explicit and Implicit Associations between Religion and National Group Membership." *Politics and Religion* 6: 373–401.

Jacobson, Moses Perez. 1913. *Is This a Christian Country?* Shreveport, LA: M. L. Bath.

Jaher, Frederic Cople. 2002. *The Jews and the Nation: Revolution, Emancipation, State Formation, and the Liberal Paradigm in America and France*. Princeton, NJ: Princeton University Press.

2010. "American Exceptionalism: The Case of the Jews, 1750–1850." In *Why Is America Different? American Jewry on Its 350th Anniversary*. Ed. Steven T. Katz, 28–53. Lanham, MD: University Press of America.

Jansen, Giedo, Geoffrey Evans, and Nan Dirk De Graaf. 2013. "Class Voting and Left–Right Party Positions: A Comparative Study of 15 Western Democracies, 1960–2005." *Social Science Research* 42: 376–400.

Jastrow, Marcus. 1868. *Sermons Delivered in the Synagogue, Rodef Shalom, Julianna Street, on Thanksgiving Day, November 26th, 1868*. Philadelphia: The Congregation.

Jelen, Ted G. and Kenneth D. Wald. 2018. "Evangelicals and President Trump: The Not So Odd Couple." In *God at the Grass Roots, 2016*. Ed. Mark J. Rozell and Clyde Wilcox, 19–30. Lanham, MD: Rowman & Littlefield.

*Jewish Advocate*. Undated. "Clipping of *Jewish Advocate* Credo." Cyrus Adler Papers. Box 3 Folder 10. Katz Library, University of Pennsylvania.

"The Jewish Congress vs. The American Jewish Committee." 1915. New York: Jewish Congress Organization Committee.

*Jewish Exponent*. 1887 (September 23). "Sermons on the Constitutional Centennial." 8–9.

1938 (January 28). "On Behalf of World Jewry." 4.

Jewish Link Staff. 2017. "OU's Allen Fagin Takes Questions on Education Policy." Orthodox Union. Retrieved from ou.org/news/ous-allen-fagin-takes-questions-education-policy/ (accessed July 12, 2017).

*Jewish Messenger*. [Anonymous articles. Also published under the name *American Hebrew & Jewish Messenger*]

1859 (November 4). "Address: Plan." 132.

1860 (December 28). "A Day of Prayer." 196.

1861 (December 27). "Display Ad #4."

1863 (January 16). "Grant's Order: Our True Course." 20.

1864 (December 16). "The Constitutional Amendment." 180.

1892 (October 21). "Model Celebration." 798.

1911 (November 24). "Thanksgiving Day." 111.

Joseph, Samuel. 1969. *Jewish Immigration to the United States from 1881 to 1910*. New York: Arno Press and the *New York Times*.

Kammen, Michael G. 1986. *A Machine That Would Go of Itself: The Constitution in American Culture*. New York: Alfred A. Knopf.

Katz, Nathan. 1996. "Understanding Religion in Diaspora: The Case of the Jews of Cochin." *Religious Studies and Theology* 15: 5–17.

Kazin, Michael. 2006. *A Godly Hero: The Life of William Jennings Bryan*. New York: Alfred A. Knopf.

Kazis, Josh Nathan. 2016 (November 8). "Why So Many Ultra-Orthodox Jews Will Vote for Hillary Clinton – Not Donald Trump." *Tablet*. Retrieved from http://forward.com/news/353644/why-so-many-ultra-orthodox-jews-will-vote-for-hillary-clinton-not-donald-tr/ (accessed July 22, 2017).

Keith, Bruce E., David Magleby, Candice J. Nelson, Elizabeth Orr, Mark C. Westlye, and Raymond E. Wolfinger. 1992. *The Myth of the Independent Voter*. Berkeley: University of California Press.

Kellstedt, Lyman, John Green, Corwin Smidt, and James Guth. 2007. "Faith Transformed: Religion and American Politics from FDR to George W. Bush." In *Religion and American Politics: From the Colonial Period to the Present*. Ed. Mark A. Noll and Luke E. Harlow, 269–296. New York: Oxford University Press.

Kettner, James H. 1974. "The Development of American Citizenship in the Revolutionary Era: The Idea of Volitional Allegiance." *American Journal of Legal History* 18: 208–242.

1978. *The Development of American Citizenship, 1608–1870*. Chapel Hill: University of North Carolina Press.

Key, V. O. 1949. *Southern Politics in State and Nation*. New York: Alfred A. Knopf.

Kirchik, James. 2016 (March 14). "Donald Trump Is Turning Me Liberal." *Tablet*. Retrieved from tabletmag.com/jewish-news-and-politics/198487/do nald-trump-is-turning-me-liberal (accessed August 9, 2017).

Kiron, Arthur. 1996. "'Dust and Ashes': The Funeral and Forgetting of Sabato Morais." *American Jewish History* 84: 155–188.

Klapper, Melissa R. 2007. *Small Strangers: The Experiences of Immigrant Children in America, 1880–1925*. Chicago: Ivan R. Dee.

Klein, Max D. 1912 (December 6). "Rabbi Klein's Thanksgiving Sermon." *Jewish Exponent*, 9.

Kleinfeld, Daniel J. 1999. "Staging a Nation: Mordecai Noah and the Early Republic." In *The Selected Writings of Mordecai Noah*. Ed. Michael Joseph Schuldiner and Daniel J. Kleinfeld, 69–76. Westport, CT: Greenwood Press.

Kliger, Sam 2011. Russian-Jewish Immigrants in the U.S.: Identity, Politics, Religion, and the Future. Paper presented to the conference on the Contemporary Russian-Speaking Jewish Diaspora, Cambridge, MA.

Kloppenberg, James T. 1998. *The Virtues of Liberalism*. New York: Oxford University Press.

Kohler, Kaufman. 1888. "Three Elements of American Judaism." *The Menorah* 5 (November): 314–322.

1908. "Strife and Triumph of America and the Jew." Kaufmann Kohler Papers. 1851-1959. MS-29, Box 6, Folder 10. American Jewish Archives, Hebrew Union College, Cincinnati.

1918 (April 6). "The Attitude of Reform Judaism toward the Recent Occurrences in Palestine." *Reform Advocate* 56: 199–200.

Kohler, Max J. 1915 (January 29). "Our Union and Kindred Organizations." *Sentinel* 17: 3.

1930. "The Fathers of the Republic and Constitutional Establishment of Religious Liberty." In *God in Freedom: Studies in the Relations between Church and State*. Ed. Luigi Luzzati, 670–705. New York: Macmillan.

1933. "Letter to Julian Mack, September 28, 1933." Max J. Kohler Papers. Box 15, Folder 10. Center for Jewish History, New York.

Kolsky, Thomas A. 1990. *Jews against Zionism: The American Council for Judaism, 1942–1948*. Philadelphia: Temple University Press.

Koopmans, Ruud. 1999. "Political. Opportunity. Structure. Some Splitting to Balance the Lumping." *Sociological Forum* 14: 93–105.

Korn, Bertram W. 1949. "Jewish 48'ers in America." *American Jewish Archives* 2: 3–20.

Kosmin, Barry A. 1992 "The Permeable Boundaries of Being Jewish in America." *Moment* 17 (August): 30–38, 51.

Kotler-Berkowitz, Laurence. 1997. "Ethnic Cohesion and Division among American Jews: The Role of Mass-Level and Organizational Politics." *Ethnic and Racial Studies* 20: 797–829.

2002. "Social Cleavages and Political Divisions: A Comparative Analysis of British, American and South African Jews in the 1990s." *Journal of Modern Jewish Studies* 1: 204–233.

2017. "The Structure of Political Divisions among American Jews." *Contemporary Jewry* 37: 5–27.

Kramer, Michael P. 2003. "Beginnings and Ends: The Origins of Jewish American Literary History." In *Cambridge Companion to Jewish American Literature.* Ed. Hana Wirth-Nesher and Michael P. Kramer, 12–30. New York: Cambridge University Press.

Kramnick, Isaac, and R. Laurence Moore. 1996. *That Godless Constitution.* New York: W. W. Norton.

Kriegshaber, V. H., David Marx, and Leonard Haas. 1911. "Letter to A. O Bacon, November 11, 1911." Mayer Sulzberger Papers. Box 1, FF 8. Katz Library, University of Pennsylvania.

Kristol, Irving. 1999. "On the Political Stupidity of the Jews." *Azure* No. 8 (Autumn). Retrieved from azure.org.il/article.php?id=299 (accessed September 16, 2016).

Kuhn, Thomas S. 1970. *The Structure of Scientific Revolutions.* Chicago: University of Chicago Press.

Lacorne, Denis. 2011. *Religion in America: A Political History.* New York: Columbia University Press.

Lahav, Pnina. 1981. "American Influence on Israel's Jurisprudence of Free Speech." *Hastings Constitutional Law Quarterly* 9: 21–108.

Lambert, Frank. 2003. *The Founding Fathers and the Place of Religion in America.* Princeton, NJ: Princeton University Press.

Laponce, Jean A. 1988. "Left or Centre? The Canadian Jewish Electorate, 1953–1983." *Canadian Journal of Political Science* 4: 691–714.

Laskier, Michael M. 2000. "Israeli Activism American-Style: Civil Liberties, Environmental, and Peace Organizations as Pressure Groups for Social Change, 1970s-1990s." *Israel Studies* 5: 128–152.

Lauder, Ronald S. 2018 (August 13) "Israel, This Is Not Who We Are." *New York Times.* Retrieved from www.nytimes.com/2018/08/13/opinion/israel-ronald-lauder-nation-state-law.html (accessed August 13, 2018).

Layman, Geoffrey C., Thomas M. Carsey, John C. Green, Richard Herrera, and Rosalyn Cooperman. 2010. "Activists and Conflict Extension in American Party Politics." *American Political Science Review* 104: 324–346.

Lazerwitz, Bernard. 1986. "Some Comments on the Use of Distinctive Jewish Names in Surveys." *Contemporary Jewry* 7: 83–91.

Lederhendler, Eli. 2009. *Jewish Immigrants and American Capitalism, 1880–1920: From Caste to Class.* New York: Cambridge University Press.

Leege, David C., Kenneth D. Wald, Brian S. Krueger, and Paul Mueller. 2002. *The Politics of Cultural Differences: Social Change and Voter Mobilization Strategies in the Post-New Deal Period.* Princeton, NJ: Princeton University Press.

Leeser, Isaac. 1861 (January 17) "The Prospect." *Occident*, 1.

1867. *Discourses on the Jewish Religion.* Philadelphia: Sherman.

1868a. *Discourses on the Jewish Religion*, Vol. 4. Philadelphia: Sherman.

1868b. *Discourses on the Jewish Religion*, Vol. 6. Philadelphia: Sherman.

Leibovitz, Liel. 2016 (July 18). "When Trump Speaks at AIPAC, Let's All Walk Out." *Tablet.* Retrieved from tabletmag.com/scroll/198637/when-trump-speaks-at-aipac-lets-all-walk-out (accessed September 15, 2017).

Leibowitz, Yeshayahu. 1992. *Judaism, Human Values and the Jewish State.* Ed. and trans. Eliezer Goldman. Cambridge, MA: Harvard University Press.

Levey, Geoffrey Brahm. 1996. "The Liberalism of American Jews – Has It Been Explained?" *British Journal of Political Science* 26: 369–401.

Levinger, Elma Ehrlich. 1954. *Jewish Adventures in America: The Story of 300 Years of Jewish Life in the United States.* New York: Bloch.

Liebman, Charles S., and Steven M. Cohen. 1990. *Two Worlds of Judaism: The Israeli and American Experiences.* New Haven, CT: Yale University Press.

Lilienthal, Max. 1865 (December 22). "Oration: Delivered by the Rev. Dr. M. Lilienthal, on Thanksgiving Day." *Israelite*, 196.

Lilla, Mark. 2007. *The Stillborn God: Religion, Politics and the Modern West.* New York: Alfred A. Knopf.

Lipset, Seymour Martin. 1960. *Political Man.* Garden City, NY: Doubleday Anchor.

1963. "The Study of Jewish Communities in a Comparative Context." *Jewish Journal of Sociology* 5: 157–166.

1967. *The First New Nation.* Garden City, NY: Doubleday Anchor.

Lipset, Seymour Martin, and Earl Raab. 1995. *Jews and the New American Scene.* Cambridge, MA: Harvard University Press.

Lipset, Seymour Martin, and Everett Carll Ladd. 1971. "Jewish Academics in the United States: Their Achievements, Culture and Politics." *American Jewish Year Book* 72: 89–128.

Loeffler, James. 2015a. "Nationalism without a Nation? On the Invisibility of American Jewish Politics." *Jewish Quarterly Review* 105: 367–398.

2015b. "The Particularist Pursuit of American Universalism: The American Jewish Committee's 1944 'Declaration on Human Rights'." *Journal of Contemporary History* 50: 274–295.

Lorberbaum, Menachem. 2012. "Israel's Constitutional Tragedy." *Touro Law Review* 29: 289–294.

*Los Angeles Times* Poll. 1988. *Statistics Sheet for Study # 407/408 American and Israeli Jews.* Los Angeles: *Los Angeles Times.*

Lupu, Ira C., and Robert W. Tuttle. 2008. "Ball on a Needle: Hein v. Freedom from Religion Foundation, Inc. and the Future of

Establishment Clause Adjudication." *Brigham Young University Law Review* 115–168.

Luz, Ehud. 1988. *Parallels Meet: Religion and Nationalism in the Early Zionist Movement (1882–1904)*. Philadelphia: Jewish Publication Society.

Mack, Julian. 1911. "Letter to Mayer Sulzberger, January 20, 1911." Mayer Sulzberger Papers. Box 1, FF2. Katz Library, University of Pennsylvania.

Mandel, Bethany. 2016 (May 25). "The Outrageous Jewish Hypocrisy of Ivanka Trump – Not to Mention Donald and Melania." Forward. Retrieved from f orward.com/opinion/341323/the-outrageous-jewish-hypocrisy-of-ivanka-trump-not-to-mention-donald-and-m/ (accessed September 15, 2017).

Manza, Jeff, and Ned Crowley 2017 "Working Class Hero? Interrogating the Social Bases of the Rise of Donald Trump." *The Forum*. 15. Retrieved from degruyter.com/view/j/for.2017.15.issue-1/issue-files/for.2017.15.issue-1.xml (accessed April 23, 2018).

Marcus, Jacob Rader. 1958. "The Periodization of American Jewish History." *Publications of the American Jewish Historical Society* 47: 125–133.

  1967. *The American Colonial Jew: A Study in Acculturation.* Syracuse, NY: Syracuse University Press.

  1989. *United States Jewry, 1776–1985.* Detroit: Wayne State University Press.

  ed. 1996. *The Jew in the American World: A Source Book.* Detroit: Wayne State University Press.

Marshall, Louis. 1907. "Letter to Edward Lauterbach, February 9, 1907." Louis Marshall Papers, P-24. Box 1, FF 1. Center for Jewish History, New York.

  1908a. "Letter to Oscar Straus, March 10, 1908." Louis Marshall Papers 1905–1933, P-24. Box 1, Folder 2. Center for Jewish History, New York.

  1908b (February 13). "The Question of the Hour." *Israelite*, 1.

  1908c (February 20). "The Question of the Hour, Part 2." *Israelite*, 1.

  1911a. "Letter to Francis B. Harrison, March 31, 1911." Mayer Sulzberger Papers. Box 1, FF 4. Katz Library, University of Pennsylvania.

  1911b. "Memorandum of Conference on the Passport Question, November 17, 1911." Mayer Sulzberger Papers. Box 1, FF 8. Katz Library, University of Pennsylvania.

  1911c. *Russia and the American Passport.* New York: Union of American Hebrew Congregations.

Maslow, Will. 1948. *How Israel Will Be Governed: An Analysis of the Draft Constitution.* New York: American Jewish Congress.

Mayer, Jeremy D. 2004. "Christian Fundamentalists and Public Opinion toward the Middle East: Israel's New Best Friends?" *Social Science Quarterly* 85: 695–712.

Mazrui, Ali A. 2004. "Muslims between the Jewish Example and the Black Experience: American Policy Implications." In *Muslims' Place in the American Public Square: Hope, Fears, and Aspirations.* Ed. Zahid Hussain Bukhari, Sulayman S. Nyang, Mumtaz Ahmad, and John L. Esposito, 117–144. Walnut Creek, CA: Rowman & Littlefield.

McAdam, Doug. 1982. *Political Process and the Development of Black Insurgency, 1930–1970*. Chicago: University of Chicago Press.

McAdams, Erin S., and Justin Earl Lance. 2013. "Religion's Impact on the Divergent Political Attitudes of Evangelical Protestants in the United States and Brazil." *Politics and Religion* 6: 483–511.

McDaniel, Jason A. 2014 "The Politics That Places Make: Contextual Effects and the Future of Political Behavior Research." *International Journal of Humanities and Social Science* 4:1. Retrieved from ijhssnet.com/journals/Vol_4_No_5_1_March_2014/1.pdf (accessed November 9, 2014).

McGarvie, Mark Douglas. 2004. *One Nation under Law? America's Early National Struggles to Separate Church and State*. DeKalb: Northern Illinois University Press.

Medding, Peter Y. 1977. "Towards a General Theory of Jewish Political Interests and Behavior." *Jewish Journal of Sociology* 19: 115–144.

1989. *The Transformation of American Jewish Politics*. New York: American Jewish Committee.

1992. "The 'New Jewish Politics' in the United States." In *The Quest for Utopia: Jewish Political Ideas and Institutions through the Ages*. Ed. Zvi Gitelman, 119–154. Armonk, NY: M.E. Sharpe.

Mellman, Mark S, Aaron Strauss, and Kenneth D. Wald. 2012. "*Jewish American Voting Behavior 1972–2008*." Washington, DC: Solomon Foundation.

Mendelsohn, Ezra. 1993. *On Modern Jewish Politics*. New York: Oxford University Press.

Mendes, H. Pereira. 1906. "Address." In *The Two Hundred and Fiftieth Anniversary of the Settlement of the Jews in the United States*, 58–60. New York: New York Co-operative Society.

Menocal, Maria Rosa. 2002. *The Ornament of the World: How Muslims, Jews, and Christians Created a Culture of Tolerance in Medieval Spain*. Boston: Little, Brown.

Meyerson, Michael. 2012. *Endowed by Our Creator: The Birth of Religious Freedom in America*. New Haven, CT: Yale University Press.

Michels, Tony. 2010. "Is America 'Different?' A Critique of American Jewish Exceptionalism." *American Jewish History* 96: 201–223.

Migdal, Joel S. 2001. *Through the Lens of Israel: Explorations in State and Society*. Albany: SUNY Press.

Mogahed, Dalia, and Fouad Pervez. 2016. *American Muslim Poll: Participation, Priorities, and Facing Prejudice in the 2016 Elections*. Dearborn, MI: Institute for Social Policy and Understanding.

Moore, Deborah Dash. 1994. *To the Golden Cities: Pursuing the American Jewish Dream in Miami and L.A.* New York: Free Press.

Morais, Nina. 1881. "Jewish Ostracism in America." *The North American Review* 133: 265–275.

Morais, Sabato. 1861 (October 4). "For the National Fast Day." *Jewish Messenger*, 52–53.

1862. "A Sermon for the Thanksgiving Day." Sabato Morais Papers. Box 11, Folder 5. Katz Library, University of Pennsylvania.

1863. "A Thanksgiving Sermon 1863." Sabato Morais Papers. Box 11, FF5. Katz Library, University of Pennsylvania.

1876a. "For the 4th of July 1876." Sabato Morais Papers. Box 11, FF5. Katz Library, University of Pennsylvania.

1876b (December 8). "A Thanksgiving Sermon." *The Jewish Messenger*, 2.

Undated. "On the Sabbath of the Three Weeks, It Being Also the 4th of July." Sabato Morais Papers. Box 11, FF5. Katz Library, University of Pennsylvania.

Morsink, Johannes. 1999. *The Universal Declaration of Human Rights: Origins, Drafting, and Intent*. Philadelphia: University of Pennsylvania Press.

Moyers, Bill, and Robert S. Rifkind. 1996. *"The Stakes in the Fight for the First Amendment."* New York: American Jewish Committee.

Mueller, Ignatius. 1899 (January 5). "A Thanksgiving Day Sermon." *The American Israelite*, 5.

Nathan, Benjamin. 1864 (December 11). "Letter to Isaac Leeser." Isaac Leeser Papers. Box 11, FF5. Katz Library, University of Pennsylvania, Philadelphia.

Nejaime, Douglas, and Reva B. Siegel. 2015. "Conscience Wars: Complicity-Based Conscience Claims in Religion and Politics." *Yale Law Journal* 124: 2516–2591.

Non-Partisan Conference to Consider Palestinian Problems. 1924. *Verbatim Report of the Proceedings of the Sessions Held Febr. 17th, 1924 at New York City [by the] Non-Partisan-Conference to Consider Palestinian Problems: Together with an Appendix Containing Official Documents Relating to the Jewish National Home in Palestine*. New York: Non-Partisan Conference to Consider Palestinian Problems.

Oates, Kathryn. 2010. "Group Efficacy: Religious Interests in the Court." PhD thesis, Department of Political Science, University of Florida.

*Occident*. [Anonymous articles. Published under the full title, *Occident and American Jewish Advocate*]

    1845 (January 1). "The Israelites of South Carolina." 496–509.

    1855 (February 1). "Politics." 25–31.

    1863 (January 1). "Are We Equals in This Land?" 25–30.

    1867 (May 1). "Religious Liberality." 8–12.

    1868a (July 1). "Cincinnati." 47.

    1868b (March 1). "Rishuth III." 529–533.

Pease, Donald E. 2009. *The New American Exceptionalism*. Minneapolis: University of Minnesota Press.

Peled, Yoav. 1992. "Ethnic Democracy and the Legal Construction of Citizenship: Arab Citizens of the Jewish State." *American Political Science Review* 86: 432–443.

Pencak, William. 2011. "Anti-Semitism, Toleration, and Appreciation: The Changing Relations of Jews and Gentiles in Early America." In *The First Prejudice: Religious Tolerance and Intolerance in Early America*. Ed. Chris Beneke and Christopher S. Grenda, 241–262. Philadelphia: University of Pennsylvania Press.

Pew Research Center. 2013. *A Portrait of Jewish Americans*. Washington, DC: Pew Research Center. Religion and Public Life Project.

2014 (July). "How Americans Feel about Religious Groups." Retrieved from http://www.pewforum.org/files/2014/07/Views-of-Religious-Groups-07-27 -full-PDF-for-web.pdf (accessed July 3, 2017).

2015. *America's Changing Religious Landscape*. Washington, DC: Pew Research Center.

Philipson, David. 1915. *Max Lilienthal, American Rabbi; Life and Writings*. New York: Bloch Publishing Company.

1919. *Centenary Papers and Others, by David Philipson*. Cincinnati, OH: Ark Publishing Company.

Phillips, Kevin P. 1969. *The Emerging Republican Majority*. Garden City, NY: Doubleday-Anchor.

Pianko, Noam. 2012. "'Make Room for Us': Jewish Collective Solidarity in Contemporary Political Thought." *Journal of Modern Jewish Studies* 11: 191–205.

Podhoretz, Norman. 2009. *Why Are Jews Liberals?* New York: Doubleday.

Pomorski, Chris. 2016 (May 23). "How Republican Jewish Hawks Feel about Donald Trump." *Tablet*. Retrieved from tabletmag.com/jewish-news-and -politics/202615/some-of-my-best-friends-are-jewish (accessed September 17, 2017).

Pool, David de Sola. 1912. "The Passport Question." *The Maccæbean* 23 (January): 20–24.

1917. "The Jew as a Citizen of England." In *Judæn Addresses*, 127–131. New York: Bloch.

"Positive and Negative Liberty." 2016. *Stanford Encyclopedia of Philosophy*. Retrieved from plato.stanford.edu/entries/liberty-positive-negative/ (accessed September 15, 2017).

"Preliminary Conference of the American Jewish Congress: Report of Proceedings, March 27–28, 1916." New York: American Jewish Congress.

Przybyszewski, Linda. 2000. "The Religion of a Jurist: Justice David J. Brewer and the Christian Nation." *Supreme Court History* 25: 228–242.

Public Religion Research Institute. 2010. *American Value Survey, 2010. Public Religion Research Institute*. Washington, DC: Roper Center.

Rabinove, Samuel. 1990. "How – and Why – American Jews Have Contended for Religious Freedom: The Requirements and Limits of Civility." *Journal of Law and Religion* 8: 131–152.

Ramsay, David. 1789. *A Dissertation on the Manner of Acquiring the Character and Privileges of a Citizen of the United States*. Charleston, SC: unidentified.

*Report of Proceedings of the American Jewish Congress, Philadelphia, December, 1918*. New York: American Jewish Congress.

Research Institute on Peace. 1961. *In Vigilant Brotherhood: The American Jewish Committee's Relationship to Palestine and Israel*. New York: American Jewish Committee, Institute of Human Relations.

Rieder, Jonathan. 1985. *Canarsie: The Jews and Italians of Brooklyn against Liberalism*. Cambridge, MA: Harvard University Press.

Robinson, Ira, ed. 1985. *Selected Letters of Cyrus Adler*. Philadelphia: Jewish Publication Society of America.

Rosenberg, Victor. 2002. "Refugee Status for Soviet Jewish Immigrants to the United States." *Touro Law Review* 19: 419–450.

Rosenswaike, Ira. 1960. "An Estimate and Analysis of the Jewish Population of the United States in 1790." *Publications of the American Jewish Historical Society* 50: 23–67.

Rosenthal, Steven T. 2001. *Irreconcilable Differences*. Hanover, NH: Brandeis University Press.

Rosenwald, Julius. 1912. "Letter to Herbert Friedenwald, April 22, 1912." Mayer Sulzberger Papers. Box 1, FF 10. Katz Library, University of Pennsylvania.

Ruben, Bruce. 2003. "Max Lilienthal and Isaac M. Wise: Architects of American Reform Judaism." *American Jewish Archives Journal* 55: 5–29.

2011. *Max Lilienthal: The Making of the American Rabbinate*. Detroit: Wayne State University Press.

Rubinstein, W. D. 1982. *The Left, the Right and the Jews*. London: Croom Helm.

Rudin, A. James. 1986 (September 21). "Pat Robertson and 'Our America'." *New York Times*, E25.

Runciman, W. G. 1969. *Social Science and Political Theory*. London: Cambridge University Press.

Sachar, Abram Leon. 1927. *Factors in Modern Jewish History: A Syllabus*. Cincinnati, OH: Department of Synagogue and School Extension, Union of American Hebrew Congregations.

Sanger, Adolph L. 1876 (December 1). "Religious Liberty." *Jewish Messenger*, 5.

Santoro, Wayne A., and Gail M McGuire. 1997. "Social Movement Insiders: The Impact of Institutional Activists on Affirmative Action and Comparable Worth Policies." *Social Problems* 44: 503–519.

Sarna, Jonathan D. 1981. *Jacksonian Jew: The Two Worlds of Mordecai Noah*. New York: Holmes & Meier.

1989. *American Jews and Church-State Relations: The Search for "Equal Footing"*. New York: American Jewish Committee, Institute of Human Relations.

1998. "The Cult of Synthesis in American Jewish Culture." *Jewish Social Studies* 5: 52–79.

2004. *American Judaism: A History*. New Haven, CT: Yale University Press.

2012. *When General Grant Expelled the Jews*. New York: Schocken.

Sasson, Theodore. 2010. "Mass Mobilization to Direct Engagement: American Jews' Changing Relationship to Israel." *Israel Studies* 15: 173–195.

Schanfarber, Tobias. 1906 (April 12). "Church and State." *Israelite*, 1.

Schappes, Morris U., ed. 1971. *A Documentary History of the Jews in the United States*. New York: Schocken.

Schiff, Jacob H. 1911 (February 16). "Telegram to Meyer Sulzberger." Mayer Sulzberger Papers (ARC MS25). Box 1, FF 11. Katz Library, University of Pennsylvania.

Schnapper, Dominique, Chantal Bordes-Benayoun, and Freddy Raphaël. 2010. *Jewish Citizenship in France: The Temptation of Being among One's Own*. New Brunswick, NJ: Transaction Publishers.

Schneerson, Menachem. 2014. "Rabbi Menachem M. Schneerson, 'Letter on the Question of Prayer in the Public Schools,' 1964." In *American Jewish History: A Primary Source Reader*. Ed. Gary Phillip Zola and Marc Dollinger, 298–301. Waltham, MA: Brandeis University Press.

Schultz, Debra L. 2001. *Going South: Jewish Women in the Civil Rights Movement*. New York: New York University Press.

Schultz, Kevin M. 2006. "Religion as Identity in Postwar America: The Last Serious Attempt to Put a Question on Religion in the United States Census." *Journal of American History* 93: 359–384.

Sears, David O., Richard R. Lau, Tom R. Tyler, and Harris M. Allen, Jr. 1980. "Self-Interest vs. Symbolic Politics in Policy Attitudes and Presidential Voting." *American Political Science Review* 74: 670–684.

Segal, Zeev. 1992. "A Constitution without a Constitution: The Israeli Experience and the American Impact." *Capital University Law Review* 21: 1–62.

Selengut, Charles. 2017. *Sacred Fury: Understanding Religious Violence*. Lanham, MD: Rowman & Littlefield.

Sewell, William H. 1999. "The Concept(s) of Culture." In *Beyond the Cultural Turn: New Directions in the Study of Society and Culture*. Ed. Victoria E. Bonnell and Lynn Hunt, 35–61. Berkeley: University of California Press.

Shain, Yossi. 2000. "American Jews and the Construction of Israel's Jewish Identity." *Diasporas* 9: 163–201.

Shalev, Eran. 2009. "'A Perfect Republic': The Mosaic Constitution in Revolutionary New England, 1775–1788." *The New England Quarterly* 82: 235–263.

Sheskin, Ira M., and Arnold Dashefsky. 2017. *Jewish Population in the United States, 2016*. New York: Berman Jewish Data Bank.

Shimshoni, Daniel. 1982. *Israeli Democracy: The Middle of the Journey*. New York: Free Press.

Shively, W. Phillips. 1971. "A Reinterpretation of the New Deal Realignment." *Public Opinion Quarterly* 35: 621–624.

Shortle, Allyson F., and Ronald Keith Gaddie. 2015. "Religious Nationalism and Perceptions of Muslims and Islam." *Politics and Religion* 8: 435–457.

Shteyngart, Gary. 2014. *Little Failure: A Memoir*. New York: Random House.

Sigelman, Lee. 1991. "If You Prick Us, Do We Not Bleed? If You Tickle Us, Do We Not Laugh?" *Journal of Politics* 53: 977–992.

Silver, Matthew M. 2013. *Louis Marshall and the Rise of Jewish Ethnicity in America: A Biography*. Syracuse, NY: Syracuse University Press.

Silver, Nate. 2016 (May 3). "The Mythology of Trump's 'Working Class' Support." Retrieved from fivethirtyeight.com/features/the-mythology-of-trumps-working-class-support/ (accessed April 23, 2018).

Singer, Eleanor. 2000. "Comment." *Public Opinion Quarterly* 64: 106–107.

Sirico, Louis J. Jr. 2013. "Benjamin Franklin, Prayer, and the Constitutional Convention; History as Narrative." *Legal Communication and Rhetoric* 10: 89–124

Sisk, Gregory C., Michael Heise, and Andrew P. Morriss. 2004. "Searching for the Soul of Judicial Decision-Making: An Empirical Study of Religious Freedom Decisions." *Ohio State Law Journal* 65: 491–614.

Smith, David T. 2015. *Religious Persecution and Political Order in the United States*. New York: Cambridge University Press.

Smith, Goldwin. 1891. "New Light on the Jewish Question." *North American Review* 153 (417): 129–143.

Smith, Rogers M. 1988. "The 'American Creed' and American Identity: The Limits of Liberal Citizenship in the United States." *The Western Political Quarterly* 41: 225–251.

1997. *Civic Ideals: Conflicting Visions of Citizenship in U.S. History*. New Haven, CT: Yale University Press.

Smith, Tom W. 1999. "The Religious Right and Anti-Semitism." *Review of Religious Research* 40: 244–258.

2005. *Jewish Distinctiveness in America*. New York: American Jewish Committee.

Solomon, Abba A. 2011. *The Speech, and Its Context: Jacob Blaustein's Speech 'The Meaning of Palestine Partition to American Jews' Given to the Baltimore Chapter, American Jewish Committee, February 15, 1948*. Privately published.

Sorauf, Frank J. 1976. *The Wall of Separation: The Constitutional Politics of Church and State*. Princeton, NJ: Princeton University Press.

Sorin, Gerald. 1985. *The Prophetic Minority: American Jewish Immigrant Radicals, 1880–1920*. Bloomington: Indiana University Press.

Sorkin, David. 2010. "Is American Jewry Exceptional? Comparing Jewish Emancipation in Europe and America." *American Jewish History* 96: 175–200.

Spector, Stephen. 2009. *Evangelicals and Israel: The Story of American Christian Zionism*. New York: Oxford University Press.

SSRS. 2017. "*AJC 2017 Annual Survey of American Jewish Opinion. Topline Report*." Glen Mills, PA: SSRS.

"Statement of the President at a Conference at the White House, Wednesday Afternoon, February 15, 1911." Mayer Sulzberger Collection ARC MS25. Box 1, Folder 3. Katz Library, University of Pennsylvania.

Steinhart, S. 1855 (December 7). "Correspondence of the Israelite." *The Israelite*, 181.

Stephens, Brett. 2016 (November 22). "Trump's Neo-Nationalists." *Wall Street Journal*. Retrieved from wsj.com/articles/trumps-neo-nationalists-14797741 29 (accessed September 15, 2017).

Stone, Kurt F. 2010. *The Congressional Minyan: The Jews of Capitol Hill*. Metuchen, NJ: Scarecrow Press.

Stonecash, Jeffrey M. 2000. *Class and Party in American Politics*. Boulder, CO: Westview Press.

Stow, Kenneth R. 1992. *Alienated Minority: The Jews of Medieval Latin Europe*. Cambridge, MA: Harvard University Press.

Strain, Christopher B. 2017. *The Long Sixties: America, 1955–1973*. Hoboken, NJ: Wiley Blackwell.

Straus, Oscar S. 1879 (May 9). "The Rights of American Citizens." *Israelite*, 4.

1885. *The Origin of Republican Form of Government in the United States of America*. New York: Putnam.

1887. "The Development of Religious Liberty in America." *Westminster Review* 128: 38–47.

Stroock, Sol M. 1917. "The Jew as a Citizen in France." In *Judaean Addresses: Selected*, 131–136. New York: Bloch Publishing Company,

Sulzberger, Mayer. 1904. "Address on the 250th Anniversary of the Landing of the Jewish Pilgrim Fathers by M.S." Mayer Sulzberger Papers. Box 19, Folder 3. Katz Library, University of Pennsylvania, Philadelphia.

1911 (February 8). "Circular on the Russian Passport." Mayer Sulzberger Papers. Box 1, FF3. Katz Library, University of Pennsylvania.

Sulzer, William. 1911. "Letter to Mayer Sulzberger, May 1, 1911." Mayer Sulzberger Papers. Box 1, FF 5. Katz Library, University of Pennsylvania.

Susser, Bernard. 1981. "On the Reconstruction of Jewish Political Theory." In *Public Life in Israel and the Diaspora*. Ed. Sam N. Lehman-Wilzig and Bernard Susser, 13–22. Ramat Gan, Israel: Bar-Ilan University.

Sussman, Lance Jonathan. 1995. *Isaac Leeser and the Making of American Judaism*. Detroit: Wayne State University Press.

Tarshish, Allan. 1959. "The Board of Delegates of American Israelites (1859–1878)." *Publications of the American Jewish Historical Society* 49: 16–32.

Teller, Judd L. 1955. "America's Two Zionist Traditions." *Commentary* 20: 343–352.

Tenenbaum, Joseph. 1945. *Peace for the Jews*. New York: American Federation for Polish Jews.

Therborn, Göran 2006. "Why and How Place Matters." In *Oxford Handbook of Contextual Political Analysis*. Ed. Robert E. Goodin and Charles Tilly, 509–533. New York: Oxford University Press.

Tighe, Elizabeth, Leonard Saxe, Raquel Magidin de Kramer, and Daniel Parmer. 2013. "American Jewish Population Estimates: 2012." Waltham, MA: Steinhardt Social Research Institute, Brandeis University.

Tingsten, Herbert 1937. *Political Behavior: Studies in Election Statistics*. London: P. S. King.

Tobin, Gary, and Sid Groeneman. 2003. *Surveying the Jewish Population in the United States*. San Francisco: Institute for Jewish and Community Research.

Twohig, Dorothy, ed. 1993. *The Papers of George Washington, Presidential Series*. Charlottesville: University Press of Virginia.

*The Two Hundred and Fiftieth Anniversary of the Settlement of the Jews in the United States*. 1906. New York: New York Co-operative Society.

Union of American Hebrew Congregations. 1905. *Thirty-First Annual Report*. Cincinnati: May and Kreidler.

1916. *Forty-Third Annual Report*. Cincinnati: Kriedller and May.

United States. 1918. *Papers Relating to the Foreign Relations of the United States [1911]*. Washington, DC: Government Printing Office.

1924. *Restriction of Immigration. Hearings before the Committee on Immigration and Naturalization, House of Representatives, Sixty-Eighth*

*Congress, First Session, on H.R.5, H.R.101, H.R.561 [H.R.6540].* Washington, DC: GPO.

United States Department of Commerce and Labor. Bureau of Immigration and Naturalization and Sons of the American Revolution. 1908. *Information for Immigrants Concerning the United States, Its Opportunities, Government and Institutions.* Washington: Government Printing Office.

Uslaner, Eric M. 2015. "What's the Matter with Palm Beach County?" *Politics and Religion* 8: 699–717.

Uslaner, Eric M., and Mark Lichbach. 2009. "Identity versus Identity: Israel and Evangelicals and the Two-Front War for Jewish Votes." *Politics and Religion* 2: 395–419.

Van Der Waal, Jeroen, Peter Achterberg, and Dick Houtman. 2007. "Class Is Not Dead–It Has Been Buried Alive: Class Voting and Cultural Voting in Postwar Western Societies (1956–1990)." *Politics & Society* 35: 403–426.

Verba, Sidney, Kay Lehman Schlozman, and Henry E. Brady. 1995. *Voice and Equality.* Cambridge, MA: Harvard University Press.

Verhoeven, Tim. 2013. "The Case for Sunday Mails: Sabbath Laws and the Separation of Church and State in Jacksonian America." *Journal of Church and State* 55: 71–91.

Voorsanger, Jacob. 1906. "The Influence of Americanism upon the Jew." In *The Two Hundred and Fiftieth Anniversary of the Settlement of Jews in the United States,* 183–193. New York: New York Co-operative Society.

Wald, Kenneth D. 2006. "Toward a Structural Explanation of Jewish-Catholic Political Differences in the United States." In *Jews and Catholics in Dialogue and Confrontation: Religion and Politics since the Second World War.* Ed. Eli Lederhendler, 111–131. New York: Oxford University Press.

2008a. "Paths from Emancipation: American Jews and Same Sex Marriage." In *Faith, Politics and Sexual Diversity.* Ed. David Rayside and Clyde Wilcox. 239–254. Vancouver, BC: UBC Press.

2008b. "Homeland Interests, Hostland Politics: Politicized Ethnic Identity among Middle Eastern Heritage Groups in the United States." *International Migration Review* 42: 273–301.

2012. "Stunning Stability: A Consistent Jewish Vote for 60 Years." *Sh'ma: A Journal of Jewish Ideas* (January): 1–2.

2014. "The Choosing People: Interpreting the Puzzling Politics of American Jewry." *Politics and Religion* 8: 4–35.

2016. "Religious Influences on Catholic and Jewish Supreme Court Justices: Converging History and Diverging Paths." In *Wiley Blackwell Companion to Religion and Politics in the U.S.* Ed. Barbara A. McGraw, 442–453. Malden, MA: Wiley Blackwell.

Wald, Kenneth D., and Allison Calhoun-Brown. 2018. *Religion and Politics in the United States.* 8th edn. Lanham, MD: Rowman & Littlefield.

Wald, Kenneth D., and Andrea Peña-Vasquez. In press. "Cultural Foundations of Right-Wing Politics in the United States: The Case of the Tea Party Movement." *Survey Journalen.*

Wald, Kenneth D., and Clyde Wilcox. 2006. "Getting Religion: Has Political Science Rediscovered the Faith Factor?" *American Political Science Review* 100: 523–530.

Wald, Kenneth D., and Graham Glover. 2007. "Theological Perspectives on Gay Unions: The Uneasy Marriage of Religion and Politics." In *The Politics of Same-Sex Marriage*. Ed. Craig Rimmerman and Clyde Wilcox, 105–131. Chicago: University of Chicago Press.

Wald, Kenneth D., James L. Guth, Cleveland R. Fraser, John C. Green, Corwin E. Smidt, and Lyman A. Kellstedt. 1996. "Reclaiming Zion: How American Religious Groups View the Middle East." *Israel Affairs* 2: 147–168.

Wald, Kenneth D., and Lee Sigelman 1995. Jews' Views of Preferential Treatment: The End of Tribalism? Paper presented to the annual meeting of the Society for the Scientific Study of Religion/Religious Research Association, St. Louis, MO.

  1997. "Romancing the Jews: The Christian Right in Search of Strange Bedfellows." In *Sojourners in the Wilderness: The Religious Right in Comparative Perspective*. Ed. Corwin Smidt and James Penning, 139–168. Lanham, MD: Rowman & Littlefield.

"Walker Takes the Lead in GOP Race." 2015 (February 24). Press release, Public Policy Polling. Retrieved from publicpolicypolling.com/pdf/2015/PPP_Relea se_National_22415.pdf (February 28, 2015).

Ward, Erik K. 2017 (December 3). "Forcefully Opposing Anti-Semitism Must Be a Core Principle of the Movement to Combat White Supremacy." *Tablet*. Retrieved from www.tabletmag.com/jewish-news-and-politics/2506 08/forcefully-opposing-anti-semitism-must-be-a-core-principle-of-the-move ment-to-combat-white-supremacy (accessed December 8, 1917).

Wasserman, Lewis M., and James C Hardy. 2013. "US Supreme Court Justices' Religious and Party Affiliation, Case-Level Factors, Decisional Era and Voting in Establishment Clause Disputes Involving Public Education: 1947–2012." *British Journal of American Legal Studies* 2: 111–162.

Waxman, Dov. 2016. *Trouble in the Tribe: The American Jewish Conflict over Israel*. Princeton, NJ: Princeton University Press.

Webb, Clive. 2001. *Fight against Fear: Southern Jews and Black Civil Rights*. Athens, GA: University of Georgia Press.

Webber, Michael J. 2000. *New Deal Fat Cats: Business, Labor, and Campaign Finance in the 1936 Presidential Election*. New York: Fordham University Press.

Weinrib, Lorraine E. 2003. "'Do Justice to Us!' Jews and the Constitution of Canada." In *Not Written in Stone: Jews, Constitutions and Constitutionalism in Canada*. Ed. Michael Gary Brown, Daniel Judah Elazar, and Ira Robinson, 33–68. Ottawa: University of Ottawa Press.

Weisberg, Herbert F. 2012. "Reconsidering Jewish Presidential Voting Statistics." *Contemporary Jewry* 32: 215–236.

Wenger, Beth S. 1999. *New York Jews and the Great Depression: Uncertain Promise*. Syracuse, NY: Syracuse University Press.

  2010. *History Lessons: The Creation of American Jewish Heritage*. Princeton, NJ: Princeton University Press.

White, John Kenneth. 1990. *The New Politics of Old Values*. Hanover, NH: University Press of New England.

White, Richard H. 1968. "Toward a Theory of Religious Influence." *The Pacific Sociological Review* 11: 23–28.

Whiteman, Maxwell. 1987. *American Jewish Life and the Constitution*. Philadelphia: Congregation Mikveh Israel and the National Museum of American Jewish History.

Whitfield, Stephen J. 1993. "Paradoxes of Jewish Survival in the United States." In *What Is American about the American Jewish Experience?* Ed. Marc Lee Raphael, 91–107.Williamsburg, VA: College of William and Mary.

Wiernik, Peter. 1912. *History of the Jews in America, from the Period of the Discovery of the New World to the Present Time*. New York: Jewish Press Publishing Company.

Wieseltier, Leon 2009 (September 8). "Because They Believe." The *New York Times*. Retrieved from http://www.nytimes.com/2009/09/13/books/review/Wieseltier-t.html (accessed November 29, 2017).

Wineburg, Robert J. 2007. *Faith-Based Inefficiency: The Follies of Bush's Initiatives*. Westport, CT: Praeger.

Winter, J. Alan. 1992. "The Transformation of Community Integration among American Jewry: Religion or Ethnoreligion? A National Replication." *Review of Religious Research* 33: 349–363.

Wise, Isaac Mayer. 1872 (February 9). "A Defense of the Constitution." *Israelite*, 8.

   1907 (July 4). "Independence Day, 1907." *Israelite* 4.

Wise, Stephen S. 1916. "Zionism, Religion and Americanism." *The Maccæbean* 28 (June), 125–126.

Wohl, Alexander. 1991. "Metamorphosis: The Court, the Bill, and Liberty for All." *ABA Journal* 77: 42–48.

Wolf, Jacob. 1870 (February 11). "Israel in America." *The Israelite (1854–1874)*, 8.

Wolf, Simon. 1911. "Letter to Louis Marshall, July 17, 1911." Mayer Sulzberger Papers. Box 1, FF 6. Katz Library, University of Pennsylvania.

   1918. "Jewish Nationalism at Versailles." Simon Wolf Papers, 1868–1925 (P-25). Box 2, Folder 8. New York: Center for Jewish History.

   1926. "Judaism Patriotism Fraternalism." In *Selected Addresses and Papers of Simon Wolf: A Memorial Volume, Together with a Biographical Sketch*, 281–283. Cincinnati, OH: Union of American Hebrew Congregations.

Woocher, Jonathan S. 1986. *Sacred Survival: The Civil Religion of American Jews*. Bloomington: Indiana University Press.

Woods, Patricia J. 2004. "It's Israeli after All: A Survey of Israeli Women's Movement Volunteers." *Israel Studies Forum* 19: 29–53.

Yerushalmi, Yosef Hayim. 2005. *Servants of Kings and Not Servants of Servants: Some Aspects of the Political History of the Jews*. Atlanta: Tam Institute for Jewish Studies, Emory University.

Young, Christopher J. 2011. "Barnet Hodes's Quest to Remember Haym Salomon, the Almost-Forgotten Jewish Patriot of the American Revolution." *American Jewish Archives Journal* 63: 43–62.

Zeitz, Joshua M. 2007. *White Ethnic New York: Jews, Catholics, and the Shaping of Postwar Politics*. Chapel Hill: University of North Carolina Press.

Zenner, Walter P. 1990. "Jewish Retainers as Power Brokers." *The Jewish Quarterly Review* 81: 127–149.

Zola, Gary Phillip, ed. 2014. *We Called Him Rabbi Abraham: Lincoln and American Jewry, a Documentary History*. Carbondale: Southern Illinois University Press.

Zuckerman, Alan S. 1999. "Political Science and the Jews: A Review Essay on the Holocaust, the State of Israel, and the Comparative Analysis of Jewish Communities." *American Political Science Review* 93: 935–945.

2005. "Returning to the Social Logic of Politics." In *The Social Logic of Politics: Personal Networks as Contexts for Political Behavior*. Ed. Alan S. Zuckerman, 3-20. Philadelphia: Temple University Press.

# Index